PENGUIN BOOKS

A GUIDE TO CENTRAL EUROPE

After studying History of Art at Christ's College, Cambridge, and the Courtauld Institute of Art, Richard Bassett travelled extensively in Central Europe, teaching at the University of Trieste and lecturing for the British Council at the University of Zagreb. He has also worked for a season as principal horn of the Ljubljana Opera House.

Richard Bassett is now *The Times'* Vienna correspondent and travels regularly to Hungary, Romania and Czechoslovakia. He is also a contributor to the *Spectator*.

RICHARD BASSETT

A GUIDE TO
CENTRAL EUROPE

PENGUIN BOOKS

Penguin Books Ltd, 27 Wrights Lane, London w8 5tz (Publishing and Editorial)
and Harmondsworth, Middlesex, England (Distribution and Warehouse)
Viking Penguin Inc., 40 West 23rd Street, New York, New York 10010, USA
Penguin Books Australia Ltd, Ringwood, Victoria, Australia
Penguin Books Canada Ltd, 2801 John Street, Markham, Ontario, Canada l3r 1b4
Penguin Books (NZ) Ltd, 182–190 Wairau Road, Auckland 10, New Zealand

First published by Viking 1987
Published in Penguin Books 1988

Copyright © Richard Bassett, 1987
All rights reserved

Made and printed in Great Britain by
Richard Clay Ltd, Bungay, Suffolk
Filmset in Monophoto Ehrhardt

CONTENTS

CONTENTS

LIST OF ILLUSTRATIONS

LIST OF MAPS

ACKNOWLEDGEMENTS

It is my pleasure to thank two institutions, the Leverhulme Trust and *The Times*, who have allowed me to research at length into the diverse lands which together make up Central Europe. I am particularly indebted to Mr Ivan Barnes, Foreign Editor of *The Times*, the late Mr Charles Douglas-Home and his successor as Editor, Mr Charles Wilson, all of whom encouraged me in one way or another to travel east of Vienna.

In Austria, my understanding of the historical background owes much to conversations with Herr Gottfried Pils and Prince Peter Altenburg. In Trieste, Signor Giorgio Voghera and his friends Claudio Magris and Piero Kern were equally helpful. My awareness of Slovenia and the small but unique culture which exists on that side of the Julian Alps is largely the result of talks I had in the course of one summer with Professor Edo Ravnikar. In Hungary, I am grateful for the hospitality extended to me by the former British Ambassador and his wife, Mr and Mrs Peter Unwin. I should also like to take this opportunity to thank many friends in Czechoslovakia and Transylvania whose names they would none the less not thank me for publishing.

In England, I am especially grateful to Miss Caroline Mauduit, who braved the rigours of travel in Transylvania and Slovakia to secure many of the photographs in this book. Richard Hudson, Victoria Spička, Gertrude Felderer and Bridget Tempest also helped in several ways at various times. I am grateful also to Arabella Friesen who, one spring afternoon, high above the Bay of Trieste, finally discovered the elusive path which creeps down from the carso to the white crenellations of Miramar castle.

Any errors, however, which occur in the following pages are entirely my responsibility.

Vienna, 1986

INTRODUCTION

The term Central Europe, redolent of the picturesque intrigues of an Anthony Hope novel, is no longer a fashionable one. The precise geographical frontiers of the area have never been easy to define. But as this book is the first guide since 1915 to attempt to describe the cities of what was once the Habsburg empire, some lines must be drawn on the map.

These lines do not correspond entirely to the frontiers of the old Austrian empire, which in its vastness ruled parts of Alpine, Mediterranean and Balkan Europe as well as that large piece of land which is called Mitteleuropa. What links the cities and villages described in the following pages is not simply history but a single cultural heritage. The Habsburgs governed these lands for centuries, their administration and army welding together the peoples of some twenty nations.

Much has been written about the injustice of this rule, the suppression of nationalism, the crude Magyarization policies of the Hungarians and the arrogance of the imperial ruling class. But for all its evils, by the time of its collapse in 1918, the Danube monarchy was a more liberal place than either the Kaiser's Germany or the Tsar's Russia had been.

Moreover, uniformity of education and administration created a cultural unity, forging over centuries a similarity of mentality and outlook which cut across racial barriers and which, fuelled to a certain extent by the Catholic Church's strength, was capable of imprinting its stamp on those who belonged to Protestant, Jewish, Moslem or Orthodox faiths.

This Central European mentality is still, after forty years of communist rule over much of this part of the continent, thriving. The Austrian says '*Küss die Hand*'. In the Tatra mountains, the Slovak equivalent is '*Boskavam*'. The Magyar is no less chivalrous with his Hungarian '*Kézet cókolom*'. Even in Dubrovnik, the Ragusan observes these old gallantries when he says '*Slugace*', which for all its abruptness actually means 'I [your] most humble servant bow to you'.

Those who travel around Central Europe will recognize other traces of a shared political and cultural background. It may be as intangible as the way in which a person walks or gesticulates or it may be the pedantic labelling of every house with an enamel plaque announcing the street as well as the number.

A more obvious example is the architectural heritage of Central Europe. For hundreds of years neither borders nor language problems prevented an artist or architect from working throughout this part of the continent. An architect who designed a church in Trieste could the following year build a triumphal arch in Vienna. Fischer von Erlach designed churches in Vienna and stables in Bohemia. In the nineteenth century the most successful architectural partnership in history, Helmer and Fellner, were able to furnish designs for theatres in almost every city between Vienna, Carlsbad and Fiume.

In the musical world the links were even more varied: Mahler, a Moravian, made his name in Slovenia; a Beethoven Symphony was first performed in Ljubljana; some of Lehár's best tunes were composed when he was a young officer stationed in Istria.

Cuisine in Central Europe is also remarkably consistent. Dumplings, if traditionally Bohemian, enjoy great favour in Austria. How often has the weary traveller in Eastern Europe been restored by a plate of *Palatschinken*, those sweet pancakes, originally Hungarian but to be found in every city mentioned in this book?

Although forty years of learning Russian as a second language has imprinted a new dimension onto the outlook of many young East Europeans, German is still useful: a few words of the Teutonic language will stand the traveller in good stead as far east as the Carpathians. Ironically, the Russians were able to glide almost effortlessly into the offices and corridors vacated by the old Habsburg empire and learnt much from the way Vienna governed these lands. The sixty-seven words of German command which every conscript in the Habsburg armies had to know have been replaced by a hundred Soviet phrases, for Russian is the official language of command in the armies of the Warsaw Pact.

The old bureaucracy also flourishes too under its new masters, and though the consequences of having to deal with it vary enormously between a democratic western capital like Vienna and a communist city like Prague, anyone who has experienced both would be hard put to deny certain unmistakable similarities in the thinking which prevails.

Not all of Austria is linked, however, with Central Europe, and if the

Danube Austrian of Vienna has much in common with the Hungarian or Czech, his brother Austrians in Salzburg or Innsbruck have far more in common with their Alpine brethren in Bavaria or Switzerland. It is no coincidence that the Viennese prefer the Hungarians to many of the inhabitants of their own country's provinces.

But if the tapestry of Central Europe is made up of similar patterns, it still boasts many different materials, and old racial hatreds die hard. The '*divide et impera*' tactics of the Austrians have been inherited by the Russians, who encourage national identity even if this nurses chauvinism. An important part of this policy is the systematic education of many of these peoples so that their joint cultural legacy is ignored, papered over by the rhetoric of international Marxism. None the less, a mentality cannot be broken simply by the rewriting of history, or by the importing of Russian into school curricula or Crimean champagne into Bohemian supermarkets, and those who travel in the countries described on the following pages will realize that they have far more in common with their neighbours in Central Europe than the Central Europeans have with their remote masters in Moscow.

This guide, for reasons of space, can serve only as a glimpse of a most fascinating part of the world, and only a visit will persuade the reader of the validity of the term Central Europe as an expression of cultural identity. But anyone who journeys to two or more of the places described here will be struck by the familiarity of the theme, though this is not to say that the variations played upon it are not of considerable ingenuity. The Puszta of Hungary, the Tatra mountains, the ethnic survival of Saxons in Transylvania, the magnificent remains of the Austrian Riviera near Trieste are all as different from each other as any traveller would hope, and yet a thread of similarity runs through them all.

In many of these places there is an opportunity to sample superb wines and foods; in others communism has provided an economy pitifully inefficient in supplying even the most basic foodstuffs. At times frustration and anger will furrow the brow, for the authorities can be far from enthusiastic in dealing with foreigners. But with luck and some humour the experiences and sights of Central Europe will make up for this.

On the whole, Central Europeans, whether Hungarians, Czechs or even Viennese, are a friendly lot. Those travellers who secure rooms in private houses will find a standard of hospitality and kindness rare in many parts of Western Europe, where commercial enterprise and material values have taken their toll.

However, life in that part of Central Europe which lies behind the iron curtain has its pressures, and we who live in the west cannot easily contemplate them or appreciate the problems which often the simplest actions can provoke. In the cities where intellectual life is often kept on a tight leash, a western traveller is a welcome sight for some but a cause for apprehension in others. Black-marketeering, common in parts of Czechoslovakia and rife in Transylvania, may, by its facility and frequency, delude the traveller from the west into thinking that this is a peccadillo tolerated by the state. In some ways it is, but anyone from the west who is unfortunate enough to be caught will experience the full severity of the security machinery (something which will detract considerably from the pleasures of the journey, for a brush with the law rarely leaves a pleasant taste, least of all in this part of the world). Nevertheless, a visit to the eastern lands of Central Europe should cause little anxiety. It is perhaps the only advantage of a highly controlled police system that violence and crime are rare even in a large city. Budapest, Prague and Carlsbad are all as safe at night as a Dorset village.

A great many of the monuments to this unique culture are unfortunately far from well looked after and those roses which can be admired may be surrounded by untended verges. None the less, Central Europe, even though tinged with melancholy, is a treasure chest of art, architecture, music and all the other things which collectively make up European culture. If this book can assist in any small way in helping the traveller chart its riches, it will have succeeded in its purpose.

1

VIENNA

I

There can be no better place to begin a tour of Vienna, or indeed of Central Europe, than at the heart of the Austrian capital: St Stephen's cathedral (Stefansdom). Exercise of the kind needed to reach the viewing room of its south tower is not normally to be recommended, but there is much in Vienna that conduces to long hours of indolence, and a quick march up the tower's 533 steps will happily ward off any feelings of guilt during subsequent hours spent in the city's cafés.

From the top, the view (alas, owing to the high number of suicides, possible only through iron bars) offers a glimpse of lands where more than once the fate of Austria and indeed of Europe was decided. To the north the Vienna Woods cluster round the hills of Kahlenberg and Leopoldsberg. It was from here in 1683 that the armies of Jan Sobieski poured down on the Turks who were besieging the city, driving the infidel back and so commencing the long and tortuous decline of the 'sick man of Europe', as Tsar Nicholas was to call Turkey over two hundred years later.

To the east the flat fields of the Marchfeld can be seen. A more undistinguished landscape would be difficult to imagine, but it was here that in 1278 Count Rudolf of Habsburg defeated King Ottokar of Bohemia, who, incidentally, was the monarch responsible for rebuilding the cathedral after the first St Stephen's was destroyed by fire in 1258. This victory not only gave Rudolf Vienna, it also marked the beginning of 640 years of Habsburg rule in Austria.

This was not the only battle to be fought on the Marchfeld. In 1809 over 300,000 troops were locked in one of the most sanguinary campaigns of the Napoleonic wars when, at the battle of Aspern, the Habsburg Archduke Karl inflicted the first defeat the French emperor had known on land. Six weeks later, at the battle of Wagram, Napoleon repulsed a

5

second Austrian attack over the same ground and won a bloody victory, but at the cost of a quarter of his troops. For years afterwards the land of the Marchfeld was soft underfoot.

Such conflicts suggest that the Habsburgs were a military family bent on supremacy through sheer force of arms. In fact nothing could be further from the truth. *'Bella gerant alii. Tu Felix Austria nube'* ('While others wage war, you, happy Austria, marry') was the phrase coined to express the way in which the ruling house acquired its land: through well-considered dynastic marriages in the centuries following Rudolf's victory on the Marchfeld.

In front of the woods of the Lobau and the Marchfeld rises the imposing Belvedere Palace, with its lawns and green copper domes (see p. 42). Closer to us are the gables of the Franciscan church, to the right of which, with its flags flying, is the yellow Hotel Imperial. The large boulevard which runs in a ring from the Imperial, past the domes of the Hofburg Palace visible from the south window, marks the fortifications of the city during the Turkish sieges. When they were demolished in the 1850s, the grand palaces, museums and parliament buildings were erected, giving Vienna a grandeur to match Paris and London.

Also from the south window, the Karlskirche, with its twin Trajan columns and green copper dome, can be seen. When it was begun in 1716 it lay on the glacis outside the fortifications. Even St Stephen's, now at the heart of Vienna, lay outside the old city, whose earliest walls ran along the Graben (literally 'the ditch'), now a road which runs towards the large green dome of the Hofburg, almost directly beneath us.

The east view belongs to the twentieth century. To the left of the Prater wheel (immortalized in the film *The Third Man*) the vast concrete flak towers erected for the defence of Vienna in the last war rise from the green of the Augarten. They belong, in a gruesome way, to the very best – or worst – of 1940s architecture. Even today their size makes them impossible to demolish without risk to neighbouring buildings.

The north-west window (from which we spotted the Vienna Woods and Kahlenberg) brings us past the brown mass of the new city hospital to the twin mid-nineteenth-century Gothic towers of the Votivkirche on the Ring and back along the Graben.

The city below, with its Baroque domes, narrow streets and grand palais, is still the Vienna of 1918, and the cathedral, thanks to sensitive Austrian planning, still dominates the skyline.

Those who feel the need to pause after the descent from the tower can do so at the tables opposite the west door – the Riesentor, or 'giant door' – of the cathedral. The Expresso zum Stefansplatz and the Domcafé (the latter is better if it's raining) are not typical coffee-houses, but they are comfortable and offer a good view of the west façade of the cathedral and the Riesentor. Most of what can be seen from here was at least partially rebuilt in the Gothic style when the present nave was added in 1446. Later alterations gave the hitherto unfinished north tower its Renaissance cupola, while the bright tiling of the roof has rightly been called a nineteenth-century apotheosis of lavatory decoration.

A walk round the outside of the church offers a field-day for funerary monument enthusiasts. Most of the monuments date from the sixteenth and seventeenth centuries and are indispensable to anyone tracing the development of Mannerism in Austrian sculpture. All repay close examination, though one may have to keep an eye open for the horse-drawn *Fiakers* which park along the north wall, as their drivers are understandably indifferent to such researches.

On the corner of the north tower is a monument erected to the memory of one Lorenz Zimmerman, who, like thousands of other Viennese, perished in the plague of 1574. A typical *memento mori*, it is a gruesome rendering of a skeleton. Further along, there is a crucifix in a barred niche below which stairs lead down into a rather sinister darkness and the catacombs beneath the church. Today, the catacombs may be reached from inside the cathedral, but many Viennese pause here to kneel and say a quick prayer in front of the crucifix on their way to the shops.

Just beyond this is the fine Gothic pulpit from which in 1481 St Capristanus first called for the destruction of the infidel, a cry taken up with zeal by the later Habsburgs. At the corner there is a side door to the cathedral in front of which are displayed photographs of the burnt-out shell of St Stephen's after Allied bombing during the war. Such devastation might suggest that one is about to enter one of those pitifully bleak, over-restored churches often to be found in German cities. Fortunately the craftsmen here did their work with rare skill, and the gloomy darkness of the interior seems completely medieval even to the most discerning eye. The glass was of course destroyed, but rather than replace it with some expressionist design of the fifties, the Viennese wisely chose to use simple coloured panes.

To the right as one enters, behind an iron gate, is the bishops' memorial chapel; to the left, an undistinguished monument to the raising of the Turkish siege in 1683. But this unpromising beginning soon leads to more rewarding sights. Exploring the treasures of the choir and its side chapels poses a dilemma, as everything to the east of where one now stands is barred by a metal chain. Unless one is prepared to wait for a tour at the west end of the cathedral, pay roughly a pound and enjoy a guide who recites dates like a computer, there is no alternative but to slip under this chain. Even at the height of the tourist season, it will be at least fifteen minutes before one is discovered. This is more than time enough to inspect the east end, something one can do in any English cathedral where these iniquitous practices have not been introduced.

The south chapel contains the magnificent sarcophagus of Emperor Frederick I I I (1415–93), the first Habsburg to be crowned Holy Roman Emperor. It is surprisingly self-effacing, but amid the impressive red and white marble carvings and thirty-two coats of arms can be seen the letters A.E.I.O.U., a motto indelibly associated with Frederick and standing for '*Austria erit in orbe ultima*' ('Austria will outlast all other powers'), or '*Austria est imperare orbi universo*' ('It is for Austria to rule the entire world').

The choir itself is chiefly notable for the fine late fifteenth-century light-wood Renaissance stalls, containing excellent portraits of bishops. The Baroque painting above by Tobias Pock, however, scarcely merits a glance. The small north choir is rich in monuments, including ones of Duke Rudolf I V and his duchess, Catherine. Although Rudolf reigned only from 1358 to 1365 he enlarged St Stephen's and founded the University of Vienna, which explains why the red banners marked 'Universitas' lie on his tomb.

Turning to the nave, perhaps greeting some officious warder about to remove us from this forbidden area with a cheery 'Good morning', or a twenty-*Schilling* note, it is time to slip back under the chain and explore the rest of the interior.

One remarkable area is near the third pier from the west end, which features a delightful example of flowing Gothic in the pulpit attributed to Anton Pilgram of Brno in Moravia. The craftsman's portrait is sculptured looking somewhat gravely out of a window in the latticework. The same face peers out at us from an elaborate organ base on the north wall behind us, in another gorgeous late flowering of Gothic.

As in many south European churches, there is much grafting of Baroque elements onto Gothic structure to be seen, in general effect less unpleasant than one might expect. The south aisle contains a fine wooden imperial viewing box underneath which stand, quite neglected, some exquisite black wooden stalls of the late 1520s.

For those whose tastes lie in this direction, a tour of the catacombs, where the relics of the emperors are kept, and the bones of thousands of plague victims can be seen, commences opposite.

Before leaving, it only remains to pay one's respects to the greatest general who ever led an Austrian army, Prince Eugen of Savoy, who lies buried in the south aisle chapel at the west end. The soldier who saved Marlborough's life at the battle of Blenheim has a humble grave, but we shall encounter more spectacular monuments to him in other parts of the city (see p. 42).

From the catholic bustle of St Stephen's the Singerstrasse runs from the south entrance to an oasis of calm in the remarkable church and treasury of the German knights: the Deutsche Ordenskirche (the Church of the Teutonic Order) is the perfect antidote to the tiresome restrictions and crowds of the cathedral. The chapel immediately to the right of the entrance is a fine example of fourteenth-century Gothic, with splendid blind arcading and a maverick pair of monuments to the Starhemberg family in the choir, dating from the late seventeenth century. While one Starhemberg, Prince Rudiger, took charge of the garrison of the city during the siege of Vienna in 1683, his nephew Guido distinguished himself by extinguishing a fire in the Schottenhof (see p. 29) caused by a Turkish mine. Had the fire spread there is no doubt that the city would have fallen to the Turks. Above the monuments rise tier upon tier of coats of arms belonging to knights whose names are a register of Central Europe's aristocracy.

Just before the courtyard beyond the chapel is a museum upstairs containing the treasury of the order, which ecclesiologists will find far more interesting than the treasury of the cathedral. A guide-book in English is supplied by the warder for the duration of your visit. There is an impressive collection of seals, and our attention is drawn to a deed from Henry IV which promises the German knights the sum of forty marks. In another room there is a collection of plate and coconut tankards worthy of the richest Oxbridge college, while beyond this is the pearl of the collection, a seventeenth-century German shelf clock of exquisite craftsmanship.

Leaving the Ordenskirche we may take the Singerstrasse a few steps further down where, in another courtyard, one is offered in hot weather refreshments served between white wicker chairs and potted plants. Haas and Haas, who run this establishment (an extension of their shop), specialize in teas and exotic gadgetry. Their house speciality, 'iced tee' (*sic*), which bears little relation to any tea that may be familiar to Anglo-Saxons, is by far the most refreshing drink to be had in Vienna during the August heat.

From Haas and Haas or the Ordenskirche it is only a minute's walk to the Stock-im-Eisen Platz in front of St Stephen's and the Graben. This square is chiefly memorable for the stump of a larch full of nails driven into it which is preserved behind glass at the corner of the imperious Equitable Insurance building. The stump dates from 1553. Any metalsmith seeking an apprenticeship in Vienna was required to hammer a nail into the stump on entering the city.

To the right of the building runs the elegant Graben, which contains what purport to be the best shops in the capital. Toy-soldier enthusiasts will not want to miss Kober's, while the most charming miniature chocolates in delightful boxes are sold in Altmann and Kühne, who have made these delicious confections for over a hundred years.

The pleasures of window-shopping in the Graben can result in one overlooking a most spectacular Baroque monument and our first acquaintance with the genius of Johann Bernhard Fischer von Erlach, who with his son, Joseph Emanuel, gave Vienna much of its Baroque skyline. The so-called 'Pestsäule', or Plague Column (sometimes known as the Trinity Column), was designed and executed by Fischer and others between 1687 and 1693. It commemorates the end of the plague in 1679. The figure kneeling in humble expiation is a likeness of the Habsburg who commissioned the monument, Leopold I (1657–1705). We recognize here for the first time the unmistakable features of the Habsburg family. The long nose, thick lips and dropped 'Habsburg' jaw are shown to brilliant, if unflattering, effect in this sculpture. The pyramid of clouds and frenetic consoles are a hallmark of Fischer's work. Leopold, whatever his appearance, was a great patron of the arts as well as a practising musician and composer who on his death left no fewer than 155 unison and part songs.

Along the Graben there is a large orange building on the left dating from the last years of the nineteenth century which is an early example of the great *fin-de-siècle* Viennese architect Otto Wagner. Nearby is the gentleman's outfitters Knize, designed in about 1906 by Adolf Loos, who greatly admired English art, especially for its solidity. Although little of the original building is left it is still possible to see the rich wood used for the interior and the window-frames. The passion for English styles which Loos indefatigably promoted persists today in Vienna, where many shops, such as Country Life, Sir Antony and At the Home of the English Fleet, have unashamedly English images. But little has changed since Loos's day, and he would shudder in horror – as do most people brought up with Jermyn Street tastes – at the creations perpetrated here in the name of *'Englische Mode'*.

Across the street is the Peterskirche, a large Baroque church which was built between 1705 and 1708 by Fischer von Erlach's great rival, Johann Lukas von Hildebrandt. The church is based on an earlier plan of Gabriele Montani and is considered by many to be Hildebrandt's masterpiece. The interior has an extravagance which is belied by the rather unimpressive exterior, hemmed in as it is by neighbouring buildings. As in Fischer's masterpiece, the Karlskirche, the dome is an oval, but the altar has less of the fantastic sculpture and plaster-work that is the hallmark of most of Fischer's *œuvre*. Note the fine stalls and the picturesque Kaiserloge to the right of the high altar. Here as elsewhere Hildebrandt makes great use of the tent-top forms which were inspired by the sight of the Turkish camps outside the city during the siege, some twenty years before. On dark winter evenings, the interior, almost entirely lit by candles, has mystical atmosphere rare in many of the city's places of worship.

Leaving the Peterskirche a glance at No. 6 in the square reveals a plaque stating that Mozart is reputed to have written the score of *Die Entführung aus dem Serail* in this house.

At the end of the Graben is the second most elegant street in the city: the Kohlmarkt, which leads off to the left towards the large domed Michaelertor of the Hofburg. Before walking down Vienna's equivalent of Bond Street one should look up at the roofs of the buildings. There one should be able to make out the metal figure of a dashing hussar, carbine in hand, resisting an obvious overture from a larger than life *fin-de-siècle* ceramic *femme fatale* perched on the top floor of the building opposite.

Down the Kohlmarkt, No. 9 is a building designed by Max Fabiani, a good example of Jugendstil architecture. Next door lies the renowned – in Austria at least – Huber and Lerner, former court stationers who supply, as their windows show, invitations to the cream of Austria's political and social élite. English minds will doubtless question the need for the firm's name to be printed on every card, letter-heading and wedding invitation, but for the Viennese it is this alone which ensures their patronage. After passing Cartier opposite, glance at the jeweller's shop Schullner; this has a front designed by Herr Hans Hollein which is said to be a masterpiece of contemporary architecture. Vienna, in the hands of Hollein, has been turned into a focus for architecture students throughout the world.

Architecture of a rather different sort but no less attractive is to be seen further up the street at Demel, the former imperial and court confectioners. It is a long-standing and doubtless futile argument whether Demel or Sacher make the best *Sachertorte*. The recipes are different, and after years of litigation Demel finally established the sole right of calling its version 'original *Sachertorte*'. Demel's case rested on evidence that the cook who created the cake had in fact worked at Sacher's, but after some dispute had left for Demel, taking his recipe with him. Connoisseurs of these fattening affairs will notice that Demel's cake has a layer of jam between the sponge and chocolate coating. I find Sacher's creation, without the jam but with a small amount of cream, slightly superior. Those who disagree may derive satisfaction from the fact that, while both cakes are expensive, the Demel's one is rather less expensive than its rival from the hotel behind the Opera.

Sachertorte aside, the real delight of Demel is its fairyland interior. Lined with mirrors which reflect the chandeliers, it is still the most fashionable place to be seen in the city on Sundays. The rooms upstairs are occasionally open in the summer and should not be neglected, especially by those wishing to escape the tourist *hoi polloi* below. Besides cakes, Demel does some fine lunches and even if the coffee and iced tea are to be avoided, it is the best producer in Europe of savoury nibbles for drinks parties. Those who have a passion for Jugendstil will admire the period chocolate boxes designed by members of the Wiener Werkstätte before the First World War. For decades grandmothers have been delighted by the pink and blue *langues-de-chat* boxes.

At the end of the Kohlmarkt on the right stands a curious marble façade with classical columns. This almost reticent building caused a major scandal before the First World War, when its simple proportions and uncluttered exterior provoked the Archduke Franz Ferdinand (later of Sarajevo fame) into declaring from the Hofburg opposite that he would like to break every bone in its creator's body. Luckily for the architect, Adolf Loos, whose work we have already seen something of in the Graben, the Archduke's intemperate remarks were cut short by events of greater historical significance. Today, the building, which originally housed a tailor – when have architecture and the style of a gentleman's suits been more closely intertwined? – is an unprepossessing purveyor of household goods. Quite what Goldman and Salatsch, Loos's tailors, or indeed Loos himself would have said to this, we can only speculate.

Opposite stands the Michaelerkirche which, together with Loos's building, faces the imposing domed entrance to the Hofburg. The church is in many ways one of the least distinguished in Vienna. The extremely austere arches inside, dating from 1327, are unrelieved but for a heavy Baroque high altar in the main choir. Side chapels to right and left, however, contain some fine monuments, while once again a tour of the catacombs beneath the church allows another view of the remains of yet more victims of the plague. But if rather unimpressive visually, the Michaelerkirche is of significance for art-historians because its choir represents the last phase of Baroque architecture to be found in Vienna's churches. Shortly afterwards, in 1792, a cooler classical style was employed to restore the façade. Both buildings at the end of the Kohlmarkt thus had a significant role to play in the history of Vienna's architectural development.

The rather flashy Michaeler front of the Hofburg, with its vast dome which upstages both the church and Loos's building, is a hybrid creation dating from two different periods. The conception is unashamedly Baroque, but the craftsmanship is unmistakably nineteenth-century, with a heaviness redolent of much of Whitehall. Guarding the entrance are two gargantuan groups of fountain statuary, more impressive than beautiful. The one on the left is generally considered to be the finer; it represents Austria's naval power. Although that power is non-existent now, several dramatic victories were won, notably the defeat of the Italians, in the last century. The group of figures on the right of the entrance is much less imposing, perhaps appropriately, as it represents the empire's military power, a field of activity in which the Austrians were notoriously unskilled.

Passing between these figures brings one to the heart of the imperial palace. The domed space is neither interior nor exterior: the odd taxi which glides past is strangely disturbing, as if someone were driving through a church. On the left is the entrance to the imperial apartments, a tour of which is recommended. Although only a fraction of the vast collection of Habsburg furniture is on display, these twenty rooms offer an insight into life at the Austrian court which can only be glimpsed in other parts of the building. Of particular interest is the dining room, with its green wine glasses. The rules of etiquette in force here ensured that the unfortunate man who sat opposite the Kaiser sometimes went hungry. Everyone present had to eat the same course as the emperor. If, as often happened, those opposite his royal and imperial majesty had just been served their soup as the emperor finished his, they had to go without, as their plates would be instantly swept away from in front of them.

Another room which should be seen contains the gruelling gymnastic devices which kept Franz Josef's wife, the Empress Elizabeth, the fittest and indeed the most beautiful member of the imperial house. The story of 'Sissy' (as the Viennese called their empress) is typical of the family tragedy which befell Franz Josef. Estranged from her husband and oppressed by the stiff etiquette and Spanish court ceremony, this most beautiful lady spent most of her time outside Austria. A true Wittelsbach (the Bavarian royal family which was responsible for the equally unhappy spirit of King Ludwig), she enjoyed the life of the saddle, spending many months of the year hunting in Ireland and at Combermere Abbey in England. Her brutal assassination at the hands of a deranged Italian anarchist as she stepped aboard a steamer on Lake Geneva is one of the more senseless tragedies of the nineteenth century. The empress walked a further eighty paces before collapsing, and even then only whispered calmly to her distraught aides: '*Ce n'est pas la peine, merci bien.*' The dress she was wearing, with a small hole where the assassin's stiletto entered, piercing her heart, is exhibited here.

On leaving the imperial apartments, there is a chance to visit the court silver collection opposite, and what might be considered the most esoteric museum in Vienna, the International Esperanto Museum. While the latter may prove of interest only to students of this remarkable attempt to unite the peoples of the world linguistically, the court silver collection has an undeniably broader appeal. Its cases of gold plate and cutlery are dazzling, if not very sympathetically displayed. Exceptional is the enormous empire-style service, some of which was made in Milan around 1800. Less impressive is the rather quaint gothic-revival service the Emperor Francis I ate from at Laxenburg (see p. 54). Those who appreciate the excesses of Third Empire will be particularly moved by the service in the last room. However, a less overpowering display is offered nearby, with Queen Victoria's gift to the Emperor Franz Josef of a service commemorating – albeit on only one plate – the 1851 Great Exhibition. The Archduke Franz Ferdinand's set of crystal glasses is instructive. Some of the goblets are so lacking in design that the practical elegance of the Vienna Secession would indeed have had to have been invented if it had not come into existence as a result of these clumsy objects.

Continuing further into the Hofburg, one comes to the Franzensplatz, named after the Emperor Francis I of Austria, whose statue is here. He was the last Austrian emperor to enjoy the title of Holy Roman Emperor (as Francis II of the Holy Roman Empire). Francis, who reigned from 1792 to 1835, ruled in stormy times, having to contend with Napoleon's desire to redraw the map of Europe, often at Austria's expense. After three major victories, in 1805 Napoleon declared the Holy Roman Empire dissolved. Perhaps foreseeing this, Francis had in 1804 elevated Austria to the rank of empire and thus, even after his abdication as Holy Roman Emperor in 1806, he remained of equal rank with the newly created Emperor Napoleon.

If ever there was a Habsburg who kept his head when all those about him were losing theirs, it was Francis. His armies annihilated on the plains of Italy and hills of Moravia, his capital occupied by French troops, even his daughter, Marie Louise, married off to the Corsican ogre, Francis still kept cool and waited for his moment to help Europe be rid of the French emperor, which he did in 1813 at the battle of

Leipzig. Something of a severe character, Francis none the less earned the soubriquet 'Biedermeier Kaiser' for his bourgeois predilection for a simple and homely suburban life.

Behind the statue of the emperor rises the Amalientrakt of the palace. Built in the seventeenth century, the rooms here are furnished in the style of the Empress Maria Theresa, who made this part of the 'Burg' her home. Unfortunately, as this section of the palace houses the offices of the Austrian president, there is little or no chance of inspecting it. Opposite is the equally inaccessible Reichkanzleitrakt, designed by Fischer von Erlach for Karl VI in 1729, which contains former imperial apartments and some offices leading to the Chancellery.

To the left is the red and black Schweizertor, which leads to the oldest part of the palace. This impressive gateway, named after the Swiss mercenaries who once guarded it, dates from 1552 and bears the arms of the original Habsburg archduchy. The courtyard beyond contains two unexpected delights. The first, up the stairs on the right, is the Burgkapelle, where on Sundays the Vienna Boys' Choir can be heard. (Tickets have to be applied for in writing eight weeks earlier. For those who are less well organized, standing-only tickets become available on Fridays at 5 p.m.) The chancel is the only interesting feature in the chapel: it contains the oldest Gothic work in the entire Hofburg. This can be admired to a certain extent from outside, in the next courtyard, but for the moment one must avoid the temptation to go further into the Josefsplatz and stay in the Hofburg, where one may examine, opposite the chapel, the second surprise, the imperial treasury. This includes the crown of the Holy Roman Emperors and nothing less spectacular than the imperial sword and orb of Charlemagne. At the time of writing, this is temporarily on loan to the Kunsthistorisches Museum, across the Ring (see p. 18).

Retracing one's steps out of the Schweizerhof, another arcade appears on the left. Through this lies the impressive 'range' (as these façades are called) of the Hofburg, the Heldenplatz and beyond it the Ringstrasse, with its imposing buildings. The sense of space is welcome if only because very few parts of Vienna offer the chance to see so much sky.

The curved Neo-Baroque part of the Hofburg, designed by the distinguished nineteenth-century German architect Gottfried Semper, is on the left. Semper planned an identical range opposite, hoping to create a kind of imperial forum. Fortunately, his plans came to nothing, and so we can enjoy a fine view of the Burgtor, a Neo-Classical work, and beyond, Semper's domed museums, the Kunsthistorisches and Natur-historisches. To the right of these, above the trees, race the Grecian chariots on the roof of Theophil von Hansen's Neo-Grec Parliament, while beyond it, in yet another nineteenth-century style, rises the Neo-Gothic Town Hall, to complete this extravagant lesson in architectural styles.

The Semper range of the Hofburg contains a delightful museum of antique musical instruments and an impressive collection of armour, as well as the manuscript and reading rooms of the National Library. It also contains the Austrian Ethnographic Museum, which attempts, rather un-successfully, to re-create long-forgotten cultures in a foreign land. How-ever, the museum's impressive marbled vestibule is a spectacular example of Semper's ability to construct a grand but not overpowering interior.

Before embarking on more museum work, it may be a good idea to walk through the Volksgarten on the right, to admire the Neo-Classical temple at its centre and, at the other end, the imposing Burgtheater, also designed by Semper. On entering the Volksgarten, cast a glance at the buildings to the right. The two low ranges are a rare example of Viennese architectural understatement. This is ironic, for the Ballhausplatz, the minute square between the ranges, was a synonym for politics throughout the Habsburgs' reign, and indeed even later. From here Metternich entertained the Congress of Vienna in 1815. What the Wilhelmstrasse became for Prussia and Whitehall for England, the 'Ballplatz' was for Austria. Its name suggests the frivolous nature of politics in the late nineteenth century, and although the word alone was enough to cause a ripple of fear throughout the empire, in London it could provoke a wry smile in diplomatic circles, where the hidebound nature of Austrian methods were well known.

Emerging from the Volksgarten, the nearest Burgtheater wing contains early frescoes by Gustav Klimt (see p. 43). These can usually be inspected by applying to the theatre porter. On the other side of the theatre is the Café Landtmann, a suitable point at which to recover from the day's exertions, containing as it does most of the respectable English news-papers and encouraging the comfortable indolence which is the true mark of the Viennese café. Be warned, however, that even in cold weather the cloakroom lady will insist on visitors leaving their coats with her.

An hour spent in the Landtmann will prepare one for a visit to the museums on the other side of the Ring, including the important collections of the Kunsthistorisches Museum. These should not be attempted without at least two hours in hand. But even a morning would be too short a time for those who take their *Kunst* seriously.

The Kunsthistorisches Museum is one of the richest (if least well known) European art collections. The paintings were once the property of the imperial family and were assembled by the Habsburgs over three hundred years. Occasionally, some of the greatest works were lost, as, for example, when the Swedes plundered Prague during the Thirty Years War. As Prague was then the seat of government, many irreplaceable treasures were lost. Another hundred paintings had to be sent to the Dresden gallery in the eighteenth century as part of an indemnity to the King of Saxony because of a failed Austrian attempt to recover Silesia, the province that Frederick the Great of Prussia had wrenched from Maria Theresa. Other masterpieces were lost during the Napoleonic wars. But even after two world wars the gallery can boast the finest collection of Breughel the Elder in the world, a score of Rubens, Van Dycks, Velasquezes and Titians, some important Canaletto paintings and many significant works by North German masters relatively unknown in England.

The entrance hall, with its grand vestibule, contains frescoes by Gustav Klimt and Franz Matsch which, though early, and therefore conventional, are rather amusing. It is beyond the scope of this book to offer the reader a complete guide to the treasures of this museum. If time is pressing the first-floor Egyptian exhibits may be ignored. The rest of this floor, however, contains much to interest those who appreciate Renaissance bronze statues, medieval draughts sets or Bulgarian gold drinking vessels, to say nothing of the dazzling (and deservedly renowned) Cellini salt-cellar.

But it is the floor above which annually attracts the swarms of visitors who block the entrance to the small ticket desk. The stairs to this floor are long, but one is more than adequately rewarded for the climb by the paintings presented for inspection. The greatest treasures, such as the Breughels and Rubens, have enormous rooms to themselves, but many smaller treasures can be more enjoyably examined in the intimate series of rooms which break up the corridors around. Mantegna's exquisite *Martyrdom of St Sebastian* is displayed as if it were in a private study.

Bellini's *Portrait of a Woman at her Toilet* is equally accessible, while a small group of superb Holbeins fills another niche. These few paintings alone make the long walk upstairs seem worthwhile and that is even before the Titians, Velasquezes and other great works in the main rooms are seen.

The obvious resting place after a visit to the Kunsthistorisches is a Viennese café, but the nearest is across the Ring back in the Heldenplatz. The zoologically minded may prefer to linger in the building opposite the Kunsthistorisches, the Naturhistorisches Museum, which is identical in style to the art history museum and houses the natural history collections. This building seems to have been left untouched by the trendy developments which mark the interiors of so many of London's museums. Look in vain for flashing lights, animated noises, and dark, sinister rooms. Instead, there is the more terrifying experience of being greeted at the top of the stairs by a soldier-crab (mercifully stuffed) whose legs seem almost twelve feet long.

Back to the Heldenplatz to look at two equestrian statues of that rare Austrian phenomenon, the successful general. We have already met Prince Eugen, who rides towards us from the Neue Hofburg, in the cathedral. It is ironic to learn that this military genius, who not only defeated the Turks but was also Marlborough's ally at Blenheim, Oudenarde and Malplaquet, suffered the indignity of having his military services being refused, first by Louis XIV and the French court. Apparently Eugen's 'sickly appearance, poor carriage in the saddle and insignificant height' counted against him. The Austrians, far less concerned then with external appearances than they are today, saw the Savoy prince at his true worth and never lived to regret employing him.

Opposite is the more dramatic statue of the Archduke Karl. If less gifted than Prince Eugen, he at least won the distinction of being the first general to inflict a serious loss on Napoleon when in 1809 the Austrians pushed the French back from Aspern, the Marchfeld village seen earlier from the top of the cathedral. The statue captures the moment when, seeing his Hungarian grenadiers falter, the archduke seized their standard, urging them to 'put every Frenchman to the sword'. The inscriptions on the Archduke's statue – 'dedicated to the fearless leader of Austria's army' on one side and 'who fought for Germany's honour' on the other – could have served as Austria's epitaph in 1938, the year the Nazis invaded. This curious identification of Germany's designs with Austria's interests was never accepted by many Austrians when Hitler's Reich swallowed up this country in the year before the last war. But the inscription reflects the ambivalence the Austrian has towards the German. On the one hand he is more charming, and quick to accuse his northern neighbours of Prussian aloofness. On the other hand, he admires the Germans' efficiency, which the Austrian can rarely equal. The Viennese in particular have a long history of tragic mistakes in organization. But perhaps because every Austrian seems to be an amalgam of Slav and Latin as well as Teutonic blood, these people remain masters of improvisation. In any event Austrian history has for centuries been inextricably bound up with that of Germany, even though few Austrians would appreciate being referred to as Germans.

The Burgtor nearby, designed by Nobile in 1818, contains another example of Austria's close ties with Germany: inside lies the tomb of the unknown soldier. Constructed in 1935, the design for the white staircase could have been the work of Albert Speer. The reclining marble soldier is an excellent if somewhat disturbing example of thirties sculpture. As one emerges onto the Ring there are other whispers of the aggressiveness of the thirties. Two particularly hawkish, single-headed eagles have survived on the wall between the Burgtor and the Hofburg, almost all that remains of the thousand-year German Reich in this part of Vienna.

Down the Ring (that is, turning left from the Burgtor) is the Burggarten, formerly the private palace garden of the Habsburgs. It is a small, intimate but none the less charming affair enlivened at one end by an art-nouveau hot-house constructed by Friedrich Ohmann at the turn of the century. In the middle of the garden stands a fine statue of Franz Josef, Austria's penultimate emperor, who reigned for sixty-eight years, a symbol of continuity and stability. His whiskered features are as familiar to most Austrians as the silhouette of Queen Victoria is to the British. During his long reign he became a synonym for spartan living: he slept on a simple iron bed and rose each day at 3.30 in the morning to work for two hours before breakfast. His taste for simple food gave the sobriquet 'Kaiser' to a host of Viennese dishes which, though they sound very grand, usually involve the thinnest cuts of meat and the most sparing use even of simple foods (*Kaisermelange*, for example, is coffee made with two raw eggs).

From the Burggarten a gate opposite the palm house leads to the

Augustinergasse. To the right, the large building which commands attention from across the road is the opera house, erected in the 1850s by two ill-fated architects, Siccardsburg and Van der Nüll. The Viennese so loathed the eclectic French and Italian Neo-Renaissance building that they ridiculed its construction relentlessly. Van der Nüll, unable to work on the most important commission of his life while suffering a barrage of abuse in the daily press, resorted to a characteristically Viennese solution and committed suicide. Siccardsburg, a former officer in the lancers, was made of sterner stuff, but he too died shortly afterwards, a broken man. Few stories indicate so well the crass philistinism with which Vienna treated the gifted artists the city was privileged to enjoy in its long history.

The grassy triangle between the Opera and the Augustinerstrasse (the site of the Jockey Club, which before the war rivalled Brooks) leads to the Café Tirolerhof. Like many cafés in Vienna it has been restored, but there is still something of its former art-deco elegance. From its well-heated rooms a sortie to the opera or a further inspection of the Augustinerstrasse can be planned.

Buying tickets for an opera performance is an expensive business. They are best obtained from the yellow building near the entrance to the Burggarten – tickets bought from hotel porters and ticket agencies in the city inevitably cost more. However, for those with only a few Austrian *Schillings* to spare, standing places are available for less than seventy pence and are excellent value for money (many of them offer better views than many more expensive seats). To obtain one of these places the procedure to be followed, like everything in Vienna, demands rigid adherence to certain well-defined conventions. For popular performances, it is best to arrive two and a quarter hours before the curtain rises. This secures a place in the queue. After an hour you will be allowed in, where a scarf or tie attached to the railing will ensure your place until curtain-up, while you go off for a quick bite to eat at the Tirolerhof or some other suitable establishment.

Otherwise, there are many delights in the Augustinerstrasse and the Herrengasse. The large palais at the beginning of the Augustinerstrasse is the Erzherzog (Archduke) Friedrich Palais, which now houses the largest collection of drawings in Central Europe. It is known as the Albertina. The museum contains about a million exhibits, including works by Dürer, Raphael and Rubens. The empire-style reading room, which houses the desks where many of these drawings can be studied, is on the first floor. Written applications to the director are advised if serious study of a particular school is intended. Otherwise, the Albertina organizes several exhibitions each year which enables some of its treasures to be seen more easily.

The ramp to the left of the entrance leads up to a fine view of the Ring as well as a statue of Archduke Albrecht, who defeated the Italians in 1866 at the battle of Custozza.

The chief splendour of the Augustinerstrasse is the Augustine church. To enter this is to be confronted immediately with the very finest Neo-Classical sculpture in Vienna, some would say in the entire country. Facing the entrance is the haunting monument by Canova to the Archduchess Marie Christine, daughter of Maria Theresa. The anguished expression of the lion, balanced by the more aloof Victory above the melancholy cortege which enters this precise pyramid, is unforgettable. To the right of the chancel is another object of interest which should not escape inspection: the Loretto Chapel, which contains the embalmed hearts of the Habsburgs in fifty-four urns.

Apart from this, the church offers little of interest, all trace of its fourteenth-century Gothic construction having been overlaid by severe restoration by Ferdinand von Hohenburg in the 1790s. Hohenburg was really a classical architect, but he was greatly moved by the 'gothick' of Horace Walpole's house in London, Strawberry Hill, and he was largely responsible for the beginning of the Gothic revival in Austria. On Sundays, the church normally resounds to the sound of a Mozart or Schubert mass, complete with orchestra, and the scions of Austria's aristocracy pathetically wave at each other during the service.

Beyond the church is the Josefsplatz, with an equestrian statue of Joseph II in its centre. Joseph ruled only from 1780 to 1790, but he was probably the most approachable of all the Habsburgs: he it was who threw open the Prater gardens to the public. Asked why he spent so much time in the company of the 'lower orders', Joseph replied that if he spent all his time with his equals he would be confined to the Habsburg vault in the Capuchin church. Joseph's reign saw the abolition of serfdom and torture, and an increase in religious toleration, including the emancipation of the Jews and the creation of what became a forerunner of the modern welfare state, administered by an enormous civil service. But together with these reforms came the closure of some six hundred monasteries, which incensed the clerical establishment; the forces of reaction closed ranks and reversed much of the 'enlightened despot's' work once Joseph died.

The Josefsplatz contains several treasures behind its rather austere walls. The high building to the left is the National Library; designed by Fischer von Erlach, it contains his finest and most dramatic secular interior. It was begun in 1722, one year before Fischer's death. Again the oval form is predominant; running across the main axis of the library, it startles the visitor by its maverick disregard for the line of thought suggested at first by the Corinthian columns. Looking up at the frescoed ceiling, its gorgeous chaos interrupted by shafts of light from the big deep windows, it is impossible to question that this is indeed the apotheosis of Austrian Baroque.

At right angles to the library is the Winter Riding School, designed by Fischer's son, Joseph Emanuel, and begun in 1729. It is altogether a more austere work, suggesting the early classicism which was soon to make itself felt in Vienna. Morning training is held five times a week in season and offers an excellent opportunity to study the paces of the grey Lipizzaner stallions. Demonstrations of 'Haute École' have been part of Vienna's culture for over two hundred years; the Spanish school of equestrian art first arrived here in the period up to 1714, when the Habsburgs ruled Spain as well as Austria. Those who wish to see one of the rare performances can apply for tickets at the tourist office opposite, in the Augustinerstrasse, but people habitually in the saddle will learn as much, if not more, from the training sessions, during which a number of horses are quickly but effectively put through the basic steps of the school.

Opposite the riding school is the Redoutensaal, where masked balls were held before 1918, while on the other side of the road rises the imposing Neo-Classical Palais Pallavicini, with its curious caryatids designed by Hohenburg. The palais was used as the setting for the opening scenes in *The Third Man*. As well as state rooms used for official functions, it contains the Rennverein Club, which offers hospitality to members of London's Turf Club. The Palais Palffy next door was badly bombed during the war but has been restored and occasionally houses exhibitions.

In the nearby Dorotheergasse is Vienna's least changed and most characteristic café, Hawelka's. Still run by the irrepressible Frau Hawelka and her more taciturn, bow-tied husband, this establishment offers more than any other a picture of what one imagines café life must have been like. In the early morning, it is a hushed retreat in which to recover from the excesses of the night before. In the early evening it hums with the '*erste Gesellschaft*', who feel it is a good place to be seen. By nine o'clock, this rather foppish clientele gives way to a more Bohemian group who are usually fed by Frau Hawelka's delicious *Buchteln* cakes and are eventually turned out towards two o'clock the next morning.

Along the Josefsplatz towards the Herrengasse, one passes on the right another gallery of Austrian art, dedicated to modern paintings and containing the few works of the French Impressionists to be seen in the Austrian capital. Beyond this are the stables (visits are sometimes permitted – see the notice displayed) of the Lipizzaners and the Kohlmarkt which we saw earlier. The Herrengasse contains the former palaces of the imperial aristocracy, sheltering under the shadows of the Hofburg like insecure children under a maternal wing. Many of these are now government offices or museums, but their façades and courtyards are of interest.

The first on the left is the Palais Wilczek. Its courtyard has a dark, leafy calm, not unlike that of an Oxford college. A plaque on the wall commemorates two literary residents of the last century, Franz Grillparzer, the Biedermeier playwright, and Joseph von Eichendorff, one of the more gifted poets of the same period. Next door to the Palais Wilczek stands the Palais Modena, whose severe Neo-Classical façade once housed the Gestapo headquarters but which is now the office of the Minister for the Interior. Further on is the Palais Mollard Clary, constructed in 1689, and now containing several museums of little interest to anyone who is not an afficionado of taxidermy. The courtyard, however, contains a fine wrought-iron well.

A small side street to the right leads to the Wallnerstrasse, interesting for the fine Palais Caprara-Muller, which used to house the British consulate and which has a pleasant courtyard with trees. The building on the left is the former Anglo-Austrian Bank, while the two palaces to the right – the last is the Palais Esterházy – also merit a quick glance. Beyond the former bank is a curiously eclectic nineteenth-century palais whose entrance proudly displays the notice 'Freyung passage'. This leads to an arcade, recently restored, which houses the Café Central (closed Saturday afternoons). It is a popular myth that the Russian revolution was plotted here by two Russian émigrés, one of whom was called Trotsky. The palace was designed by one of Austria's second generation of Gothic revivalists, Heinrich Ferstel, a rather dull fellow responsible for many uninspired buildings along the Ringstrasse. However, the clever use of space and the richly effective 'stucco-lustro' decoration make this one of his more successful achievements.

A passage to the left of the arcade fountain leads back to the Herrengasse. Opposite is an imposing and still (despite the cruellest of readaptations) monumental Neo-Classical palais. Its Grecian-columned interior and temple-inspired ceilings have only just survived shameful conversion into a hat shop.

At the corner, turn up the Landhausgasse, where a fine Carinthian restaurant known as Bei Max daily feeds the Austrian civil servants who work in this part of the city, many of them in the Minoritenplatz, which houses a church of the same name. The square itself is most picturesque. The original gas lanterns have been preserved and the buildings to each side of the church have a noble character. To the right the vast Palais Starhemberg, once the property of the family whose ancestors were encountered in the monuments of the Deutsche Ordenskirche (see p. 9), now houses the Ministry of Education. Opposite, with a caryatid-covered portal is the rather stolidly styled Palais Liechtenstein. To the left of this stands the charming Palais Dietrichstein, which, like its heavier neighbour, houses the Austrian Foreign Office.

At the corner of the church runs a picturesque vista of arches. This 'cloister' contains several interesting, if neglected, monuments of which the severe Elizabethan lady in black staring haughtily at the pigeons is the most memorable.

This part of Vienna is invariably deserted on Saturday and Sunday afternoons, and it is poignant to recall that much of the most glittering entertaining during the Congress of Vienna took place here. Castlereagh himself had rooms in the Palais Dietrichstein.

The Minorites' church's interior, entered from the west door, is bleak and white like many Viennese churches, but it contains a unique, for Austria, piece of Rococo Gothic in its high altar, again by the ubiquitous Hohenburg. A chapel to the left of this pays tribute to the many Italians who once lived under the Habsburg monarchy, and the church today is still the Italian church in the city.

The Abraham and Sancta Clara Gasse leads from the Palais Liechtenstein to the Bankgasse, where the Hungarian embassy is housed in an impressive late-eighteenth-century palace. To its right is the Palais Batthany, probably designed by Fischer von Erlach, but uninteresting save for the rather heavy portal. The rather down-at-heel palais opposite in the Herrengasse is the former property of the Harrach family, who, like the Batthanys, Dietrichsteins and Liechtensteins, all held important positions at the Austrian court, each family having the right to be part of this most exclusive club by virtue of the sixteen quarterings their arms displayed. For some years now the Harrach Palais has stood empty, a sad reminder of the former glory of the Herrengasse.

At the end of the Herrengasse, the Palais Porcia (built in 1546) contains a delightful courtyard with blind arcades, which even the worst excesses of modern Austrian bad taste, such as ugly lamps, have failed to destroy. Next door stands the *pièce de résistance* of the entire street, the Palais Kinsky. Built by Hildebrandt in 1712 for Count Daun, it has a rich façade and a spectacular staircase (apply to the porter; the ability to speak Serbo-Croat is useful). The narrowness of the space available for Hildebrandt in no way cramped his style, as the magnificent stone panels of the balustrade indicate. Once it was possible to eat delicious goulash in the former palace stables, where a restaurant thrived under pictures of Herzog and other horses. It is now closed, but the nearby Café Central makes a suitable end to a day's sightseeing.

2

VIENNA

2

Off the well-trodden paths of the Herrengasse, Graben and Kohlmarkt, there are less well-known corners of Vienna which seem to have remained unchanged for decades and even at the height of summer afford refuge from the crowds of sightseers.

· THE NORTH-WESTERN QUARTERS ·

Opposite the west end of St Stephen's Cathedral runs the Jasomirgottstrasse. 'Jasomirgott' ('So help me God'), a common phrase in Vienna, was the nickname bestowed on Heinrich II (1141–77), the first Habsburg to establish his capital in Vienna, because of his fondness for this particular oath. It was during his rule that Austria was given the special status of a hereditary Duchy within the Holy Roman Empire.

At the end of this street stands a picturesque eighteenth-century building. By contrast, a turning to the right leads into Brandstätte, where can be seen one of the most extraordinary pre-First World War constructions in Vienna: the Zacherlhaus by Josef Plečnik (1872–1956). The large metal angel fixed to the façade was long dubbed by the Viennese the patron saint of cockroach assassins, as the house used to be the headquarters of a company dedicated to the production of D.D.T. Some eighty years after it was erected, in 1907, the building still has a startling modernity about it.

The Tuchlauben which leads off to the left has some interesting houses, too, notably a Neo-Classical chemist's and the early eighteenth-century Hochholzerhof to its right. The Steindlgasse between them weaves its way to the least changed quarters of the city. The Gösserbierklinik offers appetizing Austrian cuisine and is a suitable halting post for lunch. The nearby Kurrentgasse contains a more sophisticated restaurant called the Ofen Loch. The Steindlgasse eventually leads to the picturesque Schulhof, where the Vienna clock museum is well worth at least a cursory inspection. To our left is the Gothic choir of the church Am Hof. We should bear this medieval exterior in mind when we later turn the corner and go inside. The palais at No. 4 Schulhof is the final jewel in the square, although its courtyard is a disappointment after the rich decoration of the mellow seventeenth-century façade, which is the very finest early Baroque.

An arch to the left leads to the square Am Hof (literally 'At the Court'), so called because it was here that Jasomirgott established his court when he made Vienna his capital. The square, like so many in Vienna, has suffered the ravages of cars but it remains a pleasant space bounded to the left by the Baroque church and to the right in the opposite corner by the sixteenth-century arsenal, now the headquarters of the Fire Brigade.

The church Am Hof, with its early seventeenth-century Baroque façade pushing out into the square, is a not particularly convincing attempt at Roman Baroque spatial effects as practised by Borromini. The interior has a hopelessly cluttered and tasteless nave dating from the first half of the seventeenth century, although the choir, with its striking coffering – so unexpected after the very Gothic exterior – is rather more successful. The church today is the city shrine of the Croat population of Vienna and on Sundays is crowded with happy, devout Balkan types.

On the same side of the square, at No. 12, is the Urbanikeller. No other part of the city gives a better impression of the seventeenth-century cellars that lie underneath most of the old city than this unpretentious restaurant. To step down its wooden stairs is to enter another world and to understand why the besieging Turks in 1683 set so much store by mining underneath the city's fortifications. An entry forced here, if successful, would have had dire consequences for the future of the city.

At the centre of the square stands a monument to the Virgin Mary, erected in 1667 by Kaiser Leopold I. The quaint putti contest, albeit with little obvious commitment, the evils of war, hunger and the plague.

From this square we can move back towards the town centre to the left and perhaps stop for a quick bite at the excellent Jugendstil Black Camel, the only bar and restaurant which offers Italian-style standing service for those in need of a quick bite. But to the right, past the Austrian flag factory, there is another interesting square, the Freyung.

The uninspired church here is the Benedictine Schottenkirche (1638–48), named after its first monks, who were of Celtic origin and were referred to as Scots, although it seems more likely that they were Irish. In any event they were Benedictines whom Heinrich Jasomirgott, impressed by what he had heard of this order's piety, decided to summon to Austria in 1150. But within a year of their arrival, these monks considerably ruffled the feathers of their Viennese hosts. According to a contemporary account, 'they stuck obstinately to their language and quarrelled constantly with the inhabitants'. They were reported to be trading in furs, initiating wild dances (reels?) and, most scandalously of all, starting 'games of ball'. This was the last straw. Duke Albrecht V told the monks that their monastery would no longer be restricted to Celts. Abbot Thomas's response to this decree manifested a robust disrespect, unashamedly Irish, for the authorities. He tersely announced that if monks of any other nationality entered the building, he and his fellow Hibernians would strangle them. Some German Benedictines who did attempt to enter were given a fierce drubbing. But by 1432 the Germans had succeeded in expelling these unwelcome guests and setting up a model, if less boisterous, monastery.

The courtyard today, with its austere Neo-Classicism, shows little sign of such disturbances, and the fine library (apply to the Abbot) has a tranquillity which is still completely monastic. A statue in the courtyard commemorates Jasomirgott, while a second courtyard offers a calm if inaccessible area of green. For a glimpse of anything dating from the turbulent years of Abbot Thomas we must enter the Schotten church.

This is the French church of the city and contains several monuments to French families who either fought for or served under the Habsburgs. The Baroque decoration of the interior, the work of A. Allio, is less fussy than that of the Am Hof church and there are some fine monuments, especially a Neo-Classical black marble one on the right, to balance this bland decor. The last altar on the left contains the oldest statue of a Madonna in Vienna, while the passage beyond the choir has some masonry and fragments of fresco which are contemporary with Abbot Thomas's rowdy monks. In the crypt below lies Jasomirgott himself, in a humble tomb one cannot help feeling Heinrich would have approved of.

Leaving the church, there is another characteristic coffee house at the Café Haag in the courtyard (Schottenhof). Back past the heavy monument on the church's façade is a nineteenth-century depiction of Jasomirgott's medieval virtues, and passing the fragrant herb chemist's the street soon leads to the Palais Schönborn, another precious creation of Fischer von Erlach. It no longer boasts its fine private painting collection, but the rooms on the first floor, now belonging to the Mexican embassy, are decorated in the best Viennese Rococo.

At Renngasse No. 12 there is a charming courtyard with a touching commemorative medallion to Kaiser Franz Josef and his wife, Elizabeth. Ahead, the Wipplingerstrasse leads to the left, to the Vienna Stock Exchange, a handsome building by Theophil Hansen, the architect of the Vienna Parliament, as quiet as a sepulchre, thanks to Austria's socialism. The road to the right leads to the curious Hohe Brücke ('High Bridge'), a remarkable testament to the dramatic differences in height between the innermost fortifications and the outer ring which would have fallen away from us to our left. A plaque above the art-nouveau metalwork of the bridge relates that this was the eastern gate into the city during the days of the Babenbergs.

The Schwertgasse to the left leads to another legacy of medieval times in Passauer Square, the church of Maria am Gestade. This church, even more than the cathedral, is the perfect antidote for those exhausted by a surfeit of the Baroque. The church's name, meaning literally 'On the Steps', refers to the fact that the stairs at the west end once led almost to the Danube, which ran here until it was rerouted in the 1890s by Otto Wagner. Fishermen deposited their catches here, and for this reason the church is the patron of all those concerned with the sea. Its magnificent façade was constructed between 1394 and 1427 after the plans of Michael Weinwurm. But the oldest part of the church is the long and spacious choir which dates from the mid fourteenth century, while the impressive tower, with its rich filigree work, is about a decade later.

The interior provides another opportunity for studying different periods of Gothic. The most striking element is the way in which the narrow nave suddenly opens, off-axis, to the wide choir. This is usually inaccessible except on Sundays, but an effort should be made to walk in it, to dispel the intimate but almost cramped feeling one gets in the nave. Few Gothic churches anywhere in Central Europe offer such an atmosphere of repose. Much of the glass is medieval, an extraordinary survival for Vienna, but its height precludes any chance of appreciating it except in the bright hours of the early morning. A phonomat guide machine, not usually to be recommended, is in this church an insight not so much into the history of the church as into the mentality of post-war Vienna. The slow, lugubrious, distinguished, charming but utterly bored voice evokes some penniless aristocrat of the 1950s resorting unwillingly to earning her keep by trading old linguistic skills.

From the Salvatorgasse, where there is a small chapel with a 1520 portal whose over-restored interior must be entered from the Wipplingerstrasse, there runs the small lane known as Stoss in Himmel. The narrow but busy Wipplingerstrasse beyond it has two façades which demand attention. First is the restored but still impressive façade of Fischer von Erlach's Bohemian chancery (1708–14), with an elaborate crowning portal. Then, standing opposite this, in the former Town Hall (Altes Rathaus), a dignified building of which the oldest part dates back to the fourteenth century. By a lateral wall in the court is the Andromeda fountain (1741), the last and most beautiful work of Raphael Donner.

Across this street, at the back of the Bohemian chancery, is the Judenplatz, one of the important centres of the former Jewish ghetto. The square is attractive despite the extraordinary 1950s representation of the great German writer Lessing which stands at – one hesitates to say adorns – its centre. The Café Altstadt is an unpretentious point at which to enjoy this square. Otherwise the Kurrentgasse (see p. 27) joins the square opposite the chancery.

From the other side of the square the Jordangasse runs into the Hoher Markt, with its vast dramatic Baroque Josef Column, designed by Fischer the Elder but executed by Fischer the Younger in 1733. The Hoher Markt, alas, no longer boasts the fruit markets which once enriched every square in Vienna, and it has an emptiness which no number of cars ever seems to be able to fill.

But there remains at least something of the grandeur which the late nineteenth century imparted to the square in the shape of the large palais of the Anker insurance building of 1910, with its remarkable clock. The clock strikes up an agreeable if ultimately pedantic tune on the hour while images of different Habsburg rulers move into place. Opposite this nineteenth-century gadgetry is a small self-effacing entrance to all that remains of the first constructions of the Romans at Vindobona, as they called their settlement here. This small archaeological museum, though of interest to anyone who takes their Gibbon seriously, will probably disappoint those who have explored the ruins of Pompei and are familiar with more expansive evidence of Roman times.

Behind the Fischer von Erlach monument runs the small Judengasse, which leads to what was the heart of the Vienna ghetto. It terminates in the Ruprechtsplatz, named after the church which stands there. The Ruprechtskirche, for all the importance given to it as the city's oldest church, is none the less rather disappointing, although from its medieval walls there is a fine view over the Ring to the Leopoldstadt, the traditional settlement of the poorer Vienna Jews before 1938.

To the left of the church is the Salzamt restaurant, a popular 'alternative' hostelry favoured by the more trendy Viennese. Under the arch to the right of the church is indeed the heartland of 'alternative' Vienna. In the Seitenstettengasse, one looks in vain for a *Wienerschnitzel*. Instead, opposite the long heavily guarded entrance to the city's principal synagogue (the cameras and policemen are necessary after a terrorist attack a few years ago), there is a series of excellent and imaginative restaurants. Mapitom offers pizzas, while the Roter Engel below is renowned for its jazz and its salad bar on the first floor. Opposite the Roter Engel is the extraordinary Krah Krah, an establishment offering over seventy types of beer, including Guinness for those who are longing to escape the chill of lager.

· THE EASTERN QUARTERS ·

Round the corner to our right up the Rabensteig is the former boundary of the Jewish quarter, the Rotenturmstrasse. Crossing this is the Fleischmarkt, which is now a street rather than a market and was for centuries the centre of Vienna's Greek community, traces of whom can still be seen here. The days when the city hosted the twenty races of the Habsburg empire have long past and Vienna no longer resounds to the cries of Montenegrin fruit sellers, Triestine fishermen, Hungarian businessmen and Polish Jews in Kaftans busily pursuing their trade. Few cities have lost so much cosmopolitan splendour so quickly. If at times Vienna overwhelms us with its petty provincialism, it must be remembered that this was not always the case and that only over the last two generations have the Viennese lost the great sense of irony and charm which helped them to rule most of Eastern Europe.

Fleischmarkt No. 7 evokes the earlier days particularly well. Here are the old headquarters of Austria's most renowned grocers, Meinl. Every city in the empire had a branch of Meinl before 1918, and as the façade of this imposing building shows, the organization not only embraced the great port of the empire, Trieste, but also London and Hamburg. Further on, the courtyard of No. 16 boasts a rarity for Vienna, a vegetarian restaurant, Siddhartha, which provides highly recommended alternatives to the heavier meat dishes found in most restaurants here.

Opposite stands the recently restored brick Greek Orthodox church, a delightful gold and red-brick building whose dark interior can be inspected for a small fee. The building strikes a curiously welcome note of nineteenth-century art.

Down the Griechengasse lies a picturesque part of the city in which it is possible to imagine something of what it meant to live near the Danube. The flat land beneath once bore the river, and the narrow houses to the right and left were used for storing goods, later to become part of an international traffic of wares which stretched down to the Black Sea. The grey Neo-Classical façade with a tower is that of the old eighteenth-century Greek Orthodox church, still open from 11 to 12 on Sundays.

Back in the Fleischmarkt, above, are the impressive rooms of the Griechische Beisl, one of the oldest and most characteristic restaurants in the city. No. 15 was the birthplace of one of the gifted Austrian painters of the nineteenth century, Moritz Schwind, and the façade, dating from 1717, is picturesque. On the right stands the Vienna Chamber Opera, which is well worth a visit, although productions vary enormously in quality.

At the Postgasse, enthusiasts of Jugendstil may like to turn right and then left into the Dominikanerbastei (the former inner bastion of the city) and behold the aluminium-bolted, marble façade of Otto Wagner's post office savings bank (1904–6). Otto Wagner and his school of younger architects did more than anyone to establish Austrian architecture as the most innovative in the world at the turn of the century. It was Wagner who was responsible for 'regulating' the Danube so that it no longer flowed where the Ringstrasse now runs beneath the Fleischmarkt. His bridges and his highly decorative use of metal in the construction of the Stadtbahn stations which dot the city all deserve close examination from anyone interested in seeing how art and engineering can work together.

The post office savings bank exemplifies perfectly Wagner's practical ability to harness new materials to ensure a building which would last and yet be pleasant to work in and look at. Austrian architecture of this period is far less fussy and altogether more disciplined than French or Belgian art-nouveau. The dramatic, light interior (entered from the Georg Coch Platz behind the façade on the Dominikanerbastei) is graffiti-proof and equipped with space-age-looking ventilators which must have infuriated the conservative Viennese.

Back at the Postgasse, the buildings are less revolutionary. On the left is the Ukrainian Orthodox church, with a fairy-tale pink Rococo altar. Opposite stands the austere Neo-Classical police headquarters, while beyond, with its Baroque façade rises the Dominican church.

Constructed between 1631 and 1634, the façade is largely the work of Antonio Canevale, an Italian architect who was inspired by the equally putti-filled façade of the Graz mausoleum (see p. 67). The interior shows the same delight in cherubic heads as the façade. The stalls, with curious balls carved above them, may have been inspired by the craftsmen of Krems church (see p. 58). The Baroque confessionals are equally well constructed, while the organ loft seems to be the highest in the city.

To the right of the church, the Bäckerstrasse leads among the old buildings of the university to Dr Ignaz Seipel Platz, one of the most picturesque squares in Vienna. Opposite rises the recently restored Academy of Sciences where Haydn's *Creation* received an early performance, while to the right, facing the impressive towering Jesuitenkirche, is a plaque recording Schubert's visits to the building as a chorister between 1810 and 1813.

But it is the Jesuitenkirche, with its remarkable tiered façade of 1631, which dominates the square. As at the Dominican church nearby, there is a fine wooden door at the west end, but the interior marks an altogether more dramatic approach to the Baroque. It is one of the most impressive in the city, and certainly the best of any of the churches planned on simple lines, bereft of the dramatic effect of domes. Here, instead, is a dazzling series of marble twisted columns, which is as daring as anything in Rome. Not surprisingly, its creator, who remodelled the interior in the first decade of the eighteenth century, was an Italian, Andrea Pozzo.

On Sundays, the church is usually full of those rather absurd scarred students who, wearing little caps and sashes, represent what is supposed to be the flower of Teutonic youth. As the university church, this building has been their rallying point for decades. As an escape from these faintly disturbing sights, the small lane on the right leads to the quaintly named Schönlaterngasse ('Lane of the Beautiful Lantern'). There are many bars and cafés between the early Baroque houses of this most charming street. Enrico Panigl, boasting, in old Habsburg style, branches in Trieste and Marienbad, is the most popular.

Further up the road, No. 7a was once, says a plaque, the home of the composer Robert Schumann, while No. 7, with its curious chicken effigy, recalls a tale of 1202, when Frederick II, finding himself surrounded by enemies, was led to an escape route by the animal so quaintly depicted on the façade of this house. Fixed to the façade opposite is the '*schön*' lantern after which the street is named. From this narrow road, a door to the right leads to a spacious oasis of calm, all the more welcome for its unexpectedness. This is the picturesque courtyard of the Heiligen-kreuzerhof, containing a fine acacia tree and a small chapel of 1610 usually open on Sunday mornings. The courtyard, part of the Cistercian foundation of Heiligenkreuz (see p. 54), dates from 1667. The Bernhards chapel is earlier, although its interior was redecorated in 1730 by Antonio Tassi with the assistance of Martino Altomonte. Few Baroque interiors in the city are as intimate, and it is well worth the effort of getting the key from the porter in a neighbouring building for a glimpse of it.

Back in the Schönlaterngasse, the Café Lukas offers comfortable art-nouveau sofas and arguably the best coffee in the city, though it is in many ways the least traditional coffee-house in Vienna. The Sonnenfelsgasse at the end of the street and the small Windhaaggasse lead us to the equally picturesque Bäckerstrasse. The place to eat here is Oswald and Kalb's restaurant, which offers some of the best of Austrian cooking in pleasant surroundings, which, if cramped, are unmistakably Viennese (book in advance). Further along the road is the Weincomptoir, another popular meeting place, less chaotic than Oswald and Kalb's.

The Essiggasse to the left and the Wollzeile beyond lead to one of the more interesting if less well-known museums to be seen in the city, the Art Industry and Applied Arts Museum. Its red brick façade, designed by one of the most prolific Ringstrasse architects, Heinrich Ferstel, in the 1860s, has a South Kensington feel to it, which is quite natural, for in its own way this is Vienna's modest V. and A. The interior hall is pleasantly decorated in the Pompeian style, with an attractive imitation della Robbia well in its north-east corner. To the right are a collection of medieval vestments, some unimpressive stained glass and a series of Islamic rooms. Beyond, the most interesting rooms are those containing specimens of late German and Tyrolean Renaissance furniture and some seventeenth-century dolls-house rooms.

The first floor contains several Jugendstil rooms, beginning with the work of Josef Hoffmann, a gifted pupil of Otto Wagner, who with several other artists formed the Wiener Werkstätte, a firm renowned for producing the best of Austrian design at the beginning of this century. As the exhibits admirably show, Hoffmann and his colleagues were prepared to design everything from grandfather clocks to egg-cups. The cutlery, though impressive in design, was rarely practical. Adolf Loos, who mightily disapproved of the Wiener Werkstätte, called such things 'cutlery designed for those who have no idea how to eat'. Loos's Anglophile tastes are revealingly shown in his comfortable and rather informal sofa arrangement with Burne-Jones illustrations in the screen panels. In the following room are studies for the Klimt frieze of the Palais Stoclet, a spectacular house designed by Hoffmann in Brussels in 1906.

Across the Ring in the Karl Lueger Platz is the Café Prückel. This once glittering establishment has never fully recovered from having served as a Russian cavalry barracks after the Second World War. In damp weather the square often gives off even today a faintly discernible smell of the stable. But the Prückel remains a favourite especially with the older generation, who come in their dozens to play cards each afternoon, and few cafés manifest such a buzz of geriatric activity on a damp cold afternoon.

Back up the Wollzeile and beyond the yellow König von Ungarn Hotel is the entrance to the Domgasse, where stands the house in which Mozart first lived in Vienna. Some of its exhibits appear closely connected with the composer, while others, though interesting, have little relevance to Mozart's stay in the capital.

The Grünangergasse, at the corner of the Domgasse, has the imposing Baroque Palais Fürstenberg, whose portal is guarded by two stone greyhounds. On one side of the street, which is one of the best-preserved architectural ensembles in the city, is the Green Anchor, which eighty years ago was one of the best-known Italian restaurants in the empire. It still has considerable charm. In the summer, it is possible to sit outside in the shadow of the cathedral's soaring tower and enjoy a first-class wine list. The speciality of this restaurant, which must be sampled, is the so-called *Schlosserbuben*, a chocolate and nut pudding which is unrivalled.

The Singerstrasse beyond is dominated on the left by the handsome Palais Rottal, designed in 1750 by Franz Hillebrandt, one of the second division of Austria's Baroque architects. The façade makes effective use of pilasters without capitals, a favourite motif of the period. The entire street towards the cathedral is rich in Baroque houses, of which the grandest is the Palais Neupauer, erected in 1715 by an unknown architect.

Across the Singerstrasse, there is an even more picturesque ensemble in the form of the Franziskanerplatz. This square, with its uneven roofline and fountain – alas, usually surrounded by cars – has remained virtually unchanged for centuries. The towering chimneys of the corner houses and the elegant gables of the Franciscan church façade combine attractively with the ironwork of the Baroque house on the Weihburggasse. Flanked by a green painted wooden front is the notorious Kleines Café, the coffee-house for the 'alternative' middle-aged of the city, daily resounding to the cries of children, usually wheeled in by their unmarried mothers between shopping expeditions.

The square's fountain depicts Moses and dates from 1798. The Franciscan church, with its attached cloister, is a strange building. The roundels which mark the façade were once the only windows, as the establishment was first conceived as a house of correction from which its hapless inmates would not be permitted to look out onto the road beyond. The church was begun in 1603, but there are Gothic as well as Renaissance elements in the front. Predictably, the interior is mainly Baroque, with a high altar by Andrea Pozzo, whose work we have already admired in the Jesuitenkirche. Above stands an exquisitely carved organ which dates from the seventeenth century. A fashionable church on Sunday, it is much in demand for society weddings.

Under an archway in the south corner of the square begins the old and winding Ballgasse, which leads past various cafés to the Rauhensteingasse. No. 8, which houses one of the best bakeries in the city, is impressively Baroque, and on the site of the house next door Mozart composed his *Magic Flute* and *Requiem*, and died.

The Rauhensteingasse leads to the Himmelpfortgasse and the Café Frauenhuber, a long-established café which adheres rigidly to the rules of coffee nomenclature. It may therefore be a suitable moment to point out that simply ordering 'a coffee' is impossible in Vienna. Every shade is given a name, to say nothing of optional extras like cocoa powder, whipped cream, rum or even eggs. The term '*Melange*' will usually produce the familiar coffee with milk. But those who require a stronger cup will usually order '*einen braunen*' or, if no milk whatsoever is desired, '*eine schwarze Mokka*'. Coffee with masses of whipped cream, usually served in a glass, is known as an *Einspänner*, while different shades of the popular *Melange* can be ordered by reference to the colour of certain monastic orders' habits. Thus a *Franziskaner* is lighter than a *Capuziner*. Different cafés have slightly varying definitions, but the above will serve as a general guide in all the older establishments.

Next door to the Frauenhuber is a remarkable secular work of Fischer von Erlach, Prince Eugen of Savoy's Winter Palace built between 1695 and 1698. Much has been written about the delicate sculpture of the façade, the noble proportioning of the storeys and the dramatic use of pilasters. The palace now houses the Austrian Exchequer. Its staircase represents the culmination of Fischer's highly plastic style and manifests a break with the traditions of Roman Baroque. No Italian architect would have resorted to the curiously tortured and weird forms Fischer delights in here.

· THE SOUTHERN QUARTERS ·

At the end of the Himmelpfortgasse is a depressing sight: the busiest and alas ugliest principal thoroughfare of the city, the Kärtnerstrasse, spoiled by tacky department stores and a series of lanterns which must rank among the most hideous of any city in Europe.

Crossing over into the altogether more agreeable Neuer Markt, we should (without failing to admire the more pleasing façades above the shops) make straight for the red, restored Capuchin church (1622–32). Few façades are as dull and unprepossessing. But the door on the left gives entrance into the most hallowed quarters of imperial Vienna, the Habsburg vaults. It will be recalled that the hearts of the Habsburgs are in the Augustine church, but their tombs are mostly here. The vaults are open every day of the year and visitors are exhorted to conduct themselves in a respectful and silent manner. However, once the garish staircase into the vaults has been negotiated, the bold letters demanding 'Silentium' seem a little pointless as, unless we are very lucky, the sound of tour groups each hearing a detailed description of the personages contained within the sarcophagi will destroy any sense of mystery surrounding this macabre resting place. The lunch hour or the late afternoon, before the *Gruft* closes, are the best times to contemplate these sombre relics in peace.

We arrive at the end of the stairs in the 'old vault', enlarged in 1701. This contains the sarcophagi of the earliest Habsburgs, from Matthias (d. 1619) onwards. To the left is the new vault, added in 1748 and dominated by the Baroque hyperbole of Maria Theresa's enormous double sarcophagus in which she lies with her husband. As befits his character, an altogether far less showy sarcophagus contains the remains of Joseph II. Beyond stands the more 'empire' tomb of Francis I. To the right of this room a low dark vault contains the sarcophagi of Archduke Charles, the Austrian general who defeated Napoleon at the battle of Aspern, Maximilian, the ill-fated emperor of Mexico who met his death at the hands of a revolutionary firing squad in 1867 (see p. 218), and, opposite, the beautiful Marie Louise, the second wife of Napoleon, who died in 1847.

A room straight ahead leads to Franz Josef (d. 1916), who reigned for over sixty years, and his wife, the Empress Elizabeth. The third tomb is that of another Habsburg to die violently, Crown Prince Rudolf, victim of the hunting lodge tragedy at Mayerling in 1889. The stream of myths and stories which surround Rudolf's death are unequalled in modern royal fiction, and mystery still surrounds what is generally believed to have been a suicide pact with his mistress, Marie Vetsera (see p. 53).

Beyond, an altar marks an empty vault kept immaculately clean. A bust of Austria's last emperor, Kaiser Karl, who died in exile on the island of Madeira in 1922, marks one wall. Whether he will return from that island to lie here among his dynastic relatives is a thorny question for the Austrian government, ever wary of anything which might arouse monarchist feeling, but in the meantime an army of cleaners keep every square inch spotless.

Another Habsburg who was a contemporary of Karl's and does not lie here is the Archduke Franz Ferdinand, the heir to the Habsburg throne whose assassination was the fuse to the First World War. He had married a mere countess, much to the horror of his imperial and royal relatives, and rather than allow himself to be buried away from her, he insisted long before he met his death with her on the streets of Sarajevo that they should enjoy each other's company for ever at the castle of Artstetten along the Danube. He is reported to have dismissed the imperial vaults with the words: 'I would never have any peace lying there with electric trams rattling overhead all the time.'

From the Capuchin vaults, a brief walk past the Tirolerhof Café (see p. 21) leads to the Opera, opposite which stands the best-known hotel in the city, the Sacher. Sacher's is clearly not what it was. The unlimited credit afforded to favoured guests in Frau Sacher's time is today almost non-existent, so that the culinary delights of the restaurant (especially to be recommended is the *Kalbschnitzel Eduard Sacher*) cannot be enjoyed with credit cards. Even cheques are rarely accepted. But these slight irritations aside, the rooms of the Sacher, like its Kaffeehaus, boast a collection of paintings no hotel in the world can rival. Even Otto von Habsburg, the present heir to the Habsburg claims, peers in full-dress Austrian uniform between Biedermeier paintings on a second-floor corridor. The hall of the hotel also contains a photograph gallery, open most evenings after five o'clock, which houses portraits of the most distinguished guests who have stayed here, including members of the British military government whose officers' mess this was after the Second World War. The famous Austrian aristocratic names of Herberstein and Czernin appear as smudged signatures across the uniforms of the most dashing nobility Europe ever knew.

From the Opera, it is just a couple of minutes' walk to the Karlsplatz where, as well as some of Otto Wagner's more quaint railways stations, recently restored in vivid golds and greens, there is another monument of the fertile Jugendstil period, the Secession building, constructed by Wagner's most gifted pupil, Josef Olbrich, in 1897–8. Its copper 'cabbage' dome and very simple form enraged the Viennese, but the building served as a suitably unconventional home for the exhibitions of all the great turn-of-the-century artists. Klimt, Hoffmann and Kolo Moser all exhibited here in protest at the conservative and reactionary artists of the Academy. Today the building boasts no such talented or revolutionary exhibits and those who wish to see more of Vienna's 'golden period' should pursue the Wienzeile, past the markets and well-known Saturday morning antique fairs, to the mosaiced and highly decorative houses of Otto Wagner, a few hundred yards down on the right.

Those, however, who prefer the more sumptuous delights of the Baroque should cross the Karlsplatz to examine Fischer von Erlach's supreme ecclesiastical achievement, the Karlskirche. Few churches even of the Baroque period made as much use of the dramatic and monumental devices available to their architects as this extraordinary building. One glance is enough to convince anyone that it is a most remarkable creation.

The commission to build the church was given to Fischer by the emperor in fulfilment of a vow made to St Charles Borromeo in 1713, as thanksgiving for deliverance from the plague (see p. 10). As in Fischer's great church the Kollegienkirche in Salzburg, the façade is kept low, but here because of the breadth of the site – the façade stretches to over 180 feet in its entirety. Drawing on his immense knowledge of 'world architecture' – Fischer was the first architect to write a history of architecture – he employed Roman Trajan columns modelled on those in the Forum to flank the façade, with reliefs symbolizing the victory of faith over disease.

The actual portico is also coolly classical rather than Baroque, while the tops of the flanking columns draw on the forms of Turkish tents and mosques. After this impressive *tour de force*, the interior, though no less striking, is surprisingly much smaller than the façade suggests.

The soaring dual dome was executed after Fischer's death in 1723 by his son and is as impressive as that in the National Library.

To the façade's right is a plain modern building, the Historisches Museum der Stadt Wien, which is interesting for the light it throws on Vienna's development. A series of matchbox models of the city made with great care in the nineteenth century show better than anything what Vienna looked like before the Ringstrasse. Between the fine collection of portraits and Vienna memorabilia, there is a series of rooms showing interior decoration of the Empire and Biedermeier periods. The most interesting of the rooms is perhaps that of Adolf Loos's (see p. 11) old flat, complete with English fireplace, hearth and mahogany panelling. Nearby are some exquisite drawings by Otto Wagner as well as portraits by Klimt.

After a pleasant hour spent in the Historisches Museum, there could be nothing better than a coffee in the Imperial Hotel's café, which lies down the Ring to the right of the museum. Unlike virtually every other hotel in the Austrian capital, the Imperial was formerly an aristocratic palais and boasts a most impressive staircase, although its paintings have little to show compared with the Sacher. It was the Russian officers' mess until 1955, when the Allies left the city.

The other hotel which is part of a palais is the Schwarzenberg, behind the square of the same name nearby, which today is dominated by an enormous and it must be admitted impressive monument to Russian soldiery. It is the most vivid reminder of the Russian occupation of Vienna, which even though its effect was diluted by the presence of the other great powers, has left most older Viennese with a lasting phobia of all things communist. The chief glories of the Palais Schwarzenberg are its late Baroque rooms and its garden, both of which are open only to its guests. But in summer there can be few more enjoyable escapes from the bustle of the centre than to penetrate these charming avenues, which are the perfect foil to this architectural masterpiece, which was begun in 1697.

A side entrance in front of the town façade of the palace leads to the Rennweg and after a few minutes to an entrance into the courtyard of another of Hildebrandt's masterpieces, the Lower Belvedere (begun in 1719). From the former stable blocks stretches another series of formal gardens, which after negotiating several ramps and fountains reach the front façade of Hildebrandt's remarkable Summer Palace (1721–3) for Prince Eugen of Savoy, the great general whose Winter Palace was designed by Fischer von Erlach (p. 38).

At the top of the slight ascent (under the watchful gaze of the sphinxes) a superb view of the spires and domes of central Vienna, with the Vienna Woods in the background, can be enjoyed. Almost inevitably, depending on the time of year, the spectator will be seared by a freezing wind or gently fanned into a state of doziness by a warm one. The latter experience is due to the infamous *Föhn* wind, which is said to drive the weak to insanity and the strong-willed to suicide.

As long as it is not Monday, shelter from the wind can be found in the Upper Belvedere, which houses the nineteenth- and early twentieth-century collections of Austrian art and contains some of the greatest examples of Secession art to be seen anywhere. The ground floor usually houses examples of the country's post-war art, which can be dealt with quite briskly. Above, the principal floor is given over to examples of the Biedermeier period and later nineteenth-century artists. The works of Waldmüller, with their brightly coloured genre scenes, follow the inspiration of the Pre-Raphaelites, while the portraits of Makart have a stagy glamour which is more Italian-inspired. By far the most remarkable painter to be seen on this floor is Anton Romako, a Czech who romanized his name in the 1860s during a prolonged and addictive period of study in Rome. His work varies in quality enormously, but the portrayal of Admiral Tegetthoff standing on the bridge of the *Erzherzog Max* as that ship rammed the *Re d'Italia* at the battle of Lissa in 1866 must be one of the most dramatic and original naval pictures ever painted. Ironically, as this action was taking place, the Italian painter Ippolito Caffi was attempting to paint the battle from the bridge of the ill-fated Italian flagship, which promptly sank, consigning both crew and painter to a watery grave.

The top floor of the Belvedere begins promisingly with Klimt's view of Sonja Knijps, radiant in a pink dress. Miss Knijps's enigmatic look of anxiety tinged with longing greets the visitor at the turn of the stairs. In the same room, there is Klimt's later and almost equally seductive *Lady with a Cobra Scarf*. Almost every painting here – such as the strange portraits by Egon Schiele, culminating in the moving and calm *Self-Portrait with Wife and Child* – is worth long and unhurried study. In addition to these masterpieces, there are also works by Kokoschka, Faistauer and, rather more disturbing, Richard Gerstl, whose self-portrait is as gruesome a premonition of insanity as anything Van Gogh committed to canvas.

The prints in the gallery rooms below include a beautiful series of cartoons executed at the turn of the century for Hugo von Hofmannsthal, the great Austrian playwright, illustrating the life and achievements of the palace's founder, Prince Eugen. Here we can see clearly the deformed sickly prince being rejected by both Prussian and French courts before storming Belgrade for Austria.

From this gallery, it is possible to look down into the magnificent Marmorsaal, with its fine parquet floor and gilt mural decorations, where Austria's state treaty was signed in 1955. The Belvedere gallery contains a café, where, if there is time, strength can be gathered for a visit to the Military History Museum, housed in a brick polychromatic edifice within the equally dazzling Victorian former imperial arsenal behind the Belvedere.

These extraordinary buildings (entered through 'Objekt I') were constructed beyond the city in the 1850s so that should Vienna's student population cut up rough, as they did in 1848, artillery could be used from a distance to bombard them into submission. Although this may seem at first glance one of the least interesting museums in the city, there is much to be seen in it which was intimately connected with the fate of Austria and Europe.

The museum itself was designed by Hansen, the architect of the Austrian Parliament. The Hall of Heroes gives an interesting insight into the cosmopolitan nature of Austria's army. Among the generals here portrayed in stone are Irishmen such as Lacy, Kray and O'Donnell, some Italians such as Montecuccoli and of course plenty of well-known Germans. It is to be regretted perhaps that the 'heroes' also include General Haynau, who flogged Italian women and children during the 1848 revolutions, so outraging English opinion that when he visited a London brewery a little later the workmen promptly threw the portly officer into a barrel of ale.

In the room to our left, there is a fine display of uniforms, which, though colourful, cannot match the rich attire worn by the English and the French in the nineteenth century. Exceptions to this are of course the splendid garments of the Hungarian Life Guard. A British Silver Dragoon's helmet is all that remains of Kaiser Franz Josef's uniform as honorary colonel of the 1st Queen's Dragoon Guards, a regiment which to this day fondly remembers its former honorary Colonel in Chief.

But it is the following room which offers the most memorable symbol of what all this once meant. Here in a glass case lies the blood-stained uniform of a cavalry general. A portrait of the officer gazes enigmatically into space, while on the right stands the Austro–Daimler which bore the officer to his doom on the 28 June 1914. The officer was Franz Ferdinand, heir to the Habsburg throne, who with his wife was brutally murdered by a teenager's revolver, so precipitating one of the bloodiest conflicts in the history of mankind, a conflict which was the end for all the imperial glory we have just walked through and for much else as well. Newspaper cuttings from all over the world, including England, express the outrage that was felt at this deed, while in the room beyond loom the large howitzers which were to wreak such destruction in the years that followed.

The rooms above concentrate on Austria's achievements during the Napoleonic and Seven Years wars, happily replacing the gloom of the 'Grande Illusion' below with a colourful toy-soldier world. For those in need, the arsenal has a comfortable café.

From here it is but a few steps to the Museum of Modern Art, which houses the best of contemporary Austrian work with a small selection of foreign work. Occasionally there are exhibitions from prestigious foreign museums, such as the Metropolitan Museum of Art in New York, which recently supplied an exhibition of surrealist art. Otherwise, it must be admitted, as museums of modern art go, there is little to detain the enthusiast here for long, although some of the canvases of Georg Eisler, a pupil of Kokoschka, merit attention.

Those who wish to see more modern art should take from here the D tram back into the centre of Vienna and beyond, where an interesting collection of modern art is housed in the grand Liechtenstein Palace on the Porzellangasse in Vienna's ninth district. Open every day except Tuesday, its spacious late Baroque rooms were designed by Domenico Martinelli in 1705 and provide, with their religious frescoes by Rottmayr and Andrea Pozzo in the main saloon, an incongruous setting for a varied collection of abstract, modern and surrealist art.

At about 2.30 p.m., a bizarre electronic creation of the surrealist Tinguely fills the entrance hall with a mysterious but not unpleasant cacophany. Above, the piano nobile contains work by modern American and European surrealists. Naked bodies, collages of broken crockery, neon-lightning bolts striking bales of hay, and an entire dinner table attached to a wall and decorated with burnt-out cigarettes and stale bread, untouched since the sixties, are only the most striking of these exhibits. The staff of the museum retain a remarkable air of insouciance amid these distractions.

The top floor contains a number of fine Secession paintings, one well-known portrait of the great Austrian writer Karl Kraus by Kokoschka and a rather dull Klimt portrait of Frau Bauer-Bloch. Next door are works by Klee, Schwitters and Max Ernst and a beautifully finished Magritte.

If it is still light, it may be a pleasant alternative to the Porzellangasse to turn right at the entrance and then left up the recently restored Strudlhofstiege. These steps' insensitive restoration belies the touching words of Heimito von Doderer's poetic inscription.

Above, the Boltzmanngasse contains the American embassy in an imposing palais, while the Währingerstrasse beyond has two palaces of more than average architectural interest. Walking down into the city, on the right we come to the Josephinum, a fine palace of the 1780s designed by Isidor Canevale for the education of military medical officers which contains an interesting pathology museum with gruesome clay models. Opposite, further down the road, is the effete Palais Clam-Gallas, designed in 1835 by a rather undistinguished Neo-Classical architect called Koch.

The Southern Railway station near the Museum of Modern Art has trams back to the Schwarzenbergplatz, where at the restaurant Czardasfürstin in the nearby Seilerstätte a taste for Hungarian cuisine can be acquired.

Our tour of the inner city complete, it is time to explore some of the outlying districts of the city.

· JOSEFSTADT ·

Behind the Town Hall, where the Friedrich Schmidt Platz stands with its heavy and not very attractive eclectic buildings, lies the Josefstadt, one of the most charming suburbs of Vienna which in recent years has taken on a new lease of life as a home for many of the artistic and more creative elements of the city.

The Florianigasse leads between cafés into the heart of this area. As well as several small antique shops, the road boasts a fine Italian restaurant, known as Scarabocchio. At the corner of the Schlösselgasse stands the house where Emanuel Schikaneder, the librettist of Mozart's *Die Zauberflöte*, died.

Past the public baths of the Langegasse is the Piaristengasse, full of small shops and tailors. The street itself has a striking surprise in the form of the rather unattractively named Jodok Fink Platz, which none the less is one of the most charming squares in the city. It is dominated by the impressive Baroque Piaristen (Maria Treu) church which was designed by Hildebrandt in the late 1680s but completed by Mathias Gerl almost a century later. Its remarkable plan, spatially one of the most daring in the city, would seem to have been inspired by Borromini's

Sant'Agnese in Rome. The space wanders out of every corner in a quite un-Viennese way.

Continuing along the street, No. 41 is as forbidding a Ringstrasse palais as any to be found in the city, while No. 27, one of the last town *Heurigens* (see p. 51), offers a delightful if unassuming garden in which to enjoy a glass of wine during the early evening. To the left under an arch stands the English theatre, with its prim but elegant turn-of-the-century interior, while to the right the Rotenhof offers more Teutonic entertainment, being the home of one of the famous *Burschenschaften*, or pan-German student clubs, whose members to this day carry sabres with which to inflict on each other the requisite marks of so-called manliness and comradeship. Even in a street lined with Biedermeier houses and trees, the sight of these weapons hanging on the walls inside causes a frisson of unease to Anglo-Saxon sensibilities.

The Lerchenfelderstrasse offers a pleasing vista of towers and one very exciting twenties building. Across down the undistinguished Kellermanngasse is the Neustiftgasse, with its buildings by Otto Wagner on the right.

To the left, across the Neustiftgasse, however, is the charming St Ulrichs Platz, with the Café Nepomuk, a modern but attractive resting place. The entire square is unearthly in its abandoned but picturesque state. The church is relatively undistinguished late Baroque, but the house at No. 2, dating from the mid-1700s, is a not-to-be-missed gem with a courtyard and chapel.

The Burggasse opposite the church's west entrance is a long road offering a fine view of the centre of the city and its cathedral spire. Following the road down and taking the Spittelberggasse on the right, we shall soon reach the cobbled streets of a quarter which, if not quite in the Josefstadt, possesses a no less engaging urban ensemble. Here there are many beer houses and small restaurants sandwiched among the houses. At the far end lies the Siebensterngasse, with its Baroque inns, dominated by the vast flak towers erected under the 'thousand-year Reich' to defend the city from allied bombing in the Second World War. From here a tram or a brisk five-minute walk will bring us back to the Ring and the city centre.

47

· SCHÖNBRUNN ·

From the underground station of the Josefstädterstrasse, behind the Rathaus, a train will take us to another delightful suburb of the city: Hietzing and the exquisite park of Schönbrunn. Alighting at Schönbrunn, take the first entrance to the park, which stretches from here to the next station, Hietzing. The park, which covers 197 hectares, is laid out in the French eighteenth-century style, with formal hedges and dramatic vistas enlivened by the usual architectural fripperies of the age. In a delightful temple-like house hidden among the trees, an old lady offers glasses of water from a centuries-old spring. Behind some other bushes is an unpretentious restaurant, while nearby at the end of one vista there seems to rise from the ground a Piranesian pile of columns and entablatures. Farther on, a large basin with Neptunes, seahorses and Tritons contains a pair of suitably dramatic fountains.

But the most interesting construction in the park is the Gloriette, which sits grandly on a hill overlooking the palace. It is a dull but useful building, offering from its roof exquisite views of Vienna, views which have not changed that much since the days when Napoleon, who made Schönbrunn his headquarters in 1809, looked out from the very same spot. As in the Belvedere and parts of the Hofburg, there is an inevitable scattering of sculptured headless warriors commemorating imaginary feats of arms. Even in the summer, the park can seem quite empty towards sunset, and the Gloriette, designed by Hohenburg in 1775, loses its classical coolness, becoming bathed in a rich golden light.

The actual palace, whose origins go back to the fourteenth century, is best seen from here. Although only part of Fischer von Erlach's grandiose plans were realized – the Seven Years War interrupted his scheme to turn this into a grander palace than Versailles – and much was altered by Pacassi in the 1740s, its pleasing yellow façade is impressive under a summer sky. Close to, the detailing is rather tacky and the disastrous colour scheme of the garden flowers and yellow garden façade does not help. The interior of the palace is one of the disappointments of Central Europe. Of the 1,441 rooms, only a handful are shown, and few of these are either well decorated or possess any grandeur. Of historical value only is the extraordinary Empire Room – where has all the furniture gone? – in which Napoleon's son, the Duke of Reichstadt, died.

The former stables nearby contain a modest collection of carriages, while the road façade of the palace has two obelisks crowned by Napoleonic eagles placed there during his brief stay and never removed by the Habsburgs.

A walk across the garden brings us to Hietzing. This western part of the park contains a menagerie, the zoological gardens and the botanical gardens, with a monumental but rather inelegant palm house rarely open to the public. Most of the lawns, despite their somewhat rough surface, are not to be walked on, but on summer afternoons the keepers who are supposed to enforce this petty rule rarely exert themselves and the *Rasen* can be trod with impunity.

Leaving the Schlosspark at the western gate we come to the Hietzing village square, with its statue of Maximilian of Mexico and its Gothic church. At the start of a woody avenue – the Auhofstrasse – is the finest café in all Vienna, perhaps in all Europe: Dommayers. Dommayers deserves this accolade not so much because it was the favourite haunt of Johann Strauss or because its interior is light, unstuffy and bustling with elegance and English newspapers but because it combines these things with food of considerable quality. To breakfast here on ham and eggs or on the superb joghurts with hot blackcurrants is a delight. True, the service may seem a little aged, but patience is nowhere better rewarded in Vienna than in this establishment. The garden in summer is another agreeable feature of the café.

· THE PRATER ·

The evening dealt with in so civilized a manner, it only remains to cross the Danube Canal to discover a part of Vienna which offers considerable attraction at night, the famous Prater, with its giant wheel so brilliantly filmed in 1949 in the *The Third Man*. It can easily be reached by the underground. The square we emerge from is dominated by the imposing Tegetthoff monument, dedicated to the naval hero of Lissa (see p. 43).

Before embarking on any of the entertainments the Prater offers, we must of course first pay homage to the 'Big Wheel', the symbol of the park and as much an association with the Austrian capital as any waltz by Strauss. It was designed by a British engineer called Walter Basset, who in the 1880s, after service in the Royal Navy, designed a number of wheels for fairgrounds in Europe. This one was almost identical to one in Paris and another in Blackpool and is the only survivor of the three.

Badly damaged in the last war, it has been restored to its former glory. A touching if somewhat faded exhibition of photographs portrays its creator, resplendent in full-dress naval uniform, and the various stages of its construction, as well as predictably a couple of stills from the film which immortalized the wheel.

Equally inevitable, given that we are in Vienna, is the pace of the machine. But on an autumnal afternoon, there is no better way of escaping the high façades of the old city than to rise slowly above the richly coloured chestnuts of the Prater Hauptallee. All the green so sadly absent in the city is revealed before our eyes, the formal planning of the chestnut avenues cutting lines into the far distance.

Compared to this, the more conventional fare of ghost trains, miniature railway, helter-skelters etc. seem an anti-climax, although the tall Danube Tower nearby offers the very sixties thrill of a revolving restaurant.

3

EXCURSIONS FROM VIENNA

After touring the capital, it is time to explore the picturesque environs of Vienna. All the following excursions take a full day and are best undertaken in favourable weather.

· THE VIENNA WOODS, MAYERLING
AND BADEN ·

As most guides quite rightly point out, no tour of Vienna is complete without a visit to a *Heurigen*, one of the inns in the Vienna Woods selling the young and somewhat astringent local Heurige white wine, which customers invariably dilute with soda water. The food at these establishments is often first-class, especially the bread and Liptauer orange-coloured cheese, but in recent years many have become tourist traps which the more discerning traveller should try to avoid. Grinzing and Kahlenberg, the two most traditional locations for *Heurigens*, are now almost entirely filled with coach-loads of tourists, although during the winter a visit to Reblaus in Grinzing still provides an opportunity to savour something of the old *Heurigen* atmosphere.

A far better idea is to take the tram to Pötzleinsdorf and the bus thence to Neustift-am-Walde and walk along the Agnesweg over the hill to Sievering, a delightfully unspoilt village which contains several excellent *Heurigen*, of which Agnes is perhaps the most renowned. The delightful Biedermeier houses which make up upper and lower Sievering repay considerable study and so far its leafy calm has not been spoilt by buses of American or Italian tourists 'doing' a *Heurigen* under the supervision of some hapless girl attired in a dirndl.

To enjoy the Vienna Woods fully, however, it is essential to go farther afield and take a train from the Südbahnhof to either Mödling or Baden.

MÖDLING is a village just on the edge of the Vienna Woods over-looking the Danube plain towards Hungary. Its town museum is full of nostalgic photographs of the remarkable railway which used to run from here across the valley to Hinterbrühl. Although the town has been done up recently with rather excessive zeal, especially as regards the positioning of nineteenth-century lanterns, there are several medieval buildings. Along the main road past the museum towards the church are some with frescoed façades.

At the time of the Turkish wars, Mödling suffered terribly. The entire population was put to the sword, a tragedy recorded by numerous memorial stones to the left of the church on the hill. Although a Romanesque chapel nearby contains several fragments of frescoes, the church itself has lost much of its atmosphere because of an over-enthusiastic restoration programme.

From this church a path winds round to the left towards a fine old viaduct which once carried the railway to Vorderbrühl. It then descends between dramatic rocks, crosses the road and soon ascends to the ruined castle of Mödling, with its extensive views across the country. A further path leads along the so-called Drei Stunden Weg (Three Hours' Path), a delightful walk which can be easily accomplished in far less time, to the Husaren temple. This temple, with its Neo-Classical columns, is a kind of miniature Austrian Valhalla erected by Prince Liechtenstein as a tomb for the seven hussars who died saving his life from an attack of French cavalry during the battle of Aspern (see p. 5). It is a bleak, windy place, hauntingly beautiful in autumn. Returning to Mödling, just before we reach the town, a path to the right, described as the Beethoven Wanderweg, eventually comes to Baden; but for those who are already exhausted by walking, a train from Mödling will convey them to that town after a cake at one of Mödling's fine cafés or a meal at one of the many Italian restaurants in the centre.

BADEN is very much the Brighton of Austria, without, of course, the sea. Despite its 'casino', it is predominantly a place for the elderly, with hundreds of old-age pensioners taking the waters or listening to a military band playing Johann Strauss or Carl Michael Ziehrer, that little-known nineteenth-century composer who was responsible for the best marches ever written for the Austrian army.

Like Mödling, the town centre boasts a generously lanterned pedestrian zone, but unlike that town Baden can actually lay claim to being a former Habsburg summer residence, though one which was peculiarly Biedermeier. Near the main square there stands an unassuming Biedermeier house where the last Holy Roman Emperor, Francis, lived in the early years of the nineteenth century. Unlike his residence at Laxenburg (see p. 54), a mock castle where he could play at medieval splendour, this house was a gesture to the bourgeoisie, suggesting that, though apostolic and all highest, Francis was none the less a rather easygoing fellow.

From here there are paths through the woods to various inns, or there is a bus from the station to another place rich in Habsburg memories, MAYERLING. Of the hunting lodge which saw the tragic deaths of Crown Prince Rudolf and his lover, Marie Vetsera, in 1889, nothing remains, for the Emperor Franz Josef insisted immediately that the building should be demolished. Today, almost a hundred years after the event, the truth of that winter evening is still a matter for conjecture. It is generally accepted that the two committed suicide, and indeed this version of the events has inspired a host of films, plays and ballets. But in 1983 the Empress Zita, the last Habsburg to have enjoyed power (from 1916 to 1918), told Austrian journalists that the Crown Prince was murdered by French agents frustrated at his refusal to seize power and form an alliance with France rather than imperial Germany. The theory is plausible and one must ask why an old lady of over ninety should want to lie, but there are many historians who dispute the empress's sources and dismiss her theory as an attempt to remove the stain of suicide from the house of Habsburg, which, being a Catholic dynasty, naturally found such a conclusion abhorrent.

The Carmelite convent which is now situated between these picturesque hills contains a memorial chapel to Rudolf and a couple of rooms which attempt to give us the flavour of his character. The coloured portrait, a photograph taken shortly before his death, shows a sensitive man, smoking a cigar, who obviously possessed great personal charm. His ideas for the future of the Habsburg monarchy were advanced and his learning prodigious. Like many a crown prince destined to live out the prime of his life without any actual power, his mind was troubled both by melancholy and frustration. But the beauty of these woods around Mayerling dispel any feeling of sadness, and there is a pleasant inn nearby to satisfy the appetite before the relatively short walk to HEILIGENKREUZ. The walk through the woods is well signposted, but since the construction of the southern motorway part of it is less charming than it was. It remains, however, a pleasant excursion of about forty minutes, mainly through thick deciduous forests.

The Cistercian monastery at Heiligenkreuz is a foundation dating back to the days of the Babenberg Leopold III (ruled 1095–1136) and is situated at the foot of a Calvarian hill. Although partly destroyed by the Turks in 1683, the monastery was restored in a lavish Baroque style. The entrance court leads through a pleasing Baroque entrance into a larger courtyard, dominated by several sturdy plane trees and a Trinity column, executed by Giuliani in 1729. Behind the towerless façade of the church, however, is a surprisingly severe Romanesque interior. To hear Gregorian plainsong here in the warmer months is one of the more moving musical experiences to be had in Austria, though there seems to be a curious lack of spirit in these Cistercians, perhaps due to the foundation's complacent prosperity. Some of the monks here come from aristocratic families and, as the Heiligenkreuz foundation owns enormous amounts of land, they receive the best possible training in farming. A tour of the richly decorated dining room and other parts of the monastery is available on application to the porter. The library contains over 40,000 volumes, the most interesting of which are displayed in a frescoed corner, painted in the middle of the seventeenth century. There is also a rich treasury containing a number of priceless ivory reliefs.

The Stift restaurant with its garden offers a fine choice of wines and some excellent dishes to while away the hour before the bus returns to the less cloistered world of Baden.

From here, if there is time, an excursion can be made to LAXENBURG, a small village with a palace designed during the reign of Maria Theresa and some beautifully laid-out gardens. After visiting Mayerling it is perhaps poignant to dwell on the fact that the ill-fated Crown Prince Rudolf was born here. In the park, there are various eccentric buildings erected by the Emperor Francis. In Laxenburg, there was no need for the reserve of Baden and, as the jousting arena and the mock Gothic Franzensburg, built in the first decades of the nineteenth century, illustrate, the last of the Holy Roman Emperors, if neither Holy nor Roman, had more than his fair share of medieval pretensions.

The castle was wrecked by Russian occupying troops after the last war, but has been faithfully restored to its original splendour. The Habsburg hall contains portraits of all Francis's archducal and rather degenerate-looking relations, while a gallery nearby contains an exquisite series of painted glass windows executed in the late eighteenth century. The castle porter completes his tour with a visit to the somewhat grotesque dungeons, where the emperor had an artificial prisoner constructed to rattle his chains when he stamped his foot at a particular point on the floor. Advisers to Francis, who suffered several humiliations at the hands of Napoleon in the early years of the nineteenth century, were convinced that a few minutes spent taking his wrath out on this 'prisoner' was all that kept him sane.

· KLOSTERNEUBURG AND THE WACHAU ·

A car is probably needed to complete this excursion in a day. But for those without, and with more time, it may be better to split it up into three separate afternoons.

KLOSTERNEUBURG, best reached by train from the Franz-Josef Bahnhof, is a suitable aperitif for the spectacular sights of the Wachau. Situated on the right bank of the Danube, it is a small and picturesque town dominated by its Augustinian abbey, the wealthiest and oldest in Austria.

The church, consecrated in 1136, is a Romanesque basilica with considerable Gothic additions, as is clear from the exterior. The interior of the church was inevitably rebuilt in Baroque times and is dull and heavy, but there are the remains of some fine Gothic cloisters which date from the end of the thirteenth century. But by far the most visually exciting parts of the monastery are the palatial abbey buildings designed by Felice Donato d'Allio from 1630 to 1650. These were intended by the Holy Roman Emperor Charles VI eventually to rival the Escorial near Madrid. Even incomplete, it would be hard to find a more impressive complex so near to Vienna. Though less imposing than the great abbey of Melk further up the Danube (see p. 61), it has a rather more eccentric design than Prandtauer's masterpiece there.

On the east dome rises a vast imperial crown in magnificent green copper, while on the west dome is a no less incongruous copper archducal hat. Within the abbey is the actual archducal hat on which it is modelled. There is also a small collection of pictures, chiefly by Austrian masters. In the Leopold-kapelle is the celebrated altar of Verdun made in 1181 by Nicholas of Verdun. It contains no fewer than fifty-nine plaques of gilded bronze. The windows of the chapter room contain more medieval remains; glass dating from the end of the thirteenth century.

In front of the church is a column erected in 1381 on the cessation of the plague. Through an archway towards the town there are several charming seventeenth-century houses with painted façades, and the no less renowned Stiftskeller, which for centuries has offered the very best Austrian wines. Its cavernous vaults and tasty if somewhat expensive cuisine repay further study, not least because this is one of the few places in the Vienna area where one can appreciate a reasonable glass of red Austrian wine.

The remainder of the town, though heavily restored, boasts several picturesque and winding streets containing a few untouched Baroque houses.

From Klosterneuburg, we cross the Danube and drive or take a train to BURG KREUZENSTEIN, on the left bank of the river. This spectacular castle, erected in the last century by the wealthy Baron Wilczek, an industrialist of the first rank in imperial Austria, rivals anything the Victorians created in England. To walk from the station through the woods to the rocky hill which is the base of the castle is almost to take a step into Anthony Hope's Ruritania. The romantic skyline of turrets and bastions dominates the surrounding countryside.

Generally open most weekdays and at weekends, the castle can be visited with a guide (usually excellent). He will point out how Baron Wilczek's passion for antiquarianism and collecting resulted in several Nuremberg houses being transported intact to be re-erected in the first court of the castle, while an entire Gothic loggia was brought from the magnificent cathedral of Košice (see p. 198 ff.) in Slovakia to dominate the range of the court opposite.

The interior contains little of value but much of atmosphere, not least a chained library and chapel reminiscent of some Oxford college and an armoury of weapons which, gruesome in any context, assume a particularly sinister appearance in this mock medieval setting.

The castle was built on the remains of an old medieval structure (besieged on several occasions). The present building, so aptly designed for defence with its covered corridors, did actually suffer siege during the final weeks of the last war when the Red Army was approaching from the Bohemian marches. Until the Russians brought up heavy artillery a unit of the S.S. managed to hold the place for several days against numerically superior forces.

At the end of the long ramp which crosses the moat, now dried up, around the outside of the castle is a well-run and usually empty *Gasthaus* with a pleasant garden under whose chestnuts one can sit and contemplate the gaunt towers of this most impressive folly.

From Burg Kreuzenstein, a short drive north-east takes us to another nineteenth-century folly, the HELDENBERG ('Mountain of Heroes'). This is truly Austria's Valhalla, a unique collection of over a hundred tin busts of the great Austrian, Irish, German, French and even Serbian generals who served the Habsburgs in the stormy years 1848–9, when the empire was threatened from all sides by revolutionaries.

This bizarre monument owes its creation to the memory of Field-Marshal Radetsky who, though in his eighties, was wheeled out to deal with the emergency in Italy, defeating armies twice the size of his own by skilful manoeuvring and brilliant tactics. A man of extravagant tastes in his private life, reflecting the hedonism of a true soldier, Radetsky ran up debts of thousands of crowns. Freiherr Joseph von Parkfrieder, a tin merchant who had made his fortune supplying this material to the Austrian court, admired the marshal so much that he promised to pay all his debts if Radetsky, when he died, allowed Parkfrieder to bury his body on a hill celebrating the Austrian empire's feats of arms. Radetsky agreed, as did another general, Wimpfen, who had served as Archduke Karl's chief of staff at the battle of Aspern (see p. 5). Around these Parkfrieder proceeded to erect busts of every 'distinguished' general, officer and, when these ran out, private in the Austrian army.

The effect is impressive if grotesque. The four life-size tin knights in armour who guard what is now a home for war injured are perhaps the most guilty offenders, although the ever-enchanted metal virgins who mark the path to Radetsky's tomb run them a close second.

The tomb itself is remarkable for its errors of dates (Aspern 1805, for example) but none the less suitably severe. In Biedermeier writing above the steps, a notice warns that just 'because we are silent, it does not mean we are dead', a final salvo from the octogenarian marshal sufficient to inhibit anyone thinking of carving their initials on the wall.

It is ironic that among the decorations displayed here are Radetsky's Russian medals awarded to him in the Napoleonic wars by the Tsar. Russian troops were so impressed by these when they invaded Austria in 1945 that no damage was done to any of this bizarre statuary.

The road winds down to the Danube where, following the signs to Krems, it soon reaches the beginning of the W A C H A U, the name given to the part of the Danube valley which lies between Melk and Krems, a stretch of about twenty miles. No other river landscape in Europe can equal the Wachau for charm, beauty, art and architectural treasures. Almost every crest is crowned with some glittering abbey or castle, while the small villages along the banks of the Danube below are equally rich in medieval houses and churches.

K R E M S is typical of these. An old wine town mentioned as early as 955 as a '*Reichsfeste*' ('stronghold of the realm'), it is full of narrow streets with arcades which give the town a faintly north Italian air.

Near the Parish church of St Veit, designed by Biasino in 1620, there are a number of medieval houses, including one which boasts a fine Teutonic '*Erker*' corner window and which now serves as the Town Hall (Rathaus). From the main square, steps lead up to the oldest church in the town, the Piaristenkirche, a late Gothic building of about 1520 with a light high interior. The stalls, with their wooden ball decoration, seem to be related to those executed for the church of the Dominicans in Vienna (see p. 34) and may even be by the same hand. Unfortunately, with every visit there seem to be fewer of these eccentric devices left. The view from the church on a clear day is extensive. Opposite rise the rather oriental onion-domed towers of the enormous abbey at Göttweig, while below, the Danube winds its way between dramatic cliffs towards Dürnstein. Descending to the right we come to a small square (Täglicher Markt) with several early seventeenth-century houses (Nos. 2 and 5 are even earlier) and a quiet bar with reasonable food. Down to the left, there are more sophisticated restaurants in the Hoher Markt, a square which has in its north-east corner the plain façade of the Institut der Englischen Fräulein.

Between 1 April and 1 November it is possible to cycle along the long narrow street which links Krems with its neighbour, Stein, thanks to the convenient custom of the Austrian railways whereby cycles are available for hire at every railway station. Booked in advance (one week's notice is advised), the bicycle can be collected at Krems and left at Melk station after the ride, from where it will be returned to Krems at no extra cost.

Otherwise, the walk from Krems to Stein is no less enjoyable. On each side there are houses which will absorb any architectural historian and the long straight road which leads to the arch of the town gate is no less well endowed with places to sit and drink a glass of refreshing Wachau Veltliner.

On the left, along the Danube, are several pleasing squares, while on the right lie a number of churches which are now museums. The most interesting of these is the town museum, housed in the thirteenth-century Dominican church, on the Theaterplatz, where former cloisters house a wine museum.

Under the Kremser Tor or gate is STEIN, which if anything is even more unspoilt and picturesque than Krems. The parish church of St Nicholas and its rectory have elaborate Baroque stucco work. Steps lead up to the Frauenbergkirche, an early Gothic fourteenth-century church with a fine view. Descending to the right, there are several private wine cellars where it is possible to taste and buy some of the region's renowned white wines, which are a welcome contrast to the more acidic wines offered in Vienna.

Down in the Landstrasse are several more picturesque houses, of which the former toll house at No. 135, with its alcove and rich Renaissance decorations, is perhaps the finest.

The people of Stein are rightly proud of their town's heritage and it is possible to detect a certain contempt for the inhabitants of the nearby capital city. Despite the yearly invasion of tourists, the visitor will find these Wachau people a kind and hospitable folk who will go to enormous lengths to help and guide one through this beautiful part of the country.

From Stein, a cycling road rises up to Dürnstein. For those on foot, a small railway station offers a train at regular intervals to Dürnstein, cutting through several dramatic outcrops of rock. Between Stein and Dürnstein rises a tall classical monument erected in 1805 to commemorate a victory over Napoleon's troops here. Further on, Unter

Loiben has a Gothic church with a pleasing picture by Kremser Schmidt (1718–1801), an artist to be encountered again in Dürnstein.

DÜRNSTEIN itself is perhaps the most picturesque spot in the entire Wachau. The town is minute, boasting a population of barely a thousand souls. It is dominated by the extensive ruins of the castle (ascent twenty-five minutes) from the summit of which there is an unsurpassed view of the valley. The castle was stormed on many occasions and was finally reduced by the Swedes in 1645. As a ruin, it is thus contemporary with the remains of many English castles which had to face Cromwell's armies.

But Dürnstein is perhaps best remembered for the legend that from December 1192 to March 1193 it was the prison of Richard the Lionheart. It may be recalled that at the siege of Acre, Richard hurled the standard of the Austrian Archduke Leopold from the ramparts as he considered it an insult that any flag should fly over the Holy Land before the standard bearing the three lions of England. This unfortunate disagreement over protocol resulted in the jealous Leopold placing a price on Richard's head, with the consequence that shortly after his landing at Trieste he was apprehended and eventually conveyed to this castle. Whether, as legend relates, Blondel found his master by singing underneath the windows of the castles of the Wachau is a matter for conjecture, beyond the scope of this guide, but there can have been no more worthy setting acoustically or visually for the minstrel's songs.

Below, the actual town of Dürnstein possesses fewer buildings than its neighbours to attract the eye, but there is a fine eighteenth-century monastery, formerly a convent, near the river, while the town church contains more paintings by Kremser Schmidt. The Schloss Hotel, considered one of the top establishments in the world of its kind, has a charming terrace which in summer is a favourite venue for lunch. The black Bulgarian or Russian tugs which slowly power their way up river are perhaps the most curious examples of the river's traffic. The ships of the First Danube Steam Ship Company call at Dürnstein and offer probably the most relaxing way of seeing the Wachau between here and Melk.

But if the journey is continued by bicycle, the road to Melk offers a number of picturesque distractions.

At WEISSENKIRCHEN, there are the remains of medieval fortifications, and above the village, which is idyllically situated among vine-clad hills, there is a fourteenth-century late Gothic church. Inevitably the church, like so many in Austria, underwent insensitive Baroque conversion in the late seventeenth century. None the less, it contains some memorable paintings by two nineteenth-century artists, Rudolf Alt and Jacob Schindler, who spent much of their time painting in the Wachau.

Beyond Weissenkirchen is another charming village called ST MICHAEL. The church is a late Gothic basilica and has an interesting roof. Nearby is a curious building which at first glance seems to be a chapel. But by brushing the dust off a small squint-like window a sinister scene is revealed: on an altar lie score after score of madly grinning skulls – the debris of a fourteenth-century charnel house.

On the Danube side of the village is an impressive defensive tower that once guarded the road, which now continues to SPITZ AN DER DONAU a mile or so beyond, another picturesque wine-growing village (it has trains to Vienna). Both the old Town Hall with its frescoes and the seventeenth-century Schloss Spitz merit a visit, while high above the town rise the thirteenth-century ruins of Schloss Hinterhaus, destroyed by the French in 1809.

The road continues through Oberndorf and Willendorf to Aggsbach Markt, from where a passenger ferry crosses the Danube to the village of Aggsbach, which is again dominated by a picturesque ruin, AGGSTEIN castle. Constructed in the twelfth century, the castle was bitterly contested throughout its history until in 1529 the Turks invested it for over a month before finally setting fire to it. None the less, its kitchen, dining room and Gothic chapel as well as the small rose garden, which commands such a fine view over the Danube, are still all to be seen if one can muster enough energy for the ascent.

Having crossed the Danube, the road continues to Schönbühel, with its empire-style château and Baroque Servite monastery (suitable refreshment), before continuing six miles to the magnificent climax of the Wachau at Melk.

MELK is charming, if a little run-down. The richly decorated Baroque façade of the splendid former imperial post-office is sadly in need of repair, and the cafés nearby, though providing worthy cakes, appear a little neglected. But few people come to Melk to visit its quaint town. It is the Benedictine monastery, situated impressively some 200 feet above, which seizes the visitor's immediate attention.

From this position a Roman garrison once kept watch and the site is mentioned in the *Nibelungenlied*. In 1111, a castle built on this site in 976 was given to the Benedictines by the Babenberg Leopold III. In the fourteenth century the castle was enlarged into a fortified monastery of which the towers on the north-east side are still extant. But what really gave the building its present monumental appearance was the arrival in 1702 of Jakob Prandtauer, a relatively unknown mason from the town of St Pölten nearby. Prandtauer, unlike Fischer von Erlach and Hildebrandt, had no pretensions to being an intellectual architect. Rather he was a builder whose output up to this date had largely been the construction of rather humble houses in St Pölten. Over the next twenty-five years, he was to prove that he was more than equal to his commission, and when in 1736 the building was completed, the result was one of the finest Baroque edifices in the world.

The exterior façade which faces the town is over 400 yards in length. It reveals its severely monastic character by the absence of any articulating devices such as pilasters. The west front, overlooking the Danube, with its semi-circular terrace dominated by a vast open Serlian arch, is the architectural climax of the exterior.

The interior of the monastery can be inspected with a guide. The centre of the main building is taken up by a large staircase hall in three sections with ornamental effigies by L. Mattielli. Several rooms shown are richly decorated with marble, while the library possesses more than 72,000 volumes and nearly two thousand manuscripts, the earliest of which date from the ninth century. There is also well within reach in the corners of the main library room an excellent topographical section in English, dating mostly from the beginning of the last century. Finally, the usual 'cellar' offers some good wines and is a suitable point to retire to after the tour.

Returning to Vienna on this side of the river, the road comes to the smaller but no less interesting monastery of GÖTTWEIG, whose exotic towers could be seen from the church at Krems. This monastery was founded by Bishop Altmann of Passau in 1083 as an Augustinian establishment which in 1094 became part of the Benedictine order's possessions.

It was restored in 1580 after a fire and again in 1718, but the east wing, north wing and staircase are the work of Hildebrandt and exhibit an airy sophistication missing in Prandtauer's work. The so-called Kaiserstiege is considered one of the most beautiful Baroque staircases in Austria. The library and the stucco-decorated Fürstenzimmer can be seen on appointment with a monastery guide. The monastery church has an elaborate Gothic choir with fifteenth-century glass and some fine Baroque choir stalls.

Outside, Göttweig, more than Melk, has a castle-in-the-air feeling, with its long, exposed courts. The informality of the buildings and the well-kept lawns are reminiscent of a Cambridge college or a cathedral close. On a rainy day, it is almost as if one of these has been flown high up into the clouds and set down on to this commanding position with some Baroque decoration.

Inevitably, another fine cellar awaits to round off the day's exertions and leave a lingering taste of Wachau Veltliner.

· THE NEUSIEDLER LAKE AND EISENSTADT ·

Burgenland is unlike any other part of Austria. Its position as the country's easternmost province makes it more akin to Hungary than to Austria in many respects. Its villages have an atmosphere more rural and simple than anything in Styria or Lower Austria.

Until 1921, this part of the country was in the Hungarian half of the old Habsburg empire. Its cession to Austria by the Treaty of Trianon after the First World War was an ironic gesture generally believed to have been made to please the French president Clemenceau rather than any ill-treated minority. Today, the Burgenland ('Land of Castles') still has a population who in their diminutive size physically resemble Hungarians rather than Alpine Austrians.

It is a melancholy fact that this is one of the poorest parts of Austria. There is little industry here and (mercifully for the visitor) little organized tourism, so that the area remains one of the least spoilt in Europe.

A visit to the NEUSIEDLER LAKE introduces us perfectly to the tranquil, almost unnatural, calm of the province. Trains for Neusiedl am See leave almost every hour (at fifteen minutes past) from the Ostbahnhof. The rather slow journey can be broken at BRUCK AN DER LEITHA, the town which marked the former frontier with Hungary.

Schloss Bruck dates from the eleventh century but has enjoyed several interesting restorations, first by Lukas von Hildebrandt, who lavished his sophisticated Baroque on its courtyards, and then in the nineteenth century, when it was decided to convert the castle *à la* Kreuzenstein (see p. 56) into the last word in Neo-Gothic. The park, though partly encroached on by the town, still shows signs of its English-style gardens.

Leaving Bruck, the railway pierces the Leitha hills and then turns to the east, where the shimmering waters of the lake can be seen through the thick belts of reeds which surround it. One of the largest lakes in Europe, it is fed only by a sluggish river known as the Wulka. Extreme variations in the water level here have been observed from the earliest times. In 1861, the lake dried up completely, allowing a brief attempt at building on its bed. But in the early years of this century, the waters rose so high that they lapped against the walls of Rust. Even today, when the wind blows for several days from the same direction it drives all the water into one corner of the basin, a phenomenon first recorded by Pliny.

The country east of the lake has been likened to that of the eastern steppes, with pools and warm salt lakes. Near Frauenkirchen, a small hamlet which boasts a Franciscan monastery, the climate is almost tropical, allowing almond trees and other plant life to flourish. The wines of this area are renowned throughout Central Europe, Burgenland providing almost the only consistently good red wine in Austria. As early as 1364, the wine-growers of Rust were granted the privilege of using the royal coat of arms as their trademark and most of the villages around the lake will offer excellent open carafes of home-made wine.

Around the edge of the lake, the thick belt of reeds is a natural home for all kinds of wildfowl and the ornithologist will find many interesting species of heron, bittern, moor hens and wild geese.

Perhaps the best place from which to enjoy the lake is RUST, a small free town renowned for its picturesque architecture. Almost all the houses are worth inspection, their elegant gables crowned with the nests of storks which gather here each year. A fine view can be had from the church tower (ascent 10 *Schillings*).

At Rust there is abundant opportunity to sample the red wine of the area. The food, too, is usually good and, because of the province's relative poverty, available at half Viennese prices.

From Rust, it is barely twenty minutes by car or bus to EISEN-STADT, the capital of Burgenland. Time was, not so long ago, when this was perhaps the least spoilt town in Austria. Sleepy, dreamy, fanned by warm winds from the Hungarian plain, Eisenstadt was both the most isolated and most romantic of provincial capitals. Today, the zealous building programmes of the sixties and seventies have changed all that and old Biedermeier buildings nestle between the ugliest office blocks.

But Eisenstadt should not be neglected, if only because its name is inevitably linked with that of Joseph Haydn. The town still enjoys the patronage of the once great Esterházy family, for whom Haydn composed much of his work, and their castle dominates the upper part of the town.

This seventeenth-century Schloss is a curious edifice, with enormous consoles and a general feeling for the grotesque which is almost oriental. Its heavy rooms are open most mornings and in the summer there are concerts in the fine marble saloon. The architect, Carlo Carlone, introduced here certain Baroque motifs from Bohemia, such as the faces along the stringcourse, when between 1663 and 1672 he transformed what had been a medieval castle into the yellow barrack we see today. The magnificent park contains a fine monument by Canova in the Leopoldinen temple, while the nearby town church possesses a monument to Haydn which, according to tradition, was erected on the insistence not of the inhabitants but of a certain Lord Grey.

From here the narrow street parallel to the main road running into the town from the castle offers the best clue to what Eisenstadt was like before the late sixties. In addition to several charming Baroque and nineteenth-century houses, it contains what must be the most picturesque consulate in Europe. A suitably pink and white Rococo palais boasts the proud tin shield of the 'Consolato Italiano'. On closer inspection, it seems that this illustrious building is open for consular business for only one hour a week. But who cares? The Italian government should be congratulated for flying their flag at a time when other countries are closing consulates by the dozen.

Opposite this is an inn kept by a rotund and jolly man where the wine is of the deepest red. The owner will take great delight in telling you how it has been made free from any artificial colouring. Its inky colour and full body testify to his sincerity. Such hospitality is suitable preparation for the train journey back to Vienna and the return to the less sleepy world of urban Central Europe.

· SEMMERING AND GRAZ ·

There could be no greater contrast than that between the flat impoverished Burgenland on the one hand and the mountainous Semmering and elegant prosperity of Styria's capital, Graz, on the other. The Semmering Pass is reached from Vienna by the oldest of the Alpine railways, constructed in the 1850s to link the capital with Austria's great port on the Adriatic, Trieste. Railway enthusiasts will probably feel the countless viaducts and tunnels make the journey worthwhile even if there is little time to spend at Semmering. The railway ascends at Gloggnitz (best views to the left), past the Schloss of that name. As the line describes a wide circuit round the north slope of the mountains, a fine view opens of the bold Rax mountains to the right.

At Klamm rises the old castle of Prince Liechtenstein, once the key to Styria but now half-destroyed. The next tunnel often divides misty weather from brilliant sunlight and, as the train makes another turn, a picturesque retrospect of Schloss Klamm can be seen. In ideal conditions the sun cuts through the fog at this point to give the effect of a castle in the air, seemingly suspended from the sky above a sea of white clouds.

As the train gathers speed, there is a fine view of the rocky Adlitzgraben before it reaches Breitenstein and then, after two more tunnels, Semmering itself.

Up to the Second World War, SEMMERING was Vienna's favourite weekend resort. For the Hungarians, it was the nearest place to ski if they were to avoid the Carpathians, which they lost in 1920 to the Slovaks. These two factors, combined with the area's pleasing climate – it is often sunny here when Vienna is enveloped in fog – gave Semmering a unique popularity before the war. Today all that has changed, and the resort, though still favoured by some Viennese in the winter – or at least those who are unable to drive further west – has a deserted air, its enormous hotels boarded up, its streets as quiet as a remote village.

The air is still champagne, and there is no more exhilarating way of escaping from Vienna than to ascend to Semmering and walk down through the woods to Breitenstein or take the chair-lift up to Archduke

Johann's view, with the long narrow valleys of Styria unfolding underneath into the distance. The inn near this view point offers reasonable sustenance, though the *Apfelstrudel* must be the worst in Austria.

In the town itself, some new life has been breathed into one of the oldest hotels, the Pannhans. Much of the decor is almost a parody of Alpine art-deco, but it still has something of the atmosphere of pre-war Semmering, although it rarely seems more than a tenth full.

Over the Semmering lies Styria, and GRAZ, the second largest city in Austria and with Salzburg the most enjoyable of the provincial Austrian capitals.

The station and its immediate environs were bombed during the war and were rebuilt with little inspiration, but the Annenstrasse soon leads to the small dolomite plug which is the Schlossberg, around which huddles the largest concentration of Baroque architecture in Austria.

Crossing the rather muddy-looking river Mur, we soon reach the Herrengasse and the Hauptplatz. Because of the city's proximity to the Adriatic – it is barely three hours away in a fast car – several Italian artists have left their mark on the architecture of the city. Its Baroque and later art-nouveau buildings have a lightness and modest scale completely remote from that encountered in Vienna. The soft colours, yellows and greens, with white stucco work combine with the shutters guarding each window from the fierce southern sun to give Graz an atmosphere faintly Balkan in its indolence.

From the Herrengasse runs the narrow Sporgasse, with its cobbled surface, sensibly pedestrianized. Past the magnificent wooden façade of the Edegger bakery is the Biedermeier Franzensplatz with its statue of the Emperor Francis, while beyond lies the Gothic cathedral. Its interior, inevitably Baroque, was recently restored, revealing traces of several giant medieval frescoes at the west end.

Opposite the cathedral the remains of the castle have little of interest, but we should go under the arch to examine the remarkable fifteenth-century double spiral staircase, which is one of the chief architectural glories of the city. The arch to its right leads to the magnificent Stadtpark, and at the back of the cathedral stands the picturesque mausoleum, whose architecture is the clearest expression of the value Graz once had in Central Europe. Built by the emperor Ferdinand II in 1614, this remarkable Mannerist building with its gazing putti, broken pediments and romantic campanile was designed by Pietro da Pomis. The interior decoration is the work of Fischer von Erlach the elder, who was born in Graz.

From 1564 to 1619, Graz was the seat of a branch of the Habsburgs, who made the town the administrative centre of Inner Austria. The mausoleum, as Austria's oldest early Baroque building of note, is a fitting testament to this. Ferdinand II, who is buried with his wife Anna Maria in the mausoleum, was a highly complex personality. Sometimes called the begetter of the Thirty Years War, he was a fervent Catholic whose Jesuit upbringing made him a zealous opponent of Protestantism. Under his leadership, Catholic Austria crushed the flower of Protestant nobility at the battle of the White Mountain near Prague, so obliterating Bohemian culture for more than two hundred years (see pp. 147 ff.).

The Stadtpark was formerly the fortifications of the city, its layout as an 'English garden' dating from the second decade of the nineteenth century. The fortifications which had proved so formidable against the Turk even defended the city against an army of Napoleon three times larger than the defenders. Vienna's capitulation in 1809 resulted in the Napoleon demanding, as a condition of peace, the demolition of Graz's defences. The result is not only the delightful park but, at the summit of the Schlossberg, a veritable garden in the air. The view from the Schlossberg reveals the long grey Italianate university buildings beyond the park, followed by the green Leechwald woods with the yellow Baroque Maria Trost church on a rise in the distance beyond.

To the south, the hills become gentler, while west and north rise the last peaks of the eastern Alps. The Schlossberg itself is full of delightful architectural devices scattered about its gas-lit paths. At the summit rises a Belvedere, while on the principal path below stands the one part of the fortifications which the people of Graz, by contributing their personal fortunes, managed to save from Napoleon's demolition men, the clock tower, now the symbol of Graz.

At the foot of the Schlossbergstiege, steps built this century by Russian prisoners of war, is the Sackstrasse (dominated by the severe Baroque Palais Attems) and the entrance to what proclaims itself to be Europe's largest 'grotto' railway – two miles of track piercing the Schlossberg through dark and mysterious caverns. Despite the Noddy Land advertising, the thin rails have a rather sinister character which is not dispelled by the hunchback driver who shouts out in incomprehensible Styrian dialect the names of the illuminated scenes which rush by. The train rattles past the polystyrene debris of various Nuremberg-style toy houses. Terrifying dwarfs clamber out of giant boots. Witches, evil stepmothers and wolves, all rather uncomfortably realistic in their doll-like shapes, provoke a chill which the hastily issued blankets are unable to combat. Several of the tableaux have still to be completed and their darkened silhouettes only add to the impression that, by accident or design, in the heart of Graz's fortifications some Styrian civil servants have created a most ingenious and frightening ghost-train.

Back to the Hauptplatz, where numerous cafés – the most fashionable at present is the small Café Mur beyond the tram stops – offer a suitable halt.

From here, the Herrengasse (with fine frescoes at No. 5) leads to the Landhaus on the right, with a delightful Renaissance courtyard erected by Domenico dell'Allio. A notice on its façade dating from the 1580s cautions us against drawing our breadknives.

An interesting door within this courtyard leads to the impressive arsenal, where armour was stored in preparation for Turkish sieges in the sixteenth and seventeenth centuries. It is the largest collection of its kind in Central Europe and contains over 30,000 implements of war. Unlike similar collections in other European cities, this is an arsenal rather than a museum. The visitor wanders through rooms of halberds, swords and shields, stacked for easy use rather than inspection.

Between the Herrengasse and the cathedral runs a series of narrow streets all of which repay a quick reconnaissance. The Glockenspielplatz has an art-nouveau façade with a mechanical clock chiming the hour to a folk-tune.

A fitting conclusion to the visit is to wander across the park to Laufke, on the Elisabethstrasse, for lunch or dinner. Finding somewhere reasonable to stay in Graz is less easy than finding a good place to eat. The days when the Erzherzog Johann was the smartest hotel in Styria are long past. The newer Schlossberg Hotel at the end of the Sackstrasse is, if expensive, the only really personal and comfortable establishment in the city and we shall awake in the sixteenth-century rooms refreshed with the sun pouring through Biedermeier windows and the waters of the Mur below.

4

BUDAPEST

1: Pest

To sensibilities numbed by Vienna's sleepiness, Hungary comes as a shower of iced water. While the Viennese have much in common with them and the inhabitants of Prague, the Hungarians are still a race apart: energetic where the Danube Austrians are lazy, proud rather than smug, ambitious rather than lethargic and, above all, courteous.

The Magyars, unrelated in origins or tongue to any other race in Central Europe, have long considered themselves the master race of Eastern Europe. Descended from a branch of the Finnish-Ugrian people, they led a nomadic life which brought them to Hungary in the ninth century under King Árpád. Forced to live under the Turkish yoke after the battle of the Mohács in 1526 destroyed the flower of Hungarian nobility, the Magyars first became a truly autonomous force in Central Europe in 1867 with the creation of the 'Dual Monarchy'. Under this 'compromise', the Hungarians were given virtual undivided rule over vast tracts of what is today Czechoslovakia and Romania. With extravagant chauvinism, they set about constructing a capital which would outshine even Vienna.

The old town of Buda was given an imposing royal palace which would dominate the city in a way in which the Hofburg barely achieved in Vienna. On the other side of the Danube, where the old town of Pest had, because of the absence of high ground, been on several occasions razed to the ground by the Turks, new streets, ring-roads and boulevards, all in the latest variation of bombastic electicism fashionable in Vienna, were erected in the years before 1914.

When the empire collapsed, Hungary remained in theory loyal to the Habsburgs, becoming a regency ruled by a former admiral in the Austrian navy called Horthy. Unfortunately for the monarchist movement, the admiral betrayed his royal house on several occasions during the twenties in a series of events which recall an Anthony Hope novel.

The arrival of the Red Army after the Second World War all but sealed Hungary's fate as a member of the Warsaw Pact. A brief but bloody uprising in 1956 changed nothing, and today Russian soldiers can still be seen adding colour, in their quaint Tsarist-style uniforms, to the streets of the city. But the Magyars picked themselves off the floor and have shown some thirty years later that hard work and energy combined with an insuperable national pride can, even under communism, produce a thriving and relatively prosperous country.

As the visitor to Czechoslovakia and Transylvania will see, centralized communist economies do not make for an abundant supply of the luxuries that travellers expect in western countries. But in Budapest it is possible to eat, travel and be accommodated in a style which easily rivals Vienna and at a fraction of the price. Despite current price increases taxis still rarely cost more than a pound within the city, and there are a score of private restaurants where the finest cuisine can be enjoyed for far less than in any other European capital.

Unlike the Viennese, who always seems to be living in the past, there is an almost frenetic quality to the Hungarians. People run for trams in Budapest and there is no *föhn* wind to fan one into listlessness.

The city's impressiveness is perhaps best appreciated by taking an Austrian steamer on the Danube from Vienna to Budapest (apply to any IBUSZ tourist office). Sadly they are few and far between, and the usual means of river travel between the cities is a fast and rather noisy hydrofoil. None the less, the view of the two parts of the city is majestic, as one by one the great nineteenth-century bridges, erected by foreign engineers, come into sight. On the right are the towering Royal Palace and the Gellért hills; on the left, much lower, the grand Parliament buildings worthily imitating the Neo-Gothic of Westminster, and the larger hotels built in recent years with western capital, modern, but thanks to the scale of the river, which is over 400 yards wide at this point, managing to be accommodated quite comfortably and relatively harmlessly here.

Arriving by train can be equally spectacular, although for rather different reasons. It is one of the ironies of Central European rail travel that though heading east the train for Budapest leaves Vienna's western station and arrives at the Hungarian capital's eastern station, the Kéléti Pú.

This is one of the grandest stations in Europe – tall, cathedral-like and totally unlike any of the railway stations in Austria, which because of Allied bombing were all built in the fifties. The building abounds in what journalists call 'colour'. In particular, the evening brings the most picturesque peasant costumes to the platform as villagers return home from a day's shopping in the metropolis. Sometimes the express from Moscow disgorges dozens of Russian officers, immediately distinguishable from their Hungarian colleagues by the vast size of their hats. Their Mongolian-looking batmen struggle with the luggage, adding to the confusion by dropping their fur hats and bumping into astonished bystanders.

Occasionally, for a reason I have never understood, the train arrives at the charming western station (the Nyugati Pú), an altogether smaller affair constructed by Eiffel in the 1870s, with iron columns and fruity brickwork. The inhabitants of the western station are not as colourful as those of the eastern, but the building is a suitable introduction to what is the great quality of Pest, shabby nineteenth-century grandeur untarnished by the tasteless developments of the fifties and sixties.

The use of iron will remind British visitors of London railways, and it is poignant to recall that architecturally, and to a certain extent politically, in the nineteenth century Hungary always looked towards England. Her Parliament was modelled on Westminster and during the uprising of 1848 against the Austrians, British public opinion lay staunchly behind Hungary. A mutual love of horses and bravado helped to seal this Magyar–Anglo-Saxon link. When the country recently began to open itself up politically to the west, the first Nato leader to visit Budapest was a British Prime Minister.

This sympathy is reassuring when it comes to dealing with taxis and hotels or visiting the IBUSZ tourist offices on the Váci út, which rent out rooms in private houses. These private rooms are probably the most comfortable and certainly the cheapest way of staying in the city. They offer a fraction less privacy than a hotel but are far more personal. This is not to belittle Budapest's many fine hotels, which have a standard of service long considered extinct in many parts of Western Europe.

But wherever the traveller ends up, sooner or later an expedition must be made to the Vörösmarty tér (square) on the river side of Pest, where a convenient base can be established for exploring the city. Gerbeaud, the confectioners at the end of the square, is justly celebrated. Its cakes and ices rival anything in Vienna or Paris, although the coffee is not quite up to Austrian or Italian standards. The elaborate art-nouveau furniture of the interior is relieved by a fair amount of heavy wallpapering and several fine prints of paintings by eighteenth-century English masters. They strike a rather sober note among all the Secession tables with their curling bases. To take a glass of sweet Tokay and a *dobostorta* here in the early evening is the best therapy for the stress of a day's rushing round.

From Gerbeaud runs the city's Bond Street, the lower Váci út. The shops are of course not as opulent as Bond Street's, but they are filled with luxuries which are almost unheard of in other parts of Eastern Europe. The street itself is relatively undistinguished save for an occasional nineteenth-century façade of Moorish elegance. It does however have several good bookshops, and at the junction with Erzsebet körút (avenue) stand two churches.

The first, in the Petőfi tér, named like the Vörösmarty tér after a Hungarian poet, is the Hungarian Orthodox church, built between 1891 and 1894 in a style some would describe as bastard Louis Seize. There are none the less some not unattractive stalls inside.

Below this, near the Elizabeth Bridge, the newest of the impressive links over the river between Buda and Pest, is the inner city parish church, an older and altogether much grander building. Dating originally from the twelfth century, it enjoyed considerable embellishments during the fourteenth, fifteenth, seventeenth and nineteenth centuries, although much dates from the 1720s. The wall of the southern tower contains some Roman masonry, while inside is an interesting relic of Turkish rule, a *mihrab*, or prayer niche, which faces east. The rest of the interior is a dark mixture of Gothic and Baroque, with fine funerary monuments and Renaissance niches.

In front of the church the square, dwarfed somewhat by the road leading to the Elizabeth Bridge, has some of the earliest known parts of the original Roman settlement and an impressive if noisy view of the Danube.

From the bridge, an avenue eventually arrives at the large Franciscan church, bland Baroque of the early 1730s. More interesting perhaps is the quaint Moorish arcade opposite, which houses a respectable coffee-house with wicker seats, while the Carpathia Restaurant, not far from the Franciscan church, will provide more lasting sustenance. The food is wholesome, although sometimes it temperamentally suffers from mediocre cooking as well. The decoration is nothing short of spectacular, as the whole place has retained its original nineteenth-century stencilled Gothic patterns.

Almost in front of it, the Váci út continues, becoming a less mercantile, more residential thoroughfare. On the right is a charming 1720 chapel, while No. 73 has a picturesque courtyard.

The façade of No. 66 also repays closer inspection. It is typical of the decrepit but dignified houses of the Pest professional classes. After several tin-soldier and toy shops, at the end of the street appears one of the most spectacular edifices in Central Europe, the Budapest market. Its soaring nineteenth-century metal columns, high walkways and ramps are all embraced by pointed brick lancets which evoke Liverpool Street station and are the perfect backdrop to the myriad Hungarian housewives who swarm about to secure their daily needs. Fish gaze out at us in their hundreds from large tanks; we step neatly aside or collide with box-loads of chickens; the most exotic and wildest of mushrooms are scattered across long tables guarded by friendly but toothless women in head-scarves. Forming a bright and gaudy pattern, the red peppers, the traditional spice of Hungary, reputed to cure diseases and restore fertility, hang in their thousands.

Back along the Váci út, to the right in the Nyáry Pál út is an impressive brick temple constructed in the 1920s. Further on is Egyetem Square, with the university church, a rather more inspiring building constructed in the 1730s. Opposite, beyond the southern end of the Károlyi Mihály útca, is the principal building of the university. The interior of the university church repays a visit for its well-preserved eighteenth-century frescoes and the opulent woodwork of its chancel. A sombre metal wreath clings to the floor of the second chapel from the right of the altar, in remembrance of Hungary's war dead.

From here the Henszlemann road leads to another picturesque square at the head of which stand the two nineteenth-century laboratories of a certain Herr Moser, a celebrated chemist.

In the Magyar út, to the right past some more rather shabby but still excellent examples of Hungarian Ringstrasse, is Kálvin tér, dominated by the large Neo-Classical Calvinist church. This is in many ways typical of the many Calvinist churches dotted around Hungary. Built in the second decade of the nineteenth century, it has an austere feel to it. Its architect, Josef Hofrichter, was responsible for many of Pest's Neo-Classical buildings.

No. 9 Kálvin tér should not be overlooked if only because its courtyard offers a glimpse of pre-Ringstrasse Pest – a leafy Biedermeier calm in contrast to all the traffic roaring about the square.

Opposite stands the Neo-Classical National Museum, probably the most popular of the city's many museums with the Hungarians, if only because it houses the most prized possession of the country, the royal crown of Hungary. With the sword, sceptre and orb, it is usually guarded by no less than six Hungarian policemen in a darkened chamber which would do justice to a communist martyr rather than a relic of imperialism. The sobriety of this setting is somewhat diminished by the stuffed turtles and gaily coloured rocks which make up the adjoining rooms' natural history sections. Only very recently recovered from America, the crown, with its unforgettable crooked cross (acquired when it was once hidden in medieval times), remains a potent symbol to the Magyars, commanding respect from the most fervent Hungarian communist in the country.

Beyond the geological section runs a series of rooms which in their own way merit almost as much attention as the crown jewels. There are some dramatically displayed pieces of armour and a heavy sword given to King Wenceslas by Pope Julius II. The child's suit of armour belonging to the infant Louis II is an impressive example of craftsmanship in metal, while some miniature pistols in a case nearby are reputed to have belonged to Jan Sobieski during the relief of the siege of Vienna (see p. 5). In the same room is a set of magnificent stalls taken from the ruined church of Nyírbátor and a funerary monument dated 1635 depicting 'a knight who led a pious life during tumultuous times'. Beyond this is the bright Maria Theresa room, with the dashing uniform her son wore as a child in 1745.

The Biedermeier room is full of curiosities, such as a funereal-black obelisked piano and a fine painting of the opening of the magnificent Chain Bridge in the 1840s (see p. 82). The Clark brothers, who were the engineers responsible for the bridge, strike a suitably Scottish note of sobriety in their civilian dress against the glitter of the brightly uniformed Hungarians.

Right of the muscum is Bródy Sándor út, a road of peculiarly Pestian charms. No. 4 has some fine frescoes dating from the end of the nineteenth century on the façade, while No. 6 has an impressively dark entrance hall. But it is No. 14 which reflects best the architecture of a nineteenth-century capital anxious to employ up-to-date materials. Here in the courtyard is a dramatic space boasting three classical orders beautifully rendered in iron.

Further along the road, No. 30 contains the Háry Börözo tavern, an unpretentious restaurant with reasonable food and good wine. Until a year ago, this establishment boasted the services of a gipsy violinist of the old school, with a penetrating gaze and superb musicianship. There were no tawdry costumes or bullying for requests and tips, just a discreet bow followed by the slow raising of his professorial drawn features. But even without him, this is a comfortable haunt.

Turning left along Puskin út, there are more interesting houses. To the left of Rákóczi út, a large boulevard, is the Múzeum körút. At the corner here is the old-fashioned Hotel Astoria with a pleasant café, while near it at Múzeum körút 13 is another of the city's many fine second-hand bookshops. In the nineteenth century, Budapest was a well-known centre of the book-trade in Central Europe and it still boasts many establishments which have valuable German and English books for a fraction of what they would cost in the west.

From the Astoria, the Tanács körút passes the brick synagogue, designed partly by the distinguished Vienna architect Otto Wagner (see p. 11) in the 1860s. In appearance, it is not unlike the equally picturesque brick Greek Orthodox church in Vienna's Fleischmarkt (see p. 33).

Left down the Bárczy út is the large Baroque Town Hall, originally a hospital for army invalids and designed in the late eighteenth century in a rather barrack-like style by A. E. Martinelli.

Further along the Tanács út are two rather more interesting buildings. The first is the Lutheran church on Deák tér, a Neo-Classical building of simple proportions designed by Mihály Pollack between 1799 and 1809.

The second is the much more overpowering St Stephen's cathedral, which rises above along the Bajcsy Zsilinszky út, an imposing Neo-Renaissance structure, heavy and not particularly beautiful. Its size – it has a floor area of 5,000 square metres – makes it one of the largest ecclesiastical buildings in Eastern Europe, but one feels that the Hungarians have never really taken to it. It was designed by two distinguished Hungarian architects, Ybl and Hild, in the middle of the last century, but its construction took over fifty years, giving the entire edifice a rather unhappy history. Few buildings of such size offer quite as great a sense of anti-climax as the interior, part of which is painted in nursery colours.

Withdrawing up along the great avenue unpronounceably called Népköztársaság, there is a chance to admire a more successful example of Ybl's work in the Opera, which was restored in 1984 to all its magnificent former glory. Unlike the Vienna State Opera, which was restored in the fifties (see p. 20), when it seemed fashionable to give such an interior an up-to-date appearance, the Budapest house has been renovated true to its original style, with mirrors, varnished wood and a buffet full of intimate alcoves to sit in. At present tickets are difficult to obtain, so great is the Magyar's passion for opera, but within the next year the Hilton Hotel and even the box office will apparently be able to supply some tickets, at least for the less popular productions.

Further up the avenue from the Opera is the most renowned café in the country, the Café/Restaurant Hungaria, a fabulous art-nouveau creation originally called the Café New York, a name which, in view of its brashness, would still suit it. Lunch is often excellent here, but dinner, where quite often the cuisine seems to take second place to an elaborate cabaret, can be disappointing. A simple coffee and cake is perhaps the easiest way of enjoying these novel surroundings, which evoke an atmosphere faintly reminiscent of that once enjoyed in London's Café Royal.

From the crossroads of the avenue with the square named November 7 tér, the underground line will take us to Hősök tér and the city park. The underground itself is of some interest, being the oldest on the continent. The line leading to the park from Vörösmarty tér, our initial point of departure, still contains its original mid-nineteenth-century detailing, but most of the other lines have more recent origins and are modelled on the flashy abstract Russian example. (It should perhaps be pointed out here that at present the price of underground travel is a 1 forint – $1\frac{1}{2}$p – coin placed into a box on descending to the platform.)

Hősök, or Heroes Square, is dominated by the Museum of Fine Arts to the north and the equally Neo-Classical Artists' House on the southern side. Between these distinguished classical structures rises the Millenary Monument, erected at the turn of the century to commemorate the Kingdom of Hungary's survival into the new century, and the thousandth anniversary of the Magyar conquest. Many others were built throughout Hungary's part of the empire, and though those which would now rest on Czech or Slovak soil have been demolished, there are several still to be found in Hungary.

Designed by Albert Schickedanz in 1896, its colonnade is an elegant backdrop for an extravagant equestrian statue of Prince Árpád, the first leader of the Magyar tribes who led them in their conquest of the flat plain beyond the Carpathians. It was his great-grandson Stephen who was canonized later for introducing the country to Christianity. In front of Árpád stand some seven chieftains of the Magyar tribes who swore to follow him, while on both sides of this tableau stand various other figures of historical importance in Magyar history. A more modern monument commemorating Hungarian dead in the last two wars stands in the middle of the square.

All this can be taken in at a glance. What is perhaps important now is to visit the Museum of Fine Arts before it closes at tea-time. The gallery is well-stocked with Italian Renaissance paintings, although there is nothing here to compare with the best works in the Kunsthistorisches in Vienna. None the less, admirers of Raphael should not miss the Esterházy Madonna or his portrait of a young man. There is also a fine portrait of Caterina Cornaro by Bellini and a large portrait of St James by Tiepolo as well as several Titians and Tintorettos. Those who are interested in the Dutch school will enjoy the Crucifixion by Memling or Van Dyck's double portrait. One room, indicative of the sympathy felt by the Hungarians towards the British, contains a fine series of portraits by Reynolds and Gainsborough. These and a smaller collection in Transylvania (see p. 128) would appear to represent the only serious interest Central Europe felt for the work of British painters.

Modern painting is modestly represented by the works of Monet, Renoir and Cézanne, while a modern sculpture gallery contains some interesting work of the great Jugoslav sculptor Meštrović. Several other rooms are devoted to classical and Renaissance sculpture, and the drawings collection is particularly rich in Renaissance work.

If refreshment is needed before visiting the Artists' Exhibition Hall on the opposite side of the square, the Restaurant Gundel behind the gallery on the edge of the park will offer a hearty lunch, a rather formally served dinner or the Hungarian equivalent of high tea: chocolate, nut and cream pancakes, washed down with a bottle of sweet medicinal Tokay. The pancakes are called '*palacsinta*' ('*Palatschinken*') and make a fitting climax to any Hungarian dinner if they have not already been eaten earlier in the day.

At the Artists' Hall there are usually exhibitions of Hungarian contemporary art or the ubiquitous travelling exhibition of English watercolours arranged by the British Council.

The park which stretches away from here is pleasant to stroll in. There are several imposing bathing establishments constructed in the grand style fashionable in the early years of this century, but the most interesting building is a sham Transylvanian castle, a perpetual reminder to the Hungarians of their lost province, which though never exclusively populated by Magyars is none the less their spiritual homeland and the birthplace of their finest romantic poet, Petőfi. This picturesque folly, with its grand courtyards, now houses an agricultural museum which contains a wide range of implements formerly used on the large Magyar estates. As the building is itself of such architectural interest, a half-hour spent wandering between the nineteenth-century forerunners of the combine harvester and other farming memorabilia is quite rewarding.

Some fifteen minutes' stroll across the park is the less pretentious Transport Museum, with Hungary's contribution to the development of rail, road, sea and air transport.

A taxi hailed by the quaintly dressed doorman of the Gundel restaurant will take us most comfortably and easily to the last great museum in Pest, the Museum of Applied Arts on the Üllői út, a long boulevard to the south. Unfortunately situated for any of the traditional sights of the city, the museum is however an essential part of any itinerary which attempts to capture the best of Hungarian art.

As in most places in Central Europe, the fashion for art-nouveau ran riot in the years before the end of the last century. The Applied Arts Museum, designed by the highly gifted but eccentric Ödön Lechner in the 1890s, attempts a peculiarly Hungarian brand of this style, completely different from anything happening at the same time in Vienna, or for that matter in Paris or Brussels. Its pyrogranite roof tiles and extravagant use of terracotta, glazed in the manner of English arts and crafts architects such as Halsey Ricardo, distinguish the building immediately. The white interior, relying for effect on the curved lines which seem essential to Lechner's style, is the perfect setting for the wide range of Jugendstil objects which at the time of writing are being installed in the recently restored interior.

From Üllői út, a metro line runs to Kálvin tér and thence to the Parliament, which is the last building of significance to be examined in Pest before crossing the Danube to explore Buda. The tube station to aim for is Kossuth Lajos tér, named after the Hungarian patriot of the 1848 revolution, Kossuth, whose exploits so impressed the British public that he enjoyed a comfortable exile for some months on the fringes of Holland Park.

The Parliament is the most impressive in Central Europe and was inspired both in style and constitution by the British model. It is worth recalling at this stage that whereas the Austrian Parliament, a building dwarfed by the Vienna Town Hall, rarely witnessed debates of any standard during the days of the Habsburgs, the Hungarian Parliament was renowned for its rhetoric and fine speeches. Even today, while few Austrians take their own Parliament seriously, Hungarians, despite the communist regime, still regard their emasculated Parliament with solemn pride. The building was erected between 1880 and 1902 to the designs of Imre Steindl. Eight-foot-deep concrete foundations were required to reinforce the Danube bank here so that the entire structure could be supported.

Its 300-yard façade guards no fewer than ten courtyards, twenty-nine staircases and twenty-seven gates. The eighty-eight statues on the pinnacles of the façade represent Hungarian leaders and military commanders. The main entrance is flanked by grim-faced bronze lions which even Landseer might have been proud of. To see the interior, guided tours of almost an hour are organized on certain mornings of the week (inquire at any large hotel or office of IBUSZ).

Although there is little of the wilful detailing which marks so much of Pugin's work at Westminster, the entire effect is undeniably impressive. The eighty-two-foot high hall is reached after mounting a long ornamental staircase, and is crowned by a vast dome, decorated with the coats of arms of all the former Hungarian counties, many of which are now in Czechoslovakia and Romania. The symmetrical plan of the building reflects the Upper and Lower Houses, now known as the Congress Hall and the Assembly Hall, and the lobbies are adorned by pyrogranite and majolica statues. Among the several chambers shown, some attention should be given in particular to the impressive library, several of whose old leather-bound books contain English parliamentary treatises and debates.

Opposite the Parliament in Kossuth Square is the Ethnographical Museum, but this can be saved for a leisurely morning when its rich tapestries and dazzling costumes can be enjoyed more fully. As many villages in the country still have their own living remains of this great tradition, it may be considered more sensible to examine these things *in situ* in eastern Hungary.

In the nearby Roosevelt tér, there is another charming reminder of old Anglo-Hungarian friendship in the large nineteenth-century offices of the Gresham Life Assurance Company. The plaques commemorate both Hungarian and British tradesmen, who worked hard to preserve this commercial link before the First World War. The once renowned restaurant, called the Gresham, which adorned the corner of the offices is now a Chinese take-away.

On the Danube, behind the Vörösmarty tér and facing the river, is the concert house, known as the 'Vigadó', another romantic nineteenth-century building which is the venue for concerts by the accomplished Hungarian Philharmonic Orchestra.

In the summer, however, the best light musical entertainment in Hungary – some would say in all of Central Europe – is to be found on the Margaret Island, where a spacious outdoor operetta set is the stage for the works of Lehár, Kálmán and Johann Strauss, performed with a professionalism completely lacking in the Volksoper of Vienna. Of course, the dialogue is in Magyar, but this curiously is not as disconcerting as one might expect and is a small price to pay for the exquisite feeling and musicianship that the artists here bring to these much-abused works.

At the northern end of Margaret Island, twenty-five minutes' stroll from the Margit Bridge, the Grand Spa Hotel provides meals which can be eaten *al fresco*. Otherwise, after so much walking, there is probably no better place to collapse into than the Hundred Years, on the Barnabas út, which is the third turning on the right as we walk down the Váci út from Vörösmarty Square. Its intimate rooms and excellent cuisine will fortify the spirit for the coming day which, the delights of Pest being exhausted, should be employed exploring the older, less imposing, but perhaps more picturesque quarters of Buda across the river.

5

BUDAPEST
2: Buda

The best way to approach Buda after a hearty breakfast at Gerbeaud's is to walk across the great Chain Bridge. Of all the bridges which span the Danube here this is the most impressive. Its noble classical proportions were designed by William Tierney Clark and work began on 1 May 1840. It cost over £500,000 and involved an international labour force of Scots, Englishmen, Italians (mainly from Trieste) and Slavs. Significantly, perhaps, the only Hungarians involved were the nobles who raised this enormous sum and who chose so wisely to entrust its construction to a foreign engineer.

In the 1840s, the bridge was one of the engineering wonders of Europe. One contemporary traveller in Central Europe observed, 'I know of no bridge concerning which so much has been in modern times said and written as the new one over the Danube between Pest and Buda and there are certainly few works of this kind whose execution has been opposed by so many obstacles political and physical' (H. Kohl, *Austria*, 1842).

The physical problems were largely due to the sorry state of the Danube here, which in those days was a fast river given to frequent inundations of its swampy banks. It is strange to imagine that this bridge with its proud nineteenth-century iron was the first successful attempt actually to link the two towns. Before, barges tied together or pontoons were the only secure means of crossing the river. These were useless in winter because of ice floes, and from December to March communications between the towns were limited entirely to boats. In bad weather, even these were ineffective, so that the two centres were often completely isolated from each other.

Walking across 1,800 feet of the Danube is a rather nineteenth-century experience. The bridge's pedestrian walkway, with its fine corners allowing perspective views up and down the river, is both the safest as well as the most enjoyable means of crossing the river.

If the Chain Bridge, like Pest, bears the unmistakable imprint of nineteenth-century prosperity, Buda offers a less prosperous tapestry of earlier centuries, although its predominantly eighteenth-century intimacy has had to bear the brunt of nineteenth- and twentieth-century additions of less than wholly sensitive proportions.

Although Buda appears a much older settlement, it actually dates from a time later than the earliest traces of Pest. In fact Buda owes its existence to the destruction of Pest in 1241 by the Mongols. It was then that it seemed safer to build a new city protected by ramparts on the other side of the river, on the plateau on top of the steep limestone hill. A castle was erected at the southern end and a civilian town to the north. At first only timber fences protected the town, but by the early sixteenth century it was surrounded by strong ramparts.

With the annihilation of the Hungarian nobility at the battle of Mohács in 1526, Buda, with its fortifications, became part of the Turkish system of forts in Hungary. Their ability to improve and develop the city's fortifications meant that the city became Christian again only in 1686, three years after the Turks had been routed outside the gates of Vienna (see p. 5). The city was almost completely destroyed during the siege, although several of the Turks' mosque-like baths were preserved and still give parts of Buda a faintly oriental aspect. During the subsequent two centuries, a picturesque late Baroque city developed, while after 1867 the pride engendered by Hungary's new status as a monarchy with a degree of autonomy in the empire resulted in a number of grand buildings being erected near the castle and the transformation of that fortress into an elegant and impressive palace.

At the end of the bridge stands the fine tunnel which the Clark engineers went on to build through the castle hill. The pointed tunnel entrance has a rather Moscow underground flavour to it but is, despite its dramatic zigzag decoration, nineteenth-century.

Bearing diagonally right we come to the Jégverem útca, which ascends the hill from the Clark tér. The street is lit, like many in Buda, by rather antiquated gas lamps. (A rest can be taken, if necessary, at the Café Koruna at the top of the stairs.)

On the right lie the buildings of the castle, brooding darkly over the river. Much of this area was destroyed in the last war during a two-

83

month siege, when units of the Germany army made a last stand against the Russians. All the bridges were destroyed in the engagement and the castle was gutted by artillery fire.

A heavy yellow barrack of a building, recently restored, gives way to a fine view of Pest and, according to a plaque, once housed Beethoven. Beyond are some rather Piranesian ruins with a magnificent Serlian arch. At the near end of the castle hovers a vast metal eagle clutching a sword which points the way down to the castle's modest hanging gardens. Lit by lamps at night, these steps and the dark silhouette of the walls have a peculiarly haunting quality, like a deserted ballroom.

From here Pest looks particularly impressive, although the effect of recent hotel building along the Danube will be immediately apparent. Where once fine nineteenth-century establishments like the Prince of Wales Restaurant and the Queen of England Hotel graced the river, post-war reconstruction has brought the altogether less elegant though perhaps just as comfortable Forum and Duna-Intercontinental hotels.

The castle itself now houses the National Library and several museums. Part of the National Gallery here contains some Roman remains from the nearby settlement of Aquincum. The Museum of Graphic Art, which contains some excellent posters of the inter-war period as well as many Hungarian nationalist handouts of the late nineteenth century, may be found more interesting. At the time of writing there are several plans afoot to extend the galleries in the castle and so make it a new cultural centre for the city. Whatever restoration takes place, it is to be hoped that this rather undistinguished building does not lose its shabby grandeur.

Back at the entrance of the castle, there is a rather tackily restored coffee-house on the left with reasonable coffee to sustain weary limbs before the walk back towards the centre of Buda.

On the right, overlooking the Danube and Pest, is the picturesque Fishermen's Bastion, which can be reached from the eastern side of the Trinity Square (Szentháromság tér). Apart from offering the most impressive overall view from the western banks of the Danube, this extraordinary building is of considerable interest in itself, offering ambulatories, passages and staircases executed in a bastard Neo-Gothic overlaid with Neo-Romanesque elements. The Fishermen's Bastion is named after the fishermen's town below, which contained several fish markets in medieval times. Erected in the first four years of this century, the entire complex was an attempt to provide some kind of romantic setting for the Matthias church, whose tower rises above it in the heart of Buda.

Below, in a bend of the road, stands a statue of Hunyadi, who repulsed the Turks at Belgrade in 1456, while nearby is a statue of St George, a replica of the famous one erected by the Kolozsváry brothers in 1373 which stands in Prague's Hradčany castle (see p. 159).

If the weather and company are agreeable, it may be possible to while away a pleasant hour or so on the bastion, especially if there is a Russian military band playing Shostakovich marches, as there sometimes is on national holidays. If, however, time is short, it may be best to proceed straight to the Matthias church.

The Matthias church is actually dedicated to the Virgin Mary, but is so named because its southern tower bears the arms with the raven (*corvus*) of Matthias Corvinus (ruled 1458–90), who established Buda as one of the great Renaissance courts of Europe. In the thirteenth century, Buda's first parish church stood here. In the fourteenth century, it was rebuilt as a Gothic hall church but remained unfinished. The Turks predictably converted the entire edifice into a vast mosque after they had captured the city. During the siege of 1686, it was equally predictably peppered by Christian artillery. The years immediately following saw much of the interior reconstructed in a Baroque style, but what is evident today largely dates from a turn-of-the-century reconstruction in the Gothic style.

The overall impression is unmistakably Victorian. We enter by a door in the south-western wall which leads down into a heavily and romantically stencilled nave. The walls bear the Corvin motif of the raven in whose beak rests a ring, a reference to the tale of how the young Matthias realized his vocation when a raven bearing a ring disturbed his reverie in a forest. The spiral west windows are remarkable.

The presence of so many Corvin crests and the church's name are explained by the fact that he was married here in 1463. The southern porch contains several plastered coloured decorations, while the murals depict the lives of Hungarian saints. The northern aisle has a series of chapels, that nearest to the chancel containing the impressive sarcophagi of Béla III (1173–96) and his wife Anne of Châtillon, which were brought here from Székesfehérvár.

The former crypt has been converted into a lapidary museum, while the gallery of the church contains a collection of ecclesiastical art with several notable jewelled chalices. The noble south tower is also adorned by a fourteenth-century relief depicting the Virgin Mary's death.

The Trinity Square outside the west end is essentially a creation of Baroque times. Opposite stands the old Town Hall, now a scientific establishment. The statue at its corner is of Pallas Athene holding the Buda escutcheon. The Trinity Column at the square's centre, like those at the centre of Vienna, commemorates the deliverance of the city's inhabitants from plague in the eighteenth century. Damaged in the Second World War, it was restored only in 1968. The rather ugly Neo-Gothic building to the north of the statue is the former Ministry of Finance, converted now into a student hostel.

It is impossible to ignore, however much one would wish, the astonishing structure which stands just beyond the Matthias church on the Hess András tér. At first sight it seems as if a temporary set for a Magyar version of *Star Wars* has been grafted onto this most venerable part of the Hungarian capital. A medieval tower is crowned by a late twentieth-century imitation ballistic missile. An imposing eighteenth-century monastery with a façade adorned by friezes and pilasters has been filled with orange windows, most of which appear from the outside to be impossible to open. An unedifying but in contrast almost self-effacing sign announces this building to be the Budapest Hilton.

Architectural historians, students of the Central European political situation, to say nothing of any hard-line communists who may be around, are to this day mystified as to how it was possible to construct such a striking example of the worst excesses of the capitalist economy in the very heart of a communist capital. It may be that there was simply nowhere else to put the Hilton, and certainly its ancient shell makes it comparatively inoffensive in comparison with most establishments of its type. None the less, no one who ever knew Buda before the Hilton will admit that this part of it is ever likely to be quite the same again. Inside, the spaces are rather more impressive, and no one should miss the dramatic view of the Parliament through the ruins of what was a monastery chapel. Performances of operas here during the summer vary enormously in quality but the sight of the hot summer sky turning into a star-filled backdrop to the strains of Mozart can be quite magical.

From the hotel the short Szentháromság útca (Trinity Road) leads to an interior which has remained untouched since 1827 – No. 7, the

Ruszwurm Café, which, besides containing some of the most delightful empire furnishings, offers excellent cakes in its cramped, invariably overfilled, low-ceilinged rooms.

The Szentháromság útca leads to the western end of the castle hill, where there is a view over the hills towards Austria. Until 1878, these hills were rich in vines, but phylloxera destroyed them and they are now the garden suburbs of Buda.

Between here and the Hilton is the Fortuna útca, which contains the uninspiringly named but nevertheless charming Museum of Catering. Of all the museums in Budapest, this more than any other gives an impression of what it was like to enjoy Hungarian hospitality in the nineteenth century. It consists of several rooms each designed to simulate the entrance hall of a Budapest hotel from Biedermeier times onwards. Proceeding from one room to another is to discover not only the traditions of a world-famous cuisine but also to glimpse something of the opulence which accompanied travel in this part of Europe before the First World War.

Menus boasting 1889 champagne and Tokay of even earlier vintage recall a time when Budapest was an essential part of the aristocracy's playground. Many of the menus contain English names and date from a time when nearly every important hotel bore a name like Queen of England, Prince of Wales or Victoria. Even after the First World War, the best way to acquire a fashionable clientele was to name an establishment after a member of the British royal family. An elegant cheque book of the 1920s is a curious exhibit for a communist country.

The museum's chief glories are its changing exhibitions, which draw on a vast amount of stored material, including mouth-watering photographs of the Magyar chef's art. One particularly interesting room contains a fascinating reconstruction of a nineteenth-century shop. Others evoke a world of elegance which the Hungarians remain justly proud of, retaining in their speech such anachronisms as '*Kézet cókolom*' (pronounced 'chocolom'), which means 'I kiss your hand' and is easily the most heard greeting in the country.

On the right of the catering museum runs the Országház útc. Left through the Dárda útca, with its remains of the old bastion walls, is the Úri útca, almost every house of which contains an interesting façade. To the right, across the square at the end of the Úri út, are the Baroque houses of the Táncsics Mihály út. The house at No. 7 was built from the remains of several medieval houses and in 1800 witnessed a brief visit – so a plaque recalls – from that itinerant musician Beethoven. No. 9, a rather more empire affair, was used in the first half of the nineteenth century as the royal archives and once housed the Hungarian mint.

Back in Kapisztrán tér, standing rather neglected, is the solitary tower of the church of Mary Magdalene, which was the second most important church in Buda and was all but destroyed in the Second World War.

From here, the bastions lead to the War Museum, guarded by numerous rusting cannon. It concentrates on the Hungarians' heroic struggle against the Austrians and Russians in 1848, and is rather biased against the former. Many of the cabinets are filled with brightly coloured hussar uniforms, reminding one that all hussar regiments formed in the nineteenth century were originally inspired by the dash and elan of Hungarian cavalry. There are several mementoes belonging to the dozen Hungarian generals who were subsequently executed for their part in the uprising. Whatever one's attitude to war, there is no doubt that this small museum offers a unique insight into the essential romanticism of the Magyar character.

Further down along the bastion to the right is an arch beckoning us down towards the river. The square nearby, Bécsi Kapu, contains several exquisite stucco façades, recently restored in a rather jolly shade of green. These may tempt one to ignore the arch and continue exploring the castle district.

The medieval cellars of the Fortuna restaurant on the Hess Square (near the Hilton) may supply an agreeable lunch before the descent to the newer quarters of Buda. Going from the arch near the War Museum down along the gas-lit path on the right is probably the most picturesque way of accomplishing this. Deserted villas, overgrown gardens and other melancholy signs of neglect can be seen on all sides. Whether we take the tempting cross-paths to our right or continue down along the steps, eventually we shall reach the main thoroughfare of Buda, known as Fő út. This is by no means the most attractive street in Buda, but by turning left along it and continuing for some minutes we shall come to the Turkish domed mosque-like building which is the Király baths (82 Fő út). There are many baths in Budapest, the city's waters having been written about since Celtic times. The Romans called their settlement near here Aquincum precisely because of the rich abundance of thermal springs.

In the Middle Ages, hospitals were established near the medicinal springs, with the result that today many of them are still part of large complexes devoted to hydropathic therapy. The fashion for cures in the nineteenth century led to the construction of several rather imposing baths both in Pest and in Buda, but however inspiring the art-nouveau decoration of baths like the Gellért, further along the Buda side of the Danube, there is nothing more evocative of the ancient tradition of taking the waters than the Turkish structures which remain here.

Of these, the Király is easily the most intimate and charming. Its pleasures of course can be enjoyed only by men, emancipation being sadly almost unheard of in certain walks of Hungarian life. (Ladies should not be too disheartened by this, for other baths such as the Gellért and the Czászár baths cater for both sexes on most days or have an arrangement whereby men and women alternate.)

In the best of them, and certainly in the Király, it is possible to spend an essentially lazy hour contemplating between dark medieval masonry a coloured glass ceiling over six centuries old, partly obscured from time to time by clouds of steam rising from the waters. The Király, in common with nearly all the older baths, are built on artesian wells whose water comes from a great depth and is rich in dissolved radioactive salts of considerable curative power.

It has been estimated that sixteen million gallons of medicinal water stream out daily from 117 thermal springs on both sides of the Danube. Those who have never been in any way devotees of saunas and other similar experiences will be converted by a couple of hours at one of these establishments. As well as restoring one's strength, they offer a unique insight into the way in which Budapest society is organized. Like the coffee-houses of Vienna, the baths are places for regular meetings, informal discussions and a general gathering of news. Not for nothing is there a legend that the instigators of Hungary's 1956 uprising were intellectuals who plotted the entire affair in the city's baths. Those who have lived in Budapest for some time are convinced that there is a bath for almost every profession in the city. On the other hand, the bath culture would seem to be on the decline in Budapest, as more and more young people turn to 'western' ways of amusing themselves during the day and visit bars.

Back along the Fő út, there is the centre of the Danube side of Buda, Batthyány tér, a square, open on one side, commanding a view of the

Danube and the spectacular Parliament in Pest. The square has several interesting houses and a Baroque church, St Anne, which has a delicate interior. It was built in the 1740s by Mathew Nepauer and Cristoph Hamon who, judging by the oval plan with its two towers, seem to have been inspired by Hildebrandt's work on St Peter's, Vienna.

The houses at Nos. 3 and 4 are also of architectural interest, the latter being a classic example of the so-called Hungarian 'Zopf' or Louis Seize style which bridged Rococo and Neo-Classicism.

On the northern side of the square is a Franciscan church which later became a convent but which has retained several Baroque stalls.

A few steps further on from the Batthyány tér is another picturesque square, Corvin tér. The church here is not of great interest, though it has a pleasant interior. To the right under a rather impressive portal is one of the very best second-hand bookshops in Hungary, discreetly masked by the façade of what seems to be a nineteenth-century house imitating an eighteenth-century palace.

From Corvin tér, the possibilities are legion. If Buda has captured the imagination, another picturesque path will return one to the castle for tea at Ruszwurm or dinner at the Fortuna or the Hilton, whose restaurant it must be said is entirely Hungarian in character. Otherwise the underground from Batthyány tér takes one back to the bustle of Pest and another evening in the Carpathia or the Hundred Years.

In either event, it is time to choose which of the many excursions from the Hungarian capital should be made before leaving this part of Central Europe.

If time is relatively short, perhaps the easiest way to escape the noise of the capital is to take the Pioneers' Railway into the hills of Buda, where the air is fresher during the long hot and dry summers.

The most enjoyable way of reaching the hills is to take the underground to Moszkva tér and then walk past the Városmajor, a rather rank but pleasant park, before reaching the terminal of the cogwheel railway opposite the hideous Hotel Budapest. The railway was built in the 1870s and seems to have been inspired by a Swiss model. It ascends to a height of 315 metres and affords panoramic views of the garden suburbs of Budapest. Almost opposite its terminus is the first station of the Pioneers' Railway, which is staffed by the Eastern European version of the Girl Guides and Boy Scouts. With a show of authority belying their tender years, they look after this miniature railway with great pride as it winds its way around the hills for about twelve kilometres.

The János hill offers the best walks and can be ascended from several stations in about three-quarters of an hour. Its summit is crowned by a tower designed by the architect of the equally picturesque Fishermen's Bastion in Buda (see p. 84). On a clear day the view below stretches for more than fifty miles and parts of both the Great Central European plain and the Transdanubian mountains can be seen.

On Sundays and holidays a bus lettered J returns to the inner city. Otherwise it is simply a question of ascertaining the times of trains, although for obvious reasons the young staff of the Pioneers' Railway cannot keep late hours and the line generally closes around dusk.

6

EXCURSIONS FROM BUDAPEST

· THE DANUBE BEND ·

The heart of the Danube Bend is the town of SZENTENDRE, which can be reached either by the suburban electric railway from Batthyány tér in Buda or, perhaps more comfortably, by ship from the Vigadó quay in Pest. As many tourist trips. are organized by ship to this picturesque spot, it may be better to take the humbler railway, which is cheaper and will offer a better insight into the habits of the locals. The twelve-mile journey takes little more than half an hour by railway.

The Baroque character of the town is chiefly the work of the eighteenth century. Its decidedly southern atmosphere is attributed to the hundreds of Serbian and Greek exiles who, fleeing from the Turks, set up their settlements along the Danube here, and the town still retains a picturesque lack of order in its layout.

The principal thoroughfare is the Kossuth Lajos útca, which leads into the Dumtsa Jenö útca and which runs from north to south. The winding streets which can be seen from left to right of this are all worth exploring. From the station, the first church to be seen in the Kossuth Lajos út is the Baroque Požarevačka church, which was constructed in the early 1760s. Its courtyard is rich in Serbian Orthodox tombstones and there are eighteenth-century icons in the interior of the building.

Along the Dumtsa Jenö útca, the houses become more prosperous in appearance, boasting façades of Neo-Classical and Baroque decoration, which reach a sugary climax in and around the town square, Marx tér. The ubiquitous eighteenth-century cross commemorates deliverance from evil, while the most distinguished house in the square would seem to be that known as the Serbian Merchant's House (Marx tér 2–5). Its arcades were probably used for trading, while the roof has the curious dormer windows which are a common feature of houses in parts of Transylvania and in the evening look like watching eyes. Stairs on the northern side of the square lead us up to a Calvary hill, where the oldest church of the town can be seen. Although it was destroyed during the Turkish incursions and rebuilt in a Baroque style, there are still several fragments of Romanesque and Gothic architecture of interest on the exterior.

The museum nearby, dedicated to the painter Czóbel Béla, has a fair amount of rather dull art, but is not without interest.

Back in the square there are more inspiring things: the Baroque Town Hall on the corner of the Rákóczi út and the impressive Baroque church of the Annunciation. Designed in 1752 by Andreas Mayerhoffer in a markedly restrained style, it suggests first tentative attempts at Neo-Classicism. The rather Rococo portal is frescoed with a depiction of the Emperor Constantine and his mother. The interior contains interesting vaulting and an icon of the late eighteenth century. Older icons can be seen in the valuable collection of the Serbian Ecclesiastical Museum on the nearby Engels út, which rivals many collections in Jugoslavia.

In Marx tér No. 6 is the Ferenczy Károlyi museum, a palace in the Louis Seize style. It contains much of this painter's work, which at the turn of the last century was inspired by the influence of French schools. The nearby Serbian Merchant's House at the corner of Görog útca is also worth a quick visit, as it contains exhibits on the town's history with the ceramic work of Margit Kovács and some ethnographical displays.

From the Marx tér, the Alkotmány útca leads to the imposing Greek Orthodox church, built in the Baroque style between 1756 and 1764. The elaborate ironwork of the exterior is the work of the Saxon metalsmith Mathias Ginesser. The church is notable for the decorative Rococo main entrance, an equally ornate bishop's throne which dates from the same period and an icon screen of the 1770s by Vazul Ostoic.

Next to the church is another museum, of Greek Orthodox ecclesiastical art, while back in the Vörös Hadsereg is the Preobraženska church, built between 1746 and 1750 on the site of a wooden church erected in the late 1600s. The wall surrounding it is beautifully decorated by a Rococo portal of the so-called Louis Seize style with richly ornamental ironwork. Inside, most of the decoration is late Baroque, with a late Rococo iconostasis.

Among these churches there are several cafés (the Golden Dragon is recommended), but it may be more enjoyable to walk down to the Danube for some refreshment on the Sómocsi Bácszo avenue, where the Görök, or Greek tavern, offers wines, fruit juices and coffee.

From Szentendre, a bus regularly plies the short distance to another picturesque place on the Danube Bend, the ancient settlement of VIS-EGRÁD. A fortified settlement since the Romans' day, it is situated at one of the most dramatic parts of the Danube, where the river breaks through the mountains. The ruined castle which crowns the hill of Várhegy dates from the thirteenth century. The golden era of Visegrád was, however, the second half of the fifteenth century, when Matthias Corvinus (1458–90) turned Visegrád into the most splendid Renaissance court, described by contemporaries as 'an earthly paradise'. This glorious meeting-place of the arts in Central Europe was, however, to last only a generation, and the castle soon fell into ruin with the incursions of the Turks.

If it is not too hot and exercise is needed, ignore the buses which ply from the centre of the village up to the citadel and ascend from the Fő út, which runs along the Danube, to the Solomon Tower, where a café will reward your efforts before another steep incline brings you to the ruins. The view will be more than adequate compensation for these exertions. Descending along the more gentle Kalvária road, there is an extensive view of the river and the other side of the Danube.

Back in the Fő út, No. 27 is the former royal palace, with a large courtyard relieved somewhat by the striking red marble fountain at its centre. In the course of excavations here many remarkable finds have been made. On the fourth terrace a reconstruction of another red marble fountain adorns a ceremonial courtyard, while the steam and water baths of the court have also been excavated in recent years. An eighteenth-century Baroque building further along the Fő út at No. 41 was according to local sources a royal hunting lodge. As for the rest of Visegrád, it can be explored in a few minutes, for, unlike Szentendre, it has little of major architectural interest and the few churches are modest compared to those seen earlier. Even the Solomon Tower, with its King Matthias Museum, is a rather humble affair.

Nevertheless, Visegrád is the spiritual home of much that was great in the Magyar culture, and from what are now ruins flowed a conviction which was to inspire the Hungarians to extend their culture and influence over much of Eastern Europe in the centuries which followed the repulse of the infidel. The Renaissance wells and remains of late Gothic arches, with their views out across the wide expanse of the Central European plain, express what was the cradle of Christianity on the Ottoman's western frontier.

From Visegrád, it is no difficult matter to reach our last destination on the Danube bend, ESZTERGOM. By car, it is less than three quarters of an hour and there is a regular bus service along the road No. 11. But if time is short, it may be wiser to return to Budapest and then travel straight from the capital to the town by boat, as to take in most of Esztergom treasures in less than a morning would offer little relaxation.

Seen from the river, the town, dominated by the monumental cathedral with its Neo-Classical dome and colonnade, is unforgettable. Already under the Romans, this part of the Danube had been fortified as Strigonium. Its climate and calm led the Emperor Marcus Aurelius to spend much of his time in it, and he is supposed to have composed the twelve books of his *Meditations* here.

Today, Esztergom's principal claim to fame is that it is the centre of the Hungarian Catholic Church. The Primate of Hungary is officially the Archbishop of Esztergom. His cathedral is not only the largest place of worship in the country but also the grandest, with its eight giant columns of the Corinthian order articulating its principal front. The Neo-Classical opulence of the Catholic Church in Hungary will often strike the visitor here.

The first priority is to ascend the fortress hill to inspect the cathedral, and the most picturesque route is along the Rákóczi tér to Batthyány Lajos, Makarenko u. and then up some stairs to the top of Béke tér, and the colonnade.

The original church was constructed in the sixteenth century but was razed during successive sieges in the 1590s. Subsequently Isidor Canevale and the Austrian architect Franz Hillebrandt (not to be confused with Hildebrandt – see p. 11) provided designs for a new cathedral. In the end, however, it was neither of these architects who provided the building which dominates the town in such a lordly manner. Rather humbler architects were employed: Paul Kühnel, a master mason of Eisenstadt, and Johann Baptist Packh. Their original designs of 1822 were adapted by the prolific Josef Hild in 1839. The final plan is much tighter and more disciplined than originally envisaged.

Inside, the real treasure is the Bakócz Chapel, built in the early years of the sixteenth century. It is a remarkable survival of the original church and all the more precious for the relative scarcity of such architecture in the country. It strikes a welcome note of humanity amid the icy precision of all the Neo-Classical architecture. The altar, constructed of white marble by Andrea Ferrucci of Fiesole (1519) with a relief showing the Annunciation, is also worth noting. The crypt contains several late-medieval tombs of bishops, some of which are ornately decorated. The cathedral treasury, easily the richest in the land, contains the well-known treasure crucifix of Matthias Corvinus made around 1480.

Next to the cathedral on this raised plateau are the excavated remains of the medieval Royal Palace. Destroyed by the Turks, it underwent systematic excavation from the 1930s. The chapel here contains a series of frescoes executed by Burgundian masters in the 1400s. The neighbouring hall, 'of the fundamental virtues', contains some eccentric symbols of the Zodiac in its cross-vaulting. The terrace on the roof of the Royal Palace offers fine views over the Baroque roofs of the town below.

From here, a humble path descends to the town and the uninspiringly named 'Square of 1919 Heroes'. Here is another Baroque church of the 1720s, and the Museum of Christian Art, situated in part of the Archbishop's Palace, also Baroque. The museum's collection is rich in medieval manuscripts and paintings and has some Italian primitives and Flemish tapestries, but it is not a very inspiring place.

From here, the Bajcsy Zsilinszky út leads to the Balassi Bálint Museum, a charming collection of paintings, furniture and other objects illustrating Esztergom's history. The same building also houses the cathedral library, which was established over 800 years ago and includes codices dating from the eleventh to sixteenth centuries.

Along the Bajcsy Zsilinszky út is the Bath Hotel (Fürdő Szálló), which will supply a refreshing bath or some coffee and cakes.

The Bajcsy út leads to the Rákóczi tér, which offers an eccentric ensemble of Baroque buildings and the Town Hall. The restaurant at the corner of the square and Zalka Máté is a good resting point before following the Vörösmarty út (Madách tér, Galamb út and Attila út) to the Calvary church on Szent Tamás hill, a gentle rise at the back of the town, for a final glimpse of the Danube Bend before returning to the capital.

If a car is available, there are two further places of interest nearby which could be knocked off in a couple of hours. Otherwise, there is little lost by setting out to visit them both at leisure on the following day.

· GYŐR ·

The first of these western excursions from Budapest involves a picturesque town which, despite the establishment of several industries around it, still retains a pleasant Baroque centre. The second is a monastery which in size and atmosphere is unrivalled even by the great foundations of Tuscany.

Győr, or Raab as it is known to German speakers, lies eighty miles from Budapest almost exactly half-way between Vienna and the Hungarian capital and is a suitable jumping-off point for visiting Lake Balaton (see p. 132). At first sight, Győr is rather disappointing. The railway station is a reasonable essay in forties fascist, but the buildings opposite all seem to have been erected in the last ten years. One recovers hope, though, at a large imposing edifice to the right. Grey and white Neo-Baroque, it looks rather like another of Helmer and Fellner's opera houses. In fact, it is the Town Hall, and its size and tower show how important the town was in the nineteenth century.

Almost opposite, a number of parallel roads lead to the old town centre, which is a small square of Baroque and Rococo buildings. The yellow church is sophisticated Baroque in plan and was built by the Carmelites in the 1720s. Its stalls have the ball motif we have seen in Vienna (see p. 34). The rest of the square contains a number of other noteworthy houses of the same period.

From here can be seen the old fortifications of the town, which for several years withstood the Turks. The Alkotmány útca, a pedestrianized street, contains an interesting portal at No. 17. The nearby Széchenyi Square is dominated by the fading blues and whites of the Minorites church erected with great largesse in the 1750s. The interior possesses some exquisite frescoes which have avoided the restorer's heavy hand. Opposite is a red building with a pleasantly tiled roof, housing a town museum. The Jedlik Ányos útca eventually reaches a Baroque statue marking a road rising towards the cathedral. (The Dunaetel bar just below this monument will provide a glass of refreshing beer before the ascent to this rather Mediterranean-style building.)

The church bears the marks of many styles. Its main entrance has Neo-Classical lotus-leaf columns inspired by Napoleon's Egyptian campaigns, and an even grander 1938 classical door. Inside (when closed, a friendly red-faced gentleman in a house opposite the south entrance will usually open the church up) there are some more frescoes in the nave, a Gothic side chapel of 1404 with Romanesque remains, and a thirteenth-century gold bust of St Ladislaus, one of the most valuable pieces of goldsmith's art in the country.

Near the cathedral is a modern but not too offensive hotel (at the time of writing, still to be named) and a Neo-Gothic seminary. The Bishop's Palace, or Abbot's House as it is sometimes referred to, is partly Gothic. A rank garden through the entrance arch offers views of Győr island, and a small inscription on the garden wall commemorates the year 1809, when, following the only battle fought during the Napoleonic wars on Hungarian soil, the French emperor stayed at Győr. The island itself can be reached from the square with the Carmelite church, but it offers little of interest except a dramatically ruined synagogue, a Russian barracks and some leafy promenades.

Compared with the Hungarian capital, few of the eating establishments here can match the best of Hungarian cuisine or offer comfortable surroundings, so that the 15.35 train to Pannonhalma will not be too early.

· PANNONHALMA ·

It is difficult to describe the elation this monastery, set high on the last spur of a range of hills, can evoke. In the spring, with bright blue skies, one might almost be in Tuscany. Only the train, usually packed with Russian soldiers as it approaches the village below, reminds one of the east, as the Neo-Classical façade of the Benedictine's richest establishment in Hungary seigneurially rises up over the valley.

The station, whose waiting-room is entirely given over to a table-tennis court, lies about a mile from the monastery and as the sun sets the walk is suitably invigorating.

The foundations of the abbey were laid in 995 by Prince Géza and the church was consecrated in the year 1001. The entrance is between the Neo-Classical wing designed by Josef Engal and János Albert Packh in the 1820s and a curious 1940s Italian school block, which adds even more to the Tuscan atmosphere. The main entrance is straight ahead. This opens into a large hall with a staircase-well supported by slender iron columns. Downstairs are some fading but beautiful portraits of Franz Josef and some Benedictine pupils, all with a strong hint of *japonisme* in the colours, something quite rare in Central Europe.

Up the stairs and towards the tower, however, is a Gothic cloister which in turn has a Romanesque entrance to the church for the monks and a humbler door for the congregation. Here, on a wall just before the entrance, are some of the architect's original elevations for the building, showing that only a part of Packh's initial ambitious plans were executed, though what there is is splendid enough for a prince.

Inside the chapel, there broods a dark Gothic, refreshingly northern in atmosphere. In keeping with monastic practice, the church is built on three levels, one for the monks, another for the clergy and another for the laity. A crypt below the middle floor is partly Romanesque and partly Gothic. At precisely 19.05, vespers with Gregorian chants can be heard, while those who are able to avail themselves of monastic hospitality can look forward to rising with the sun for Lauds at 5.45. These services, with their earnest closely cropped monks whose life-style is rather more austere than that enjoyed by the Benedictines in England, are solemn occasions, as moving as anything in the Romanesque abbeys of France.

A rather overgrown but none the less picturesque botanical garden drops down from behind the monastery while above, the spectacular Neo-Classical library boasts, in addition to a rather dashing statue of the Emperor Francis I, 300,000 volumes.

Pannonhalma is a severe if welcome oasis of calm scholarship. It is still a fee-paying boarding school – a remarkable achievement in any communist country – and the terrace, with its incomparable views, is as good a place as any in which to contemplate a tour of the rest of Hungary.

7

EASTERN HUNGARY AND
THE PUSZTA

From Budapest eastwards, the railway and motorway pass some of the
flattest and dullest landscape in the world. The Great Central European
plain, over which the Mongol hordes swarmed, is a lonely place which
has played upon the imagination of travellers to Central Europe for
centuries. The Puszta, as this plain is called, so excited the ingenuity
of British intelligence during the last war that a plan was seriously
considered whereby the 'Fortress Europe' of the Nazis would be set ablaze
by a vast fire ignited here by thousands of balloons flown from England
laden with incendiaries. Travelling across its seemingly interminable
expanse, it seems at times that this would have been a suitable fate for so
unexciting a landscape.

Its fifty thousand square kilometres once boasted a unique way of
life, dominated by herdsmen who dressed in picturesque attire and
looked after thousands of wild horses and cattle. Although, as can be
seen in neighbouring Transylvania, this way of life is not completely
extinct, to all intents and purposes it died in Hungary after the war,
with the country's swift transition to a modern mechanized agricultural
economy.

The best place from which to explore the plain, small villages being
rare – settlements on the Puszta are never more than a few houses – is
the interesting city of DEBRECEN (trains on the eastern railway take four
hours from Budapest), whose name is synonymous with a delicious
sausage known throughout Central Europe as a '*Debreziner*'.

Debrecen has always played an important role in Hungary's history and
has been a busy trading centre since the Middle Ages. With the establishment of a Calvinist college in 1546, it became the heart of the Hungarian
reformation. It was here that the Hungarian patriot Kossuth deposed the

Habsburgs in the revolution of 1848–9. During the winter of 1944–5, Debrecen again became the capital of Hungary, as the last German units in the country were repulsed by the invading Soviet army.

Primarily an agricultural town, Debrecen has suffered a number of unfortunate planning decisions. The need to set up an 'industrial zone' has led to it becoming a far less picturesque place than it once was. Nevertheless, there is much to see, and the oldest parts of the town behind the main boulevards are a remarkably tranquil urban ensemble.

The centre of the inner town is the Vörös Hadsereg útja which, in common with most cities of the plain, is as wide as a square. The early nineteenth-century Calvinist church, situated at the north end of the road, can rightly be called the heart of the city. Its yellow mass, with an interesting if rather severe Neo-Classical façade, is fifty-five metres long – it is the largest Protestant church in Hungary. It was built to the designs of a military engineer by the name of Mihály Péchy, but his original plans were adapted by Josef Tallherr, to whom the façade's Ionic order is attributed.

Inside, the three aisles emphasize the rather austere tenets of the Calvinist church. The chancel is the work of Samuel Kiss and the pulpit's elegant proportions were a humble if worthy setting from which to depose the century-old Habsburgs.

Kálvin tér, which adjoins the Vörös avenue, is the site of the Calvinist college. This attractive building is also the work of the engineer Péchy, although the fine interiors are attributed to Károly Rabel, while the impressive library (apply to the director), constructed in 1827, is the work of a certain Josef Dohanyósi.

In the western part of the square stands the ebullient art-nouveau Aranybika (Golden Bull) Hotel, which should be first choice for refreshment and a room for the night. Although its once splendid rooms were adapted and restored with enthusiastic bad taste in the mid-seventies, this establishment still has a certain old-fashioned grandeur which one associates with the best-established hotels of Europe.

The hall contains a charming exhibition dedicated to the hotel's builder who, besides being an architect, apparently won a medal at the first Olympic Games. The nearby breakfast hall offers some quite garish modern glass amid the Jugendstil fittings, but the breakfasts themselves, with the ubiquitous Debreziner sausages, are to be recommended. A modern annexe to the hotel has rooms which are generally less comfortable than those in the older part which, though inclined to be a little noisier, have excellent balcony views over the square.

Base camp established as it were, it is time to explore the rest of the Vörös Avenue. No. 29 is the so-called small Calvinist church, a curious building with a rather ugly tower, constructed in the 1870s over an already existing church of the 1720s. The contrast inside is curious: sweets wrapped in dull paper. Nearby is the old County Hall, built in 1912, rich in Jugendstil motifs and afire with the glow of jazzy majolica.

There are several taverns along this road which are worth exploring. At night, they are filled with a curious mixture of soldiery, mainly conscripts, and hardened wizened-looking men from the plain wearing jodhpurs and riding boots.

A left turn up Béke útca, past the lovely Baroque church of St Anna, leads to an older part of the town where few houses are above two storeys and crumbling brickwork and overgrown gardens make a picturesque and tranquil scene. Unlike the main boulevards, which meet at right angles, the little streets here meander in a remarkable survival of pre-Baroque planning. Many of the gardens contain the melancholy remains of what were agricultural outhouses and, in some, chickens and other small animals are still kept. Lizt út, behind the rather eclectic nineteenth-century theatre on Kossuth út, is typical of these. From here the Vár út returns to the Kálvin Square.

To the west of the college, which houses a small museum of ecclesiastical art, is the more interesting Déri Museum in Déri tér, which has a collection of modern Hungarian art.

The only other sight of interest in Debrecen is the Botanic Gardens, on the outskirts of the town near its university complex. The suburbs glimpsed here are an impressive if rather ugly reminder of the fast rate of construction which has taken place in post-war Hungary.

From Debrecen, a branch railway line, or a tourist bus, which is quicker, runs to what is considered the most picturesque part of the great plain, Nágy-Hortobágy. The characteristics of the Puszta are here particularly well displayed: an immense treeless grassy plain enlivened only here and there by the huts of shepherds and other humble buildings surrounded by small groves of acacias. The sunrises are still a fabulous sight, although the 'Fata Morgana', or mirages, which used to be regularly seen during the months of July and August, are rarely in evidence today.

Sadly, HORTOBÁGY has suffered from Hungary's developing tourist industry and there is at first little sign of the deserted rustic or even sleepy atmosphere one would expect. Bus-loads of tourists descend and empty out to buy bottles of the excellent Hungarian schnapps known as *barack* (pronounced 'barask') or keep a local bootmaker busy with orders.

But if one travels by train, the advantage of stopping off at the less well-known settlements between Debrecen and Hortobágy can be quite rewarding. One small halt is unforgettable for the small horse-drawn railway which ferries passengers who alight here across the field to the village. At any of these stops, something of the old Puszta can be glimpsed, although the advances made in modernizing Hungary's agricultural economy since the war means that the Puszta familiar to earlier travellers is now lost forever.

Hortobágy itself, despite its development, is still well worth visiting for its excellent museum, which offers as great an insight into life on the plain as is possible today. Old farm implements and the remarkably practical as well as colourful costumes of the shepherds are displayed along with a fine collection of black-and-white photographs. Faces sandblasted by the plain's inhospitable climate gaze down, often silhouetted against a distant shimmering horizon.

Nearby is the old inn of Hortobágy (good wine) dating from the late eighteenth century, with a newer wing added in 1815. The nine-arch bridge almost opposite is a sombre affair of the 1820s.

From here, depending on transport, it should be possible to get to Szeged, the last great city of the plain, within a few hours. Alternatively it may be useful to return to Debrecen and go on to Transylvania (see Chapter 8) or linger on the great plain and then head north for the hills and the wines of Tokay. All three options are easily accomplished from here.

SZEGED is an undeniably attractive place lying on the river Tisza, or Theiss, and well connected with other parts of Hungary by rail and road. If Debrecen is renowned for its austere Calvinism, Szeged enjoys the reputation of being the centre of Hungary's paprika production, that ubiquitous condiment of Hungarian cuisine. This was not always so, however. Indeed, the name Szeged is derived from the word *szeg* or *szek*, the local earth which is impregnated by alkaline crystals. These were exposed by the dew and collected with the earth, usually in a ratio of one to three, by the peasants, who then sold it to the soda manufacturers in Szeged. The town still boasts the nineteenth-century architecture of these curious factories, although much of the town was destroyed in 1879 when the river flooded. The names of the principal boulevards – London, Paris, Brussels etc. – recall the aid which was received from those places for the reconstruction. The new city was laid out on a grid plan with extensive suburbs, which provoked the comment from one nineteenth-century traveller that Szeged, in spite of its far smaller population, was as big as London.

Most of the important buildings of the city are on the left bank, within an inner avenue called Lenin körút. Half-way between this and the river is the heart of the city, Széchenyi Square. Each side of the square has a rather heavy statue illustrating the beneficial and destructive nature of the river Tisza. The building which seems to dominate this area is a curious Neo-Rococo Town Hall; the Tisza Hotel nearby has an adequate café. Facing the river, a road to the right leads to the rather more intimate Klauzál tér where, although rather tastelessly modernized, the Royal Hotel is one of the most convenient places to stay in Szeged. But rooms in private houses tend to be more attractive and can be obtained from the tourist office in the Széchenyi Square.

From here Kárász út leads to the university in Dugonics tér and eventually the arcaded red-brick buildings of Dóm tér, at the centre of which is the vast neo-Romanesque Votive church, constructed in the years between 1914 and 1930. Like many buildings of this scale built at that time, it has a cold precision which is not without effect, although its best role is probably as a backdrop to the events of the open-air Szeged festival which takes place here annually.

The St Demetrius Tower, constructed on eleventh-century foundations, adds to this rather stagy ensemble. When the fine musical clock in the arcaded walls of the Dóm tér strikes the hours at noon, costumed figures symbolizing the rector, deans and students of the university march in front of the dial of the clock to the strains of a Hungarian folk tune.

There are several fine restaurants in the nearby Oskola út, or by walking down to the river and turning left one comes to the hotel at Roosevelt tér, with its extensive views of 'New Szeged' across the river. Roosevelt Square itself is a more than suitable place to rest as it contains a number of museums, of which the Móra Ferenc, with its collection of paintings and ethnography and 250,000 volumes, is perhaps the most important.

Contemplating the ruins of the old Szeged fortress here, it is hard to imagine that during the empire it was for years the Colditz of the Austrian army, in which Italian prisoners captured during the insurrections of the 1848–9 revolution were kept. An interesting local museum in the fortress is able to recapture this time through old prints and photographs, although the usual inordinate amount of space is devoted to the events of the twentieth-century 'revolutionary' period after the last war.

The nearby floating restaurant, Szóke Tisza, is best visited during the summer, when a slight breeze along the river comes as a relief in what can be one of the most humid parts of the Great Plain.

Continuing along the river bank, the magnificent National Theatre, yet another work of that ubiquitous nineteenth-century duo Helmer and Fellner, grandly dominates the river along with the rather less imposing Baroque Serbian Orthodox church and the picturesque Fékete house, from which any number of winding roads lead back to the Széchenyi Square.

All that now remains to be seen in the town is the magnificent former Franciscan church, which lies in the south-west of the city centre and can be best reached quickly by taxi from Széchenyi Square. According to local records this impressive Gothic edifice was begun in the late thirteenth century but was, according to a stone dated 1503 on the exterior of the south façade, finished only in the sixteenth century. Inside the decoration is Baroque and attributed to a Franciscan monk by the name of Antal Graff. The single barn-like space of the interior, with its light airy Gothic rib-vaulting, is a suitable foil to the Baroque decoration of the pulpit, side altars and other items of Graff's Baroque furniture.

Josef Aisenhut, a native of the Rhineland, is responsible for the high altar's eighteenth-century paintings, while those of the side altars depicting St John Nepomuk and St Francis are the work of a contemporary Viennese painter, Josef Hautzinger. A curious small Romanesque window in the south wall of the sacristy suggests that parts of an earlier building on this site may have been incorporated into the church. The sacristy itself contains a number of rather fine Baroque chests. A Franciscan museum attached contains several objects of ecclesiastical interest. The nearby Franciscan monastery building is of the Baroque period and has maintained a fine library.

Another church which should not be missed, especially by devotees of art-nouveau, is the New Synagogue, designed by Lipot Bauhorn at the turn of the century in the Jósika útca, near Lenin körút. Its dome is visible from most parts of the inner town. (The usual rules on headdress are applicable here; the porter will open the church for a small sum – apply at Jósika útca 10.) The interior is unforgettable for the colours of its stained glass, while a remarkable studded ark of the covenant made of Egyptian acacia will also be shown on application to the authorities.

The other side of the river is made up of newer residential blocks and the twenty-eight acres of the university botanical garden, which contains more than 1,500 tropical plants.

If a stay of longer than a day is contemplated, there is one of the most attractive bird reserves in Europe in the form of a large sodium carbonate lake known as Fehér-tó. Liveliest in spring and autumn during the time of the great migrations, this is the northernmost stopping place for several rare species. Permits to visit the reserve should be applied for in advance from the National Office for the Protection of Nature, Költo útca 21 in Budapest.

From Szeged a small road numbered 25 and then 28 leads to SZENTES, passing through typical Puszta country. It is recommended for those wishing to return to Budapest by car more slowly. Szentes itself has an interesting museum which charts the great migrations across the plain. Although a very small settlement, it has both private rooms and a reasonable hotel with thermal baths.

From Szentes, the road leads north-west towards Kecskemét and the hills, an area renowned for the quality of its vines and grapes and apricots, from which the famous *barack* aperitif is made.

Much of KECSKEMÉT's architecture is turn-of-the-century and will thrill Jugenastil enthusiasts. Its large squares and brightly coloured façades, although under attack by recent developments, still offer a pleasing townscape.

The town itself dates from the Middle Ages, having enjoyed several trading and legal privileges in the fourteenth century. Unlike most of the towns of the plain, the century and a half of Turkish rule here brought progress rather than destruction. Many of the inhabitants of the medieval villages sought refuge in Kecskemét, which was a protectorate of the Sultan. During this time the guilds of the town flourished and the place became one of the busiest trading centres in Central Europe.

The centre of the town is a pair of wide squares onto which most of the principal roads seem to converge. Szabadság tér is dominated by an exotic art-nouveau workers' club originally built as a people's house, like that in Prague near the Powder Tower. Its name, the Cifra Palace, seems just as exotic as its appearance.

Also on the square is a nineteenth-century synagogue embracing an older building of 1818. The prominent situation of this building and its obvious wealth recalls the importance of the Jews in the trade of south-eastern Europe. Every town of any note in this part of Hungary boasts a synagogue, which usually, though not always, survived the Nazis. In the early years of the war, Hungary, virtually alone of Germany's allies in Eastern Europe, spared the Jews, gipsies and other non-Aryans pursued by the Third Reich.

Quite near the synagogue is the Calvinist church, which was built between 1680 and 1684; although its rather more decorated interior is late Baroque of the early 1790s. These buildings are the main delights of this square along with other humbler buildings, although unfortunately it also contains the modern six-storey Aranyhomok (Golden Sand) Hotel.

The adjoining Kossuth tér is the administrative centre of the town, with a dazzling art-nouveau Town Hall designed by our old friend the Jugendstil architect of Budapest's Applied Arts Museum, Ödön Lechner (see p. 79). The interior is open to the public and contains several other works of art-nouveau, including a wall painting in the ceremonial hall by Bertalan Székely illustrating the Hungarian conquest.

Also near the Town Hall, on Kossuth Square, is an old church known by the locals for some incomprehensible reason as the 'ancient church', although it dates only from the last quarter of the eighteenth century. On the southern side of the square is the rather more interesting church of St Nicholas, which was first built in the fifteenth century but rather strangely rebuilt in a quixotic mixture of Gothic motifs in the eighteenth. Another Baroque church is the Piarist church in the nearby Jókai útca, built between 1724 and 1730.

Amid all these churches, a brief respite may be taken at the restaurant at the corner of Nagykőrösi and Móricz út, while for those with a taste for the High Victorian ecclesiastical, the Lutheran church built by Ybl (the architect of the Budapest Opera) is in the Arany János út.

The town has a busy air of commercial prosperity, mixed, because of its situation rather to the south of the country, with a relaxed almost Balkan approach to life. Near Kossuth tér are several smaller squares with the town's theatre and more administrative buildings.

If the journey is being continued by rail, a modest museum of modern art almost opposite the railway station could be visited for its collection of popular art.

Efforts should also be made to attend a performance at either the opera or the concert hall, as the town is renowned for its music. Zoltán Kodály (1882–1967), the great Hungarian composer, was born here and the music academy named after him has produced many of the country's finest musicians.

To the south-east of Kossuth Square, the Csongrádi út leads to a curious artists' colony established, like that at Darmstadt, before the First World War in 1909. Its buildings, however, scarcely rival those of other artists' colonies at the turn of the century and therefore are only of novelty interest.

From Kecskemét, the B U G A C puszta, some twenty-nine miles south of the town, can be reached by bus. There is something rather more primitive about the Bugac puszta than the Hortobágy. Even before the Second World War, life was rather nomadic here and though vineyards and orchards have been planted since then, the landscape has retained much of its original character. As long as it is not the height of the tourist season, a very pleasant meal with music can be had at the Bugac csárda. The nearby woods provide excellent cover for pheasant shooting and facilities are available on the presentation of a shot-gun licence and some advance notice (apply at tourist offices).

If, instead of visiting Szeged and Kecskemét, the traveller has returned to Debrecen, a short spell, if only a couple of days, should be spent in the northern more hilly part of the country. If this is the first objective after Budapest, the best way of reaching the area is to take a train to Eger (see p. 111); otherwise from Debrecen the first destination must be the small town whose name is immortalized in all histories of Hungarian cuisine for the greatness of its wine: TOKAY.

This small village, whose wines continue to enjoy the sobriquet 'King of wines, wine of kings', is still one of the least spoilt places in Hungary. No industry and relatively few new buildings have emerged to mar its simplicity and intimacy, and there are few villages in which an hour can be spent as profitably as here.

The settlement is entered near its river. Those arriving by train are met by a bus, which transfers passengers to the village centre. The village is well worth spending a night in, although accommodation is limited. There is a modern and not particularly attractive hotel near the river, but rooms in private houses are likely to be more attractive as well as cheaper. These can be found on application to the hotel porter or the tourist office in the village square. If these requests prove fruitless, the best and, in the author's experience, most effective way of securing rooms is to stop some friendly old lady and ask in German for her advice. More often than not she will knock on the nearest door and persuade the owner to offer her rooms to the strangers.

If finding rooms is not particularly a problem, food, it must be said, is not as good as it is in the main cities, although the modern restaurant of the hotel has an attractive terrace overlooking the river. Occasionally the fish can be excellent, but otherwise it is advisable to concentrate on the real joy of the place, its wine.

The glory of this wine, known as 'essence of Tokay' or *'essencia'*, is usually very difficult to obtain. It is sweet Tokay made from pressing of the finest grapes and matured for at least twelve years in a deep cellar, where a black spongy mould forms on the bottles and walls because of the moisture. Its purity and sweetness are unquestionable and indeed it lives up to its reputation of being capable of restoring a dying emperor.

Commoner than the *essencia* are the dry Tokays known as 'Szamorodni' and the sweet 'Aszubor', which is given a number of 'butts' on its bottle neck from one to six depending on the level of sweetness. Thus a 1980 Aszubor with six butts will be sweeter and richer than a 1976 with three butts. Most of the bottles to be seen for sale throughout Hungary come from the government's own consortium in the nearby village of Tolcsva. However, there are several private cellars in the region which allow tastings and possess some very fine Aszubor for modest prices. The most convenient of these is almost five minutes' walk away from the hotel. Turning left then right from the hotel out of the village, there is a private cellar on the right where an aged lady will syphon the wine from the barrel with a long test-tube device.

Along the main street, there is much of interest. As in many settlements in this part of the world, there has long been a variety of religious activities here. There are Protestant, Catholic, Lutheran and Calvinist churches, and down one road to the right the impressive if melancholy ruins of a synagogue.

Continuing along the main road past several pleasing doors of early nineteenth-century pattern on the left, we come to the main square, where the most visited church is situated on the left. It is a nineteenth-century affair with a rather austere character relieved by modern glass and a jolly congregation. Above it to the left is another church of some Protestant denomination, while below, continuing along the road, one passes another unidentifiable religious building with a lofty tower, though it is usually closed.

On the left of this principal village street, after walking for some minutes, is the museum of wine and wine-making, whose exhibits are displayed in the basement of an old house. Here there is an impressive array of machinery and earlier implements involved with the making of wine, as well as several charming old bottles of the Tokay wines made before the war. Many of these came from princely estates and bear the names of such famous aristocratic families of Hungary as Esterházy and Széchenyi. There are also several menus and posters dating from the time before the First World War, when the Tokay wine industry was launching an export drive in foreign countries, including England. Although Voltaire commemorated the wine in a book and Haydn and Schubert are both said to have composed songs praising its great restorative qualities, it would seem that mass advertising was still necessary. Ironically, this great wine was considered to possess such medicinal qualities that for many years of this century in Hungary the only way to procure the best wine was through a chemist's.

A little further on from the museum, a turning to the right leads down several picturesque streets which then lead back to the river and the hotel. Continuing further along the main road however, it may be of interest to reflect that one of communist Europe's few boarding schools is situated in the large and very school-like nineteenth-century building on the road. The British Council, always fond of arcane ventures, commendably supplies the school with an English native speaker. It is curiously reassuring to think that a few yards along these dusty roads, still used mainly by horses and carts, someone is instilling these young Magyars with a basic awareness of English literature. It is yet another example of the close connections Hungary enjoys with the Anglo-Saxon world.

Back in the village square, a small bar run by the government's Tokay wine consortium will offer a good glass of four-puttom (or butts) Aszubor.

From Tokay, a railway runs to MISKOLC, the second largest city in the country, where much of the nation's industry is concentrated. Although the city has several fine churches, it is not a place to spend a night. Cement and lime works as well as several iron industries make it a grey settlement, especially in winter.

The classical Calvinist church at the corner of Kossuth útca and Széchenyi útca is of interest, as is the Greek Orthodox church in the courtyard of Ferenc Deák tér 7, built between 1785 and 1806, which contains an exquisite iconostasis and some impressive choir stalls in the severe Zopf or Louis Seize style.

At the end of the Széchenyi útca is the 234-foot-high Avas hill, with its Calvinist church dating from the fourteenth century which has an interesting wooden ceiling and choir. The old streets on the hill contain about 800 wine cellars, for this is an area renowned for its red wines. The Hermann Ottó Museum near the church above is rich in archaeological objects found while the limestone was being excavated. At the top of the hill is a squat modern lookout with a café commanding excellent views of the city – when the smog lifts.

If there is time, an excursion should perhaps be made to Diósgyőr castle, a symmetrical series of fortifications dating from the fourteenth century. Having lost its strategic role, it was used as a hunting base for the country's kings and queens.

About one and a half miles from the village begins a romantic ravine (Hámorvolgy), watered by the brawling Garadna. From here a picturesque road winds its way along the Bükka to EGER, one of the most interesting towns in the northern part of the country and a welcome change from the overdeveloped sprawl of Miskolc.

Eger is one of the oldest settlements in Hungary and the first King of Hungary, St Stephen, founded a bishopric here at the beginning of the eleventh century. The sixteenth-century bishops of Eger liked to build extensively, but the invasions of the Turks ended this. Luckily the fortress, which had been extended most capably after the first Mongol incursions in the thirteenth century, was able to withstand the initial attacks of the Turks in 1556. Captain István Dobó, the commander of the garrison at this time, has been justly celebrated in several Hungarian poems and plays. Unfortunately, forty years later, the Turks were successful and the town was occupied for almost a century until 1687. Later, during the uprisings of Rákóczi against the Austrians, the fortress again had to be besieged.

The rest of the town is Baroque, with little sign of that rather heavy nineteenth-century architecture which is to be encountered in most towns of Central Europe. This must be partly the result of the town's isolation from the main railway lines across Hungary. Even today, it only has a branch line to the junction of Füzesabony.

The present town still bears signs of the rivalry between bishops and citizens which existed in the Baroque period, with the result that there are two centres in the town, one ecclesiastical and the other civic. The ecclesiastical centre is situated around the cathedral and Szabadzág Square and the centre of the merchants' town around Dobó István tér.

On the eastern side of this rather impressive square is the Lyceum, or training college for teachers, a Baroque building designed by Jakob Fellner and Josef Grossmann in the 1770s. The library here contains some 80,000 volumes, many of them dating from the seventeenth century. The Astronomy Institute is in the eastern wing's rather picturesque observation tower. It is worth recording that the building was erected originally as a philosophy and theological institute, but this was suppressed by the reforms of Joseph II (see p. 22) and converted into a school. Several of the rooms, including the library, have impressive ceilings painted in the eighteenth century and on the whole sympathetically restored. The building is one of the most important of its date in Hungary, and the library, with its medallions and wood carvings, is an excellent foil to the richness of the frescoes above, portraying the Council of Trent.

The Lyceum provides a worthy overture to the other splendid buildings of Eger. Opposite stands the Neo-Classical cathedral, designed by Josef Hild, Hungary's leading empire architect, in the 1830s. The exterior, with its six Corinthian columns and dome, is one of the most striking façades in Hungary. The effete statues of saints along the monumental staircase ascending to the portico were executed by the Italian craftsman Marco Casagrande between 1833 and 1846. Casagrande is also responsible for the reliefs on the façade depicting Jesus in the Temple and the Pietà.

Through the portico another colonnade leads to the three aisles. Three domes mark the ceiling of the central aisle, rather as in Sant'Antonio at the end of the Canale Grande in Trieste, designed by Hild's contemporary Peter von Nobile (see p. 214). An octagonal chapel to the right of the principal altar contains a number of somewhat mediocre frescoes of the 1880s by Férencs Szoldatics. The large marble cherubs guarding the high altar are again the work of Casagrande. All in all the atmosphere is curiously like that of many Neo-Classical churches in Italy. The paintings of the side altars, mainly the work of nineteenth-century Italian artists from Modena, reinforce this impression. The paintings in the south aisle are much earlier than the classical structure and are believed to have come from a previous church of the 1760s on this site.

From the cathedral, the park leads to an ugly bus-station, mentioned here only because it may be useful later on.

Kossuth út, leading from the bottom of the cathedral stairs to the left, should now be followed, as the street contains a wealth of Baroque houses, many of which are well worth a few moments' attention. The first house of note, No. 4, known as the Provostal House, is a magnificent Rococo palace built in 1758, possibly to the plans of the Austrian architects Matthias Franz Gerl or Franz Anton Pilgram, though the façade is attributed to one Henrick Fazola.

Inside, the most impressive room is an octagonal Festsaal, with frescoes by Lukas Huetter representing the four continents of the earth. Notice the allegorical figures chosen to represent the continents: an Indian for the Americas, a Turk for Asia, a Moor for Africa and no less a person than Maria Theresa for the continent of Europe. Other rooms are notable for the quality of Rococo stucco work on the ceilings.

Further along the street is the Franciscan church, built on the site of an earlier mosque in the 1740s, but with a façade which would seem to be rather later than this, towards the end of the century. The former

Franciscan monastery which adjoins it is also a Baroque building of considerable dignity.

Opposite this is another impressive secular palace worth examining: the former County Council hall. Designed by Matthias Gerl, in 1748, it was partly rebuilt in the 1790s and added to in the late 1830s. The Rococo ironwork with allegorical figures representing faith, hope and charity is all the work of Henrick Fazola.

The Jókai út on the left leads to the Dobó István tér, where there is a rare example of mature Baroque architecture in the shape of the former Minorites' church. The Minorites first built a church here in the second decade of the eighteenth century, but the present building dates from the years 1728 to 1730 and would seem to have been built, if the latest research is to be believed, by the remarkable Prague architect Kilian Ignaz Dientzenhofer (see p. 157).

The façade alone demands attention. Its plain rectangle is broken up by a convex façade with twin Ionic columns on large bases – very much a Roman solution. Inside, the decoration is no less impressive. Four bays, each domed, culminate in a rectangular choir with frescoes by the Pressburg (Bratislava) artist Martin Raindl. The high altar of 1771, with its sculptures, is attributed to Johann Lucas Kracker, while the choir has two paintings by Bartolomeo Altomontes.

Left of the church, down the Alkotmány út, is the Széchenyi útca with the Archbishop's Palace and monastery buildings, originally Jesuit but later Cistercian. The old chemist's at No. 14 has been operating here since 1743, and its very quaint interior is open to the public.

Nearby is another attractive church, that of the Greek and Serbian Catholics. Built in the eighteenth century, it contains a number of interesting examples of conventional Byzantine art, with an iconostasis attributed to Miklós Jankowits. From here the Sándor I. út to the right leads towards a small brook, across which is a 95-foot-high Turkish minaret. The mosque which was attached to it was destroyed when the Turks were driven from the town in the seventeenth century, but the tower was restored in the nineteenth century and still contains a gallery from which a fine view of the rooftops of Eger is available.

Beyond here on a hill to the east are ruins of the old castle of Eger (entrance on the Dózsa György tér). It has interesting casemates, and a museum is situated in the Gothic arcaded building of the medieval Bishops' Palace in the courtyard of the fortress.

From here a walk north to the Gárdonyi út leads via a café to the Gárdonyi Museum, which commemorates the siege of 1551. Alternatively, across the brook in the Dobó István tér, a bar will provide some of the very best wine in Hungary. The red wine will be familiar to most people, as it has for some years now been popular in British supermarkets under the name of 'Bulls' Blood', or Egri Bikavér. At its best it is fruity, dry and rather strong.

Most of the hotels are situated in the southern part of the town, but the most convenient is probably at the corner Kossuth Lajos út and Hibay Károly út, although it is not as quiet as those nearer the springs. At the time of writing a restaurant in the Jókai út seemed to offer the best Magyar cuisine, though, as in so many parts of Hungary, the food is not quite up to the standard of Budapest.

From Eger, the branch-line railway runs to Füzesabony for trains to either Debrecen or Budapest, where strength must be gathered before contemplating what is the most arduous part of any tour of Central Europe, Transylvania.

8

TRANSYLVANIA

The luxury and physical comforts of Hungary will be less easy to find in Transylvania. Instead, this land offers a glimpse of what most of rural Central Europe must have looked like before the war. Therein lies its charm. To see on a bright summer morning a Saxon wedding in a German village or to walk among the narrow cobbled streets of Hermannstadt (Sibiu) or Schässburg (Sighişoara) is to be able to experience an outpost of Teutonic culture which in other parts of Eastern Europe disappeared after the war.

It is questionable how long the Romanian regime in Bucharest is prepared to tolerate these blond Saxons. For the last five years a consistent policy of enforced emigration has been implemented, allowing a few thousand people each year to reach West Germany for a by no means insignificant sum paid by Bonn.

In addition, there are many Hungarians here, although their culture is not as noticeable to the ordinary traveller, who is unlikely to be able to tell the difference between them and the majority of the inhabitants, the almost equally dark-skinned Romanians.

Renowned for its legends, not least that of Dracula, Transylvania can claim to have been one of the most bitterly contested parts of Europe in the Dark Ages. Until A.D. 274 it was under Roman sway. Then the Emperor Aurelian was compelled by the Gothic hordes of the north to withdraw his troops and the Roman colonists across the Danube. From this time down to the twelfth century, the area was the scene of great battles between Ostrogoths, Huns, Longobards, Bulgarians, Magyars, Kumans and other eastern races.

During the reign of Ladislaus I, King of Hungary (1078–95), the land was united with Hungary. Geisa (Géza) II (1141–62), who perceived the importance of Transylvania as the key to Hungary's east flank, summoned Germans from the Middle Rhine to colonize and repopulate the desolated territory. These immigrants are the forefathers of the present 'Saxon' population of Transylvania.

They set to work fortifying seven towns (the Sieben Burgen) and in 1224 Andreas II of Hungary (1204–35) granted them a charter known as 'The Golden Bull' in which the rights and privileges of the Germans were theoretically safeguarded for centuries. But when Hungary lost her independence at the battle of Mohács in 1526, Transylvania became an independent principality under Turkish protection, governed by princes elected by the people but approved by the Sultan. Innumerable conflicts then arose between the Habsburgs and the Turks, and when in 1699 the latter made their peace with Vienna, they abandoned their claim to the province, which thence became part of the Austrian empire.

After 1867, when the Dual Monarchy was formed (p. 70), Transylvania became part of the Kingdom of Hungary and was ruled from Budapest. With the collapse of the monarchy after the First World War, it was assigned to Romania, who on the whole exercised considerable tolerance towards the Hungarians before 1939. But the passions engendered by the Second World War rekindled old hatreds, which it must be admitted have not been extinguished by the passage of time – there is probably no more contentious issue in Central Europe. This is partly the result of the enormous differences in wealth between Hungary and Romania today, but partly also of a deep-rooted mutual distrust fuelled by racial chauvinism which is unlikely ever to be dispelled.

As one approaches the frontier from Debrecen, past impressive airbases manned by the Russians, the villages are all kept in immaculate condition. Roads are also all well serviced, so that the contrast with rather backward Romania is as sharp as possible.

The Romanian frontier authorities seem reluctant to undermine this impression. Their uniforms look like something out of a thirties cartoon, but the Romanians are not fools and however implausible these policemen and soldiers may seem they are not to be provoked. There will hardly be any reason to, for it must be said that the average Romanian in uniform can be as hospitable as anyone else. On one trip to Transylvania, while waiting for a train at 5 in the morning, they even supplied me with freshly baked bread and liquor, all for the price of a few words on the fate of the Labour Party in Britain.

The search of luggage will of course be thorough and the customs officials do their work with relish, though not without tact. A copy of Bram Stoker's *Dracula* will invariably raise a smile, while one customs official I encountered, bearing no slight resemblance to the Prince of Darkness himself, actually spent five minutes picking out his favourite passages in the book.

This bothersome business over, both train and road lead to the first city to be encountered on Romanian soil, ORADEA, or Grosswardein as it was known in the days of the Habsburg empire. The Hungarians of course, too, had a name for the settlement – Nagy Varad.

The town is worth a couple of hours but should be avoided for the night if time is short. It is none the less one of the most pleasant towns in Central Europe and were it not for the strain that staying in Romania can impose, there would be no hesitation in suggesting spending more time here. As it is, those who are interested in turn-of-the-century architecture will be delighted by the principal square of the town. Many of the administrative buildings are brightly coloured, and an arcade with ceramic and stained-glass decoration winds its way from the square to a street parallel with it, containing several churches, including an imposing synagogue – another reminder of the important role the Jews played in this part of Europe.

From the main square, a leafy avenue leads to the river Körös (Crişul in Romanian). Across this stands the impressive opera house, designed needless to say by Helmer and Fellner (see p. 2). The building is totally in keeping with the atmosphere of the town, which, despite talk of Romanization, is uncompromisingly Central European. Both the Catholic and Greek Orthodox churches are worth a brief inspection, although like most of the buildings in the town they are only nineteenth-century structures.

Not at all Central European, however, is the absence of cafés. We may have to make do with a piece of greasy *burek*, a cheese pastry which is sold in stands at several street corners, or a bottle of undeniably East European beer. In Romania, what food is obtainable depends largely on the time of year, but meat is rationed and at the time of writing most fruits and vegetables were not easy to come by in the town. The rapid industrialization of Romania set into action by the Ceausescu government has lamentably turned what was once the most prosperous agricultural

1. The heart of Vienna, St Stephen's cathedral, with the dome of Hildebrandt's St Peter's in the foreground.

2. The Benedictine abbey of Melk, the Baroque masterpiece of Jakob Prandtauer, situated at the edge of the Wachau.

3. *The Karlskirche in Vienna, erected to designs by Fischer von Erlach as a thanksgiving for deliverance from the plague.*

4. *Schönbrunn, the Habsburgs' summer palace on the outskirts of Vienna.*

5. *Styrian green: Graz, the southernmost German-speaking city in Europe, where Teuton meets southern Slav.*

6. *Budapest's Parliament, closely modelled on that of Westminster and erected in the late nineteenth century.*

7. *The Chain Bridge, Budapest, designed in the 1840s by the English engineer William Tierney Clark.*

8. *Visegrád, overlooking the Danube in Hungary, where King Matthias Corvinus established his 'earthly paradise'.*

9. *Benedictine learning: the great library at Pannonhalma in Hungary.*

10. A Hungarian woman in traditional costume.

11. Cluj (Clausenburg) in Transylvania. In front of the cathedral, an equestrian statue of Matthias Corvinus.

12. *The Cluj opera house, erected by Helmer and Fellner at the turn of the century.*

13. *Saxon women on the way to market in Transylvania.*

14. *A view across the Charles Bridge in Prague, with Hradčany castle on the horizon.*

15. *A view across the orchards of Hradčany towards St Vitus's cathedral in Prague. On the right, the dome of the Dientzenhofers' St Nicholas.*

16. The main entrance to Prague castle, attributed to the Italian Renaissance architect Sanmicheli.

17. *Prague Baroque: an old square behind Hradčany castle. The gas lanterns were converted to electricity only last year.*

18. *Brave new Prague: Hradčany castle guards marching to take up their sentry posts.*

19. *Carpathian retreat: a typical house in the Tatras near Slovakia's frontier with Poland.*

20. *Legacy of a vanished nobility. Former steam baths in Taïranská Lomnica, high in the Tatras.*

21. Carpathian church architecture near Stará Ľubovňa.

22. *Slovak village planning. The market square at Bardejov.*

23. *The cathedral at Košice, the finest medieval building in Slovakia.*

24. *Duino, the home of the Thurn and Taxis princes and, for a few years earlier this century, the great Austrian poet Rainer Maria Rilke.*

25. *Trieste, Central Europe on the Adriatic. At the end of the canal, the church of Sant' Antonio, erected by Nobile.*

26. *Miramar castle, near Trieste, created by the hapless Archduke Maximilian, executed in Mexico in 1867.*

27. *The Austrian Riviera: grand hotels at Opatija (Abbazia).*

country in the Balkans into the most difficult land in Central Europe for finding basic foodstuffs.

Nevertheless, the display of a packet of Kent cigarettes – for some reason no other will do – will usually make the waiter in a restaurant change his mind if he had insisted that none of the articles on the menu is actually available. Chewing-gum and oranges have been known to have a similar effect, and it is no exaggeration to say that most transactions of any value in the country are carried out in this way. Ticket-collectors, hotel-keepers and waiters (but not policemen) are all familiar with this currency, which to all intents and purposes seems to have replaced the official *lei* for daily transactions.

If there is no time for Oradea, the first real city in Transylvania is CLUJ, or Clausenburg as it was known in its imperial heyday, which ever since its founding in 1272 has been an important Transylvanian settlement. This is a far less flashy place than Oradea. There is little art-nouveau and no evidence of nineteenth-century building schemes, with their full panoply of cathedrals and synagogues. The only buildings of this scale and this date are the opera house, another variation on the Neo-Baroque by Helmer and Fellner, and the Romanian Orthodox cathedral – built after the First World War – opposite.

From the station, the broad boulevard called the strada Horea runs to the town centre. To the right on a hill is the citadel erected by General Steinville in 1715. Most of the buildings here are modern. The rather older and more picturesque inner town lies across the river Someşul.

The strada Gh. Doja has a number of quaint buildings, many of which, especially on the right, have interesting courtyards. The house at No. 2 is a chemist's museum. Further on is the nineteenth-century Hotel Metropol, with its rather seedy café–restaurant, as good as any here. The road ends in the large Liberty Square.

The Roman Catholic cathedral of St Michael dominates the square and with it the large equestrian statue of Matthias Corvinus (see p. 94), Hungary's greatest king but considered on this side of the frontier to be a Romanian hero – he was born here in 1458. The statue by Fadreuz, a clumsy object, was erected in 1902.

The cathedral is not without charm and its dark Gothic interior is littered with monuments. Although restored in the nineteenth century, when the present north tower was erected, it still has a fifteenth-century atmosphere inside, with medieval stained glass diluted by some Renaissance woodwork.

Corvin strada, which is at right angles to the piata Libertea, contains the house (No. 6) where Matthias Corvinus was born, although for some reason the rooms of this unprepossessing dwelling seem to have been converted into a kind of applied arts gallery at the time of writing.

The piata Libertea is without doubt the hub of the city. The rather elegant turn-of-the-century Hotel Continental at the corner, with its domes and pediments, is the most convenient place to stay although the food on occasions has been vile. It is expensive, but since it is illegal to stay in private rooms there is little alternative.

From here across the square is the picturesque street known as 6 Martie, whose houses offer an excellent example of nineteenth-century planning. Though Cluj has tripled its population since the war and has endless suburbs every bit as inhuman as anything to be seen in Russia, the centre has been spared and the skyline, looking back down 6 Martie, is as irregular and satisfying as anyone would wish.

The road emerges at a large and dignified square called piata Victorei, which is dominated by two buildings. The Opera, a delightful Helmer and Fellner essay in Neo-Baroque, has recently been restored and has a sumptuous interior. As in most opera houses in Eastern Europe, standards of performance vary enormously according to the programme. But although it is unlikely that there will be anything here to rival the performances of Vienna or Milan – or for that matter Budapest or Prague – a visit to this opera house will afford as good an insight into the workings of cultural life in Transylvania as any guided tour.

Since 1920, most of the works performed here have been in Romanian, the old Hungarian repertoire which once enjoyed exclusive rights here having been relegated to a humbler building in the park. Occasionally the operas are political in theme. I remember one extraordinary work, the magnum opus of some Romanian revolutionary leader, resounding to the sound of machine guns and partisan massacres. The Romanian audience, which numbered less than a dozen and were easily outnumbered by the combined forces of cast and orchestra, were a colourful lot with several elegant ladies wearing hats in their boxes, adopting stiff poses redolent of an Olivia Manning novel.

Almost opposite the Opera is the Romanian Orthodox church. Work began on this vast pile soon after the First World War. The style is

Byzantine revival and the interior suitably sombre and surprisingly atmospheric for a building which was completed only in the thirties. Although there are only a limited number of services which have singing, there are few places in the country where Romanian voices are heard to worse advantage. Why the choirs of neighbouring Bulgaria should be altogether more professional is a difficult question, but the Bulgarians are Slavs, and whatever talent the Romanian has for music it is not for singing.

From the piata Victorei, the str. Petru Groza, a broad avenue, returns to the Liberty Square, from which on the left ascends the str. Universitatu which crosses the Avram str. to become the Bisericii Ortodoxe str. From the right of this runs a small road to the Botanical Gardens.

The gardens were laid out in the nineteenth century as a gift to the town by Count Miko, a Hungarian nobleman. It is still one of the richest and most charming gardens of its kind in Central Europe. The wide variety of trees are planted over a large area broken up by small ravines, not unlike the narrow chines to be found along the south coast of England. Rhododendrons and wooden bridges over streams reinforce the impression that this could be Bournemouth. A sadly – at the time of writing – dilapidated tower near the acacia hill is no longer accessible for the commanding views it must once have offered. Below stands a small but by no means uninteresting museum of botanical specimens.

Back down the str. Republici and left along the road is the large avenue dedicated to the 30th of December. No. 21 is the Ethnographic Museum, which contains a selection of Transylvanian peasant costumes, guarded by a contingent of rather sleepy old women enjoying their knitting. It is symptomatic of the Romanian approach to tourism that surprise is the most common reaction to a request for a ticket.

The Transylvania Restaurant at No. 13, further up the avenue, may be in a position to present a reasonable meal, but as usual much will depend on the circumstances and time of the year. At its best, the Transylvania is not a bad place for an omelette with chips, the least pretentious and disappointing of the many dishes offered in this corner of Central Europe.

Corvin str., on the left, in which is the birthplace of Matthias Corvinus (see p. 94), once the most sacred of shrines in the days of the Austro-Hungarian monarchy, leads to Savinesti str., which at the corner of Emil Zola str. houses a former Franciscan monastery. The monastery is still in the hands of a small community but that is only a shadow of the order which, during the eighteenth century, transformed the buildings into a wealthy Baroque foundation.

The little canal of the Someşul river runs to the left of the monastery towards the town park, at the end of which is the Hungarian opera house, a humble modern building which none the less offers the occasional performance of a Puccini opera which given the resources available is surprisingly good.

The nearby Sport Hotel, despite its heavy architecture, is the most satisfactory place to have dinner before contemplating a visit to the least touched of the seven castles which make up the Saxon settlements in Transylvania, Sighişoara (Schässburg), some miles up the valley, on the road to Sibiu (Hermannstadt).

Few places in Transylvania match SCHÄSSBURG's charm. Picturesquely situated at the entrance to the Schaas valley, it has a sleepy calm which no other town in the region can match. Here, for the first time, it is possible to see Teuton faces, pale with flaxen hair, among the inhabitants. '*Grüss Gott*' rings out more frequently than any other greeting, and the general lack of modern development in the town suggests a world rooted firmly in the past.

From the station, a road leads to the upper town, which with its pinnacles and towers might have inspired *The Prisoner of Zenda*. The streets of the lower town are a mixture of two-storey nineteenth-century Ringstrasse and the odd inter-war building, while not far from the station is a sturdy Protestant church erected in a pattern-book Neo-Gothic style in 1887.

Pleasant though all this is, it is the upper town that allows the visitor to appreciate the best of the place. A small square with a curious twenties folkloristic-style hotel (offering reasonable lunches) is the best starting point. From here, a winding path takes us under the first of a series of towers and past several rather quaint houses with courtyards dating from about the middle of the seventeenth century. The square at the end of this path contains a large Gothic church which on Sundays resounds to the music of Bach chorales sung in German. The congregation consists invariably of the over-fifties, and the old ladies here could have come from any church in Austria or Germany.

Opposite the west end of the church is a pleasant inn with an upstairs terrace. A plaque near the doorway boasts that this was the residence of a certain Vlad Dracul, and the square itself is supposed to have once been the site of this medieval tyrant's innumerable executions. Dracula, Prince Vlad V of Wallachia, lived from 1431 to 1476. There is no evidence that he was a vampire, but he was certainly cruel and at least one well-known contemporary print depicts him rather nonchalantly eating a meal surrounded by his enemies, who have been impaled on pikes. He was a great warrior and leader and has despite his cruelty retained the honour and affection of the Romanians to this day. This building offers a glass of refreshing wine and is also a restaurant, so that strength can be found for the ascent of the beautiful clock tower, which is also a museum.

At present its curator, a strange red-haired Saxon eccentric, will usually guide, in person, any visitor with a smattering of German. He is a convivial soul and like many Saxons in Transylvania he bears any hardship lightly, sustained by the inner spiritual strength which is often to be detected among the remnants of these direct descendants of King Geisa's colonists.

The museum contains several curious items dealing with the town's history, including maps, furniture and a collection of chemists' bottles. The view from the top of the tower is splendid, and there are the usual guidelines giving the directions of the world's capitals.

From the tower a number of attractive parallel streets ascend to a hill-top church. Here there is also a seminary, housed in a rather institutional building, Neo-Gothic in spirit. But the chief object of interest is the fifteenth-century church. It is rarely open and a key must be applied for at the neighbouring seminary. Inside, there are a splendid set of choir stalls and an equally beautiful ciborium, all ascribed to the sons of Veit Stoss of Nuremberg. The atmosphere is Teutonic and contrasts with the warm southern landscape outside.

From here, a path leads through the cemetery – where many Saxon names are to be found engraved on the tombstones – down the hill through some woods.

If there is time and the weather is – as it invariably seems to be here in summer – warm and sunny, there is no better way to spend the afternoon than to walk along one of the small country roads to a Saxon village. Owing to petrol restrictions traffic is minimal, and the carts and horses which occasionally pass one by are easily outnumbered by the rather picturesque pedestrians who appear round every corner hurrying to the next village.

On Sundays, many of the Saxon villages have a wedding at which the amount of colourful costume to be seen will satisfy the most ardent ethnographer. Meivdiasch (Mediaş), a small fortified town ten miles from Schässburg, is a good example, as is Schass (Şaroşu), only five miles from the town, and Teufelsdorf, on the line to Kronstadt. On a clear day there are few hills which are as beautiful as those to be encountered during such walks and the colourfully decorated houses in these villages are a happy sight. The churches in the German-speaking villages are usually Protestant, and again the words of Luther and the strains of Bach can frequently be heard on Sundays.

Although there are unlikely to be many inns in the villages, the hospitality of these people is unrivalled in Central Europe and schnapps, water, beer and bread will never be refused the traveller, especially if he is on foot. At weddings, a few words of German will guarantee a place at the subsequent banquet, a happy feast overshadowed only by the realization that this culture is ultimately doomed.

From Schässburg, the road to Hermannstadt (Sibiu), or a train as far as Karlsburg, from where connections run to Hermannstadt, can be taken.

KARLSBURG, or Alba Iulia as it is called today in Romania, is an interesting place, although it lacks the picturesque charm of much of the other parts of Transylvania. The Apulum of the Romans, the town was once the residence of the princes of Transylvania, Gabor Bethlen and György Rákóczi.

There is a curious museum of antiquities near the station, but the most picturesque and interesting part of the town is the citadel, built on an eminence commanding excellent views of the surrounding countryside. The fine brick fortifications were constructed between 1716 and 1735 by the Emperor Charles VI and recall the wars between the Austrian empire and the Turks following the relief of Vienna in 1683. The chief building of merit here is the cathedral of St Michael, built originally in the Romanesque style but substantially enlarged in the Gothic style by Hunyady Janos in 1443–4. The church contains the sarcophagi of Hunyady Janos (d. 1456), his son Ladislaus, beheaded in Buda in 1457, and Queen Isabella (d. 1556) and her son Sigismund (d. 1571).

Adjoining the cathedral is the episcopal palace, designed in the eighteenth century, while to the north there is a military academy built originally as a Protestant grammar school by Gabor Bethlen and later converted into the series of rather austere barracks to be seen today.

The church of the Jesuits nearby was converted in the nineteenth century into a gunpowder magazine and today is in an area so full of soldiers that cameras should be concealed if the guards are not to jump to all the wrong conclusions. The view from the bastions, especially from the main arch, now bereft of the fine eighteenth-century coat of arms which once adorned it, but decorated by a modern communist obelisk, is not to be missed on a clear day as the land stretches flatly for miles from here.

Back at the cathedral, a large late Baroque building nearby contains the great library which once made up the Batthyaneum, founded by Bishop Batthyány in 1794. Admission is difficult, and sullen staff seem to be everywhere. But the books are beautifully bound.

A couple of cafés nearby may tempt the thirsty, but apart from these there is little to prolong our stay in the fallen glories of the Roman Apulum.

Beyond Karlsburg, the line traverses the plain which was once the scene of the bloody battle in which Hunyady Janos routed the Turks under Mezet Beg in 1442. To the left rise the iron-ore mountains of Transylvania. Eventually, after several long bends, both road and rail reach HERMANNSTADT, the former capital of Transylvania. The town is undoubtedly one of the most picturesque places in Transylvania, although it has far more bustle to it than Schässburg.

Pleasantly situated on a hill lying on the river Cibinul, the old town is entered from the station by following the road proudly named after General Mágheru. This rises with rather dilapidated nineteenth-century houses to the right and left to the church of the Ursuline nuns. This is a Gothic structure erected according to local sources in the fifteenth century. The buttresses of the exterior certainly seem to date from this period, but the rest of the exterior is Baroque. Inside, the hexagonal choir and Gothic vaulting have survived the rather lavish alterations of the eighteenth century.

Left down the str. Mánegului is the Franciscan church, which also dates from the late fifteenth century. The north aisle façade again has impressive buttresses and Gothic windows. Inside, the altar and west façade were rebuilt in the Baroque period, but the sculpture of the Madonna with Child on the high altar is medieval.

Beyond this church lie the old fortifications, which can be examined by turning right along the str. Maternia. The wall, below which can be seen the river, was erected in the seventeenth century as a third ring of fortifications against the Turks. This brick wall has recently been restored, but it remains much as it must have been in previous centuries, while the towers further along seem to have survived successive restorations unharmed.

Turning right down the str. Gh. Lazar we soon come to the centre of the town, the large ring or piata Republica, humming with an almost Mediterranean air, especially during the early evenings when the conscripts from the nearby barracks throng through the streets in a way familiar to anyone who has lingered in an Italian café in a garrison town at the same time of day. At the corner of the square and the Lazar road is a large nineteenth-century grammar school, opposite which are a number of crowded smoky cafés.

The house at No. 10 is a Gothic building which was extended in the sixteenth century to incorporate several Renaissance features, of which the doorway with the arms of a merchant by the name of Petrus Haller is the most striking. The balustrade and staircase inside leading to several vaulted rooms are quite impressive, while the large building inside the courtyard is an old chapel (usually closed) with Gothic windows. Nearby, No. 16 is graced with a fine stone doorway reputed to be the work of Elias Nicolai, whose monogram can be seen on part of the vaulting. Inside there are traces of frescoes on some of the walls.

But the square is dominated by the large Catholic church of the 1720s, a typical Jesuit building, restrained and with a rather austere façade. The interior is undistinguished except for the ceiling, which has some jolly stucco work.

From the main square, a tower adjoining the Catholic church and constructed in 1588 connects us with the smaller ring or market square, perhaps the most delightful urban space in the entire country. To enjoy it fully, cross through the market to the sixteenth-century arcaded building opposite. There a café with surprisingly luxurious chairs offers a fine vantage point. The arcaded house which it forms part of is typical of the town, not least because it contains the famous dormer windows – more slits than actual windows – which are known in Transylvania as 'the eyes of Hermannstadt'. Indeed, walking across the square towards twilight, it is hard to imagine that the buildings here are not engaged in some traditional act of surveillance. A local guide points out that the square itself was the scene of many executions and 'revengeful acts watched by these houses', and the traveller will be impressed by the rather eerie quality of the architecture, which has survived so well the ravages of centuries, invasions and world wars included. No. 31 (6 Marte Square) is the former Town Hall, while No. 22 contains some interesting seventeenth-century frescoes on the ground floor.

Some stairs lead down past No. 31 to a beer tavern on the right beyond an old tower. The square here was once the home of many goldsmiths, while another square to the left was once called Dragonerplatz after the cavalry officers who billeted here during the wars against the Turks. Few of the streets around are paved, cars are rare, and as the children play their football matches in the road it is hard·to believe this is a part of modern Europe.

From here it is possible to return to the 6 Marte Square along the str. Karl Marx, which runs across the no more imaginatively named str. 9 Mai. This runs underneath a quaint iron bridge erected in 1859 which was for many years a favourite meeting place of merchants and others involved in the petty financial transactions indispensable to any provincial town in this part of Europe.

On the right rises the most impressive church in the town, the Lutheran church. It is a solemn Gothic building dating from the fourteenth to the sixteenth centuries and built on the ruins of a Roman basilica. The imposing bell-tower dates from 1499. The interior (key from the sacristan at the green door opposite the north aisle) is a wonderfully northern vaulted space, designed to house several hundred worshippers. On the north wall is an interesting fresco dating from the fifteenth century and attributed to Johannes of Rosenau. Situated at the west end is a beautiful cup-shaped font dating from 1438 and attributed to one, Master Leonhardus.

The so-called 'New Church', an addition of the sixteenth century, contains several interesting tombstones of Saxon counts and includes the tomb of Petrus Haller, whose house on the piata Republica has already been admired. The door to the sacristy is a fine example of the medieval locksmith's art. On Sundays there are just a few score of Saxons left to worship in this barn of a church.

From the church, past the statue of G. D. Teutsch, a nineteenth-century Protestant bishop, the road back to the main square leads to the Bruckenthal Museum, with its splendid art gallery. Bruckenthal, whose name and image appear in a window in the Protestant church as one of the town's benefactors, was governor of Transylvania from 1777 to 1787, and this grand palace was bequeathed by him to the Protestant school in Hermannstadt, who in turn were forced to hand it over to the state after the last war.

The picture gallery on the second floor is a welcome oasis of fine art in an otherwise unsophisticated country not renowned for its collections of old masters. The first room to be entered contains nothing less startling, for this part of the world, than a fine portrait by Van Dyck of Charles I with his wife. The next room contains works of the Italian school, which include a Titian and a fine Lorenzo Lotto of St Jerome as well as a number of minor Venetian paintings.

The other rooms, furnished with what one imagines to be the relics of the Baron's saloon, contain fine works by Dutch masters, including Memling. Altogether, the entire collection shows a good eye, and the room dedicated to portraits of the Bruckenthal family suggests that these merchant noblemen were well aware of what to buy in their travels to the more civilized parts of the Austrian empire.

Several other rooms contain the works of Romanian painters of the last century, many of whom, judging from the amount of Monet-inspired landscapes, would seem to have studied in Paris at the time of the French Impressionists. One Romanian beauty portrayed in blue strikes a more Edwardian note and with her dark hair and eyes must typify the ideal Romanian woman, whose appearance so captivated the society of western courts at the beginning of this century.

The palace also contains about 250,000 books, of which about half belong to the Bruckenthal collection. Many of the others have been added because of their early references to the province of Transylvania. Next to the library is a collection of coins and archaeological remains together with some cups, ciboria and vestments.

From the rear of the Bruckenthal palace runs the str. 1 Mai, a long road flanked by elegant buildings. The church at the beginning of the street is a small reformed church built in 1786. The house further on at

No. 13 strikes a grander note and has a pair of 'empire' caryatids. A narrow passage between this house and its neighbour leads to an attractive street named Xenophol, which is followed until it reaches the str. Tribunei on the right. This leads to the tall Byzantine-style Orthodox cathedral at No. 35 1 Mai Street.

Built in 1902–6, the cathedral is clearly modelled on St Sophia in Istanbul; although it has only a fraction of that great building's majesty. The suitably dark interior contains frescoes of a certain Octavian Smigelschi, who seems to have been influenced by the art of Puvis de Chavannes in the Paris Pantheon. The columns and altar are constructed in a fine local granite which at present is gleaming after a recent restoration.

Turning left from the cathedral back towards the str. Tribunei, one comes to the busiest street in Hermannstadt, the str. N. Balçescu, a delightful promenade with interesting houses on each side. No. 32 has a courtyard, as have Nos. 24 and 16, from the rambling gardens of which the original roof-line of the town, unchanged in a hundred years, can be examined with pleasure.

Further on the road at No. 4 is the Hotel Imparatul Rômanilor ('Roman Emperor'), an old establishment which has in its time housed Johann Strauss, Franz Liszt and the Emperor Joseph II. Its rooms are invariably crowded with Romanian officers, but its dining room is probably the most suitable place to end the evening before embarking for the last town to be visited in Transylvania, Kronstadt.

KRONSTADT, or Brasov as the town is now known, was founded by a German order of knights in the thirteenth century and is the most important commercial and manufacturing town in Transylvania. It lies, as Baedeker would say, in a 'charming' basin. In recent years the outskirts have been developed crudely, but the centre has the sort of isolated calm found in all Transylvanian towns east of Clausenburg.

In front of the east side of the town, to the right on leaving the railway station rises the 'Schlossberg', or castle, which is not unlike the one at Graz in Styria and was constructed partly for the same purpose – to keep the Turks at bay – but also to protect the town in the 1550s from the demands of Voivode Peter of Wallachia, a figure whose cruelty seems at times to have rivalled even that of Vlad Dracul.

From the railway station, a road with some barracks to the left eventually leads to the str. Republicii, the principal thoroughfare of the town. The houses are of more stature than those of Schässburg or Hermannstadt because they were built after a serious earthquake in the eighteenth century. The piața 23 August, dominated by the Town Hall, is nevertheless a picturesque ensemble of buildings.

The Town Hall was built in 1420, although its tower is said to be earlier. The façade, however, bears traces of the Baroque era, for the building was restored in that style in 1777. A lavish coat of arms adorns one corner of the building, while the interior contains a local museum with objects of ethnographic interest as well as several old prints which show what the city looked like in the eighteenth century. The same square contains a number of other buildings which should not be overlooked. To the south is a Greek–Catholic church with twin domes, near which is a superb Renaissance market hall dating from 1545.

The restaurant next to the Town Hall, Cerbul Carpatin, was once considered one of the very best restaurants in Romania and is still capable, despite the shortages, of supplying the finest of Transylvanian cuisine. From here the str. Maxim Gorki leads to the Catherine Gate and other parts of the original town walls. To the south, in the next road below, the str. Castelului, are more remains of the fortifications, including the bastion known in German as the Weberbastei. Today this houses a small museum dedicated to archaeological and historical objects.

By far the most impressive building in the town, however, can be found back in the Maxim Gorki str. in the form of the Protestant church which, like that at Hermannstadt, forms an indispensable feature of the townscape. Popularly called the 'Black Church' because of its smoke-stained walls, it has recently lost something of this sooty complexion in restorations. The soot is said to have coated the church in 1689, when Austrian soldiers set fire to the city to quell a revolt. It is the most impressive Gothic church in Eastern Europe, its only rival perhaps being that of Košice in eastern Slovakia (see p. 198).

Built between 1385 and 1425, the building has some traces of Romanesque influence. On the exterior of the choir wall are statues of the twelve apostles, amidst foliage which according to contemporary records was once gilded. Inside, the dark vaulting speaks a bolder language. The altarpiece is attributed to a certain Martersteig of Weimar; the choir-stalls are magnificent examples of medieval carving, while the seats of the guilds are hung with rich oriental tapestry. The buttresses and roof reinforce the picturesqueness and the church is a powerful symbol of the cultural contribution to this part of Europe made by the Saxons.

From the church, the str. Barituu and 7 Novembre lead to the dull new theatre, from which the boulevard G. Gheorghiu Dej offers several cafés and the most comfortable hotel in the town, the Carpati, unfortunately an unattractive modern high-rise affair. This part of the town contains many of the later nineteenth-century buildings which housed parts of the imperial administration, including for example fine Neo-Classical law courts, the architectural litter of Europe's most insatiable bureaucracy.

Before leaving Kronstadt, and Transylvania, some attempt should be made to ascend the Zinne (3,153 feet), which offers a spectacular view of the town and the surrounding countryside. It can be reached through a beechwood forest from the Weberbastei in about an hour. Although much of the town's developed outskirts will become visible, it is still a most worthwhile walk from which to take a final view of the land of the seven castles.

9

WESTERN HUNGARY AND LAKE BALATON

From Transylvania, the return to Hungary is welcome not least for its material comforts and the absence of daily bartering. A tour of western Hungary reveals many different aspects of Magyar history, from the Turkish minarets of Pécs on the frontier with Jugoslavia to the Baroque splendour of the Esterházy palace at Fertőd. Between these two extremes is the magnificent lake Balaton, with its delightful bathing, popular not least because the summer temperature in this part of Hungary is often the highest to be found in Central Europe. For those in need of a more relaxing sojourn after the bracing challenges of Romania, this part of Hungary is ideal.

Predictably, for a city in which trains going west leave from the eastern railway station, trains going south sometimes depart from the western railway station in Budapest, the picturesque iron-ribbed building constructed by Eiffel. From here, there are trains to Pécs and other points south.

The journey to Pécs, even in an express train, lasts a long afternoon. Though to arrive at this city in the early hours of a barmy summer evening is a delight, it may be better to take a rail or road route to the east of the Danube and break the journey in KALOCSA, an archiepiscopal residence rich in historical associations and an important centre of the paprika production. There are few more colourful sights in Hungary today than these red spices drying in the sun at every house.

Adrian Stokes, the English art-historian and writer who spent several summers visiting Hungary before the First World War, observed of Kalocsa that the high street, terminating at one end in the cathedral and in the other in open country, seemed almost a mile long. The vivid market scenes he so ably described in his book on the country can still be seen, although the amount of colourful costume is no longer as great, as the apron is gradually replaced by the trouser-suit. This great thoroughfare, the Istvan Király út, is lined with cafés and hotels, most of which are worth patronizing. At its climax rises an impressive eighteenth-century ensemble.

The Baroque cathedral, designed by Andreas Mayerhoffer, dates from the 1730s and replaced an earlier Gothic structure which had been destroyed by the Turks. The imposing building in the Baroque style of the 1760s next to it is the Archbishop's Palace, constructed a little later by a Piarist priest called Gaspar Oswald and rich in early manuscripts and books (ring the bell three times). Among these, the visitor will be shown on request a copy of a Bible reputed to have once belonged to Martin Luther. Its walls have some fine frescoes, notably those in the dining room by Maulbertsch.

The nearby folk art museum re-creates the world which must have been a familiar sight to Adrian Stokes and other travellers to Hungary before the last war – bright costumes, guarded here by ceaselessly knitting women.

There are several other Baroque buildings of note in the vicinity, most of which would appear, like the Archbishop's Palace, to be the work of Gaspar Oswald.

From Kalocsa, the line runs south to PÉCS, the fourth largest city in Hungary, situated not far from the Jugoslav frontier. In Roman times, it was the capital of Southern Pannonia. Because the remains of several Christian churches were found near the site of the present cathedral, in the Middle Ages the town was given the name of 'Quinque Ecclesiae' ('Five Churches') and to Germans it is still known as 'Fünfkirchen'. In 1367, the first Hungarian university was founded here, but between 1543 and 1686 the city was in Turkish hands, becoming an important military and religious centre for them. Several mosques and other Turkish remains have survived here to the present day.

During the eighteenth century, a number of Baroque buildings were erected. Shortly afterwards rich coal deposits found in the immediate surroundings made the city even wealthier, and in 1851 a porcelain factory was established by the family Zsolnay. Today, however, Pécs is a quiet place, tranquillized by the heat and the fine wines of the nearby Mečsek hills.

Regardless of whether arrival is by train or car, sooner or later we shall come to the Széchenyi tér, which is the heart of the city and to which no fewer than twelve roads lead. It is dominated at the centre by the largest surviving Turkish building in Hungary, the Ghazi Kassim Mosque, which for centuries has served as a Roman Catholic parish church. Its sixteenth-century masonry still exudes Islamic confidence. Inside, the Turkish *mihrab*, facing Mecca, has been preserved. The entire building is full of surprises. The Jesuits installed a number of Baroque furnishings which sit unhappily under the remains of a dome constructed at the turn of the last century but removed in the late fifties to reveal a number of Turkish details.

As well as the parish church, the main square also offers a nineteenth-century Town Hall and a curious Baroque church whose façade seems to have enjoyed the attentions of some unknown nineteenth-century eclectic architect.

The north-western part of the square is taken up by the Nagy-Lajos grammar school, a competent collection of buildings mainly Baroque. Nearby is an equally pleasing Louis Seize palace housing an archaeological museum containing remains of the 'Quinque Ecclesiae'.

Both the Pannonia Hotel and the Nádor guest house nearby will supply a refreshing cup of Turkish coffee or some no less pleasing 'Fiz' (mineral water). Past the Pannonia Hotel in Kossuth Lajos út, near the square, are the National Theatre and the Baroque Lyceum church, which has a stuffy empire interior. Returning along one of the many narrow side streets to Széchenyi tér, the Janus Pannonius út, named after a Hungarian Renaissance poet, leads from the north-western corner of the square to a part of the city which was once surrounded by fortified walls. Eventually this leads to the religious heart of the city, the Dom tér. The promenade, with its wooded paths and delightful old pavilion cafés, is a welcome shelter from the midday sun in the summer. Little seems to have changed here since the days before the First World War. Children play with hoops, cars are rare, and the ice cream is rich and sugary.

Suddenly, in the middle of the promenade, the trees part and a lawn leading to the cathedral opens up. There are several worthy buildings on the cathedral square, but our attention is immediately seized by the four-towered cathedral which, like a ship at anchor, rests on the northern part of the square.

The building's history is complex. The present sanctuary undercroft and the two sixty-metre-high western towers date from the eleventh century. The undercroft reliefs and the two eastern towers, however, are from the twelfth century, though in appearance they are not dissimilar. Inside, the chapels in the north and south aisles are fourteenth-century, while the Gothic vaulting of the nave is supposed to date from the last years of the sixteenth. The so-called Száthmary pulpit, with its Renaissance detailing, is from 1506. During the nineteenth century, the cathedral underwent a number of restorations, first in a Gothic style and then towards the end of the century in a Lombard Romanesque style. The interior is high and spacious and rich in colours from the second of these nineteenth-century restorations.

Opposite the cathedral is a collection of statues and a lapidarium with objects dating from the Roman period. On the western side of the square is the Bishop's Palace, which, though of medieval origins, was rebuilt in the Baroque style between 1780 and 1800. The fine Louis Seize archives palace to the east of the square dates from a decade later.

By contrast, opposite the south-western tower of the cathedral stands a funerary chapel of the fourth century with stone mosaics from the third century. Adjoining the eastern obelisk in the square is an entrance to another curiosity, an early Christian painted burial vault, a rare thing outside Italy.

To the west of the cathedral stands the only surviving round stone bastion of the former city walls of Pécs. It has a battered drawbridge gate and insane crenellations. To the east stands the oldest house in the city, Káptalan út 2, constructed in the fourteenth century, but rebuilt several times since. Today it houses part of the art collection of the Janus Pannonius Museum as well as the Zsolnay collection of porcelain.

In the nearby Rákóczi út stands one of the monuments to the city's oriental past, the Jakovali Hassan Mosque, the only Turkish building erected for religious purposes to have survived more or less intact. It has retained its very oriental minaret, which was usually the first feature of these buildings to be destroyed after the Turks had been routed. Its square hall is crowned by an octagonal dome, while the minaret above is dodecagonal in section, with iron railings on its balcony. The dark interior, unspoilt by the Jesuits, still seems to whisper the Koran.

At the end of the promenade in front of the cathedral, a hill rises to the west on which a number of chapels marking the stations of the cross lead to a Calvary church, rather forlorn but none the less giving an impressive view of the old town.

Another hill to the north-west has the impressive funerary chapel of the Pasha Idris Baba, constructed in 1591. After the Turks were driven from Hungary, this octagonal building became first a Jesuit church and then a hospital chapel before being finally converted in 1961 into a museum of Mohammedan funeral customs. The original masonry is still almost entirely intact.

From here, several lanes lead to leafy paths which eventually wind their way up into more hills which offer plenty of opportunity for walking in the shade.

From Pécs, a short excursion can be made to the town of MOHÁCS, which contains some notable buildings as well as, nearby, the battlefield on which in 1526 the Hungarian army was destroyed by the infidel. The memory of this sanguinary exchange still imparts a hint of sadness to what is otherwise a peaceful landscape. In Mohács there are some fine Turkish baths and an eccentric memorial church pompously commemorating the 400th anniversary of the battle, erected in 1926.

The Danube here, just before it enters Jugoslavia, is very wide and impressive.

Between Pécs and the centre of Hungary is Central Europe's largest lake, Balaton. It is fifty-one miles long and two to nine miles wide, and abounds with fish. The south shore is flat, while that on the north side is bounded by a chain of hills and volcanic peaks which yield the esteemed Somlauer wine. Since the war the area has been extensively developed for tourism and bathing, so that at the height of the summer there is a holiday atmosphere rather reminiscent of the English south coast.

The road which runs along the southern shore is crossed by a series of smaller roads which lead to some picturesque villages. A railway line from Budapest follows a similar route to that of the main road and makes frequent halts. The first of these worth briefly exploring is BALATONSZABADI, which contains several old churches, although of late tourist development has resulted in some of this village's charm being lost.

About ten kilometres further along is the most important settlement on the southern shores: SIÓFOK. As official Hungarian tourist guides proudly relate, Siófok has the largest concentration of modern hotels on the lake. This does not sound promising, but the town is an old settlement which was first seriously developed as a resort in the late nineteenth century, so that there is still a feeling of 'last year in Marienbad' about it. A lot of building was done between the wars, which was Siófok's heyday as a renowned resort for the whole of Central Europe.

The town is divided into two halves by the railway. That towards the lake is dominated by the jetties and piers from which many of the lake's ships sail, for this is the centre of Balaton shipping and the headquarters of the half-dozen grey gunboats which make up what is proudly referred to as the Hungarian Navy. Despite their size, they are well armed. The long jetty here is a favoured promenade and leads to a rose garden, fragrant and informal.

As well as post-war hotels and forbidding tourist-information buildings, there are dozens of picturesque villas, several of which provide private rooms (apply to the tourist office in Szabadság tér). The half of the town on the other side of the railway line is notable for the Beszédes József Museum (signposted), which recaptures the atmosphere of the resort before the end of the Habsburg empire in an exhibition of photographs and furniture depicting the development of the lake. But of all this veranda wistaria, few traces remain.

From Siófok, a boat regularly plies across the lake to the northern shore resort of BALATONFÜRED, the oldest spa on the northern side. Balatonfüred is protected by a range of hills which not only give the town a picturesque setting but also prevent the climate becoming too hot in summer or too ravaged by cold winds in winter.

The resort dates from Roman times – behind the classical Calvinist church there are remains of the walls of a third-century Roman villa. In the seventeenth century both French and British travellers visited the spa and gave the place a reputation which grew steadily, reaching its zenith in the Biedermeier days of the first three decades of the nineteenth century.

Thanks to accounts of the spa given by Richard Bright and John Paget, the town became favoured by Anglo-Saxon travellers eager to relax among the Hungarian noblesse. By the middle of the nineteenth century, Baedeker was able to describe Balatonfüred as 'a pleasing bath with springs impregnated with carbonic acid, beneficial in female complaints and frequented by the country's aristocracy'. Possibly the affection these nobles felt for the spa was also the result of its having been, in the 1820s, the site of the first permanent building for a Hungarian-language theatre. As if this were not enough, the place was also renowned for its shipbuilding industry, the quality of its fruit and the celebrated strength of its wines.

Again, a railway line divides the two parts of the settlement. That towards the shore is the administrative and tourist centre. Gyógy tér, half-way between the shore and the railway line, is a bustling square heavy in the rhetoric of convalescence. The Trade Union Council Sanatorium, a state hospital and the Recreation Home for miners all brightly announce their presence in bold lettering. Within a hundred yards radius of the square there are no fewer than seven therapeutic springs, giving the air a rather sulphurous tinge. The Kossuth Lajos drinking hall in the middle of the square, erected in 1853, provides an opportunity to try the 'refreshing, sour water'. I can think of few experiences more vile.

Since 1825, there have been pageants and balls here towards the end of July to celebrate St Anne's day. These generally take place around the Sanatorium on the northern side of the square. The arcades contain memorial plaques to famous visitors, including visiting English nobility. A dignified past is considered nothing to be ashamed of here, as it is in the spas of Bohemia. The Recreation Home for the miners, a fine Louis Seize building, is transformed in the summer into a ballroom for the St Anne celebrations.

From the square down to the shore runs a picturesque rock garden and park notable for a lime tree planted in 1926 by the Indian poet Rabindranath Tagore. At the foot of the tree, on a marble slab, is a short poem Tagore wrote on his departure, inscribed in English and Hungarian. In 1961, another poet, the Italian Salvatore Quasimodo, planted a tree in the Füred park, while in 1966, in less literary times, a Soviet astronaut also left his mark in this way.

Unfortunately, modern high-rise hotels have been erected at the end of the park which detract from the place's nineteenth-century elegance, but private rooms can be had in a number of villas (apply to the tourist office in the Blaha Lujza útca), while there are two excellent old hotels on the Petőfi Sándor útca, the Astoria and the Arany Csillag, both of which have first-class restaurants. Several of the streets leading away from the main square have Neo-Classical villas and there is a circular church built in the empire style at the corner of Blaha Lujza útc and Jókai útca.

Between Balatonfüred and Tihany, there are a number of country inns or *csárdas*, of which the Baricska Csárda is perhaps the best known. Visitors are admitted to the cellar where, after a tasting, they can choose their own selections of wine or *barack*, the potent Hungarian schnapps. The food that is available is usually prepared on a grill, while the ubiquitous gipsy band will be whining away, with melancholy rather than bravado.

Another of these inns is the Koloska Csárda, which is hidden in a picturesque valley above the old village near the Lóczy caves. Both these inns are brisk walks from Balatonfüred, or they can be visited by bus, although more often than not tourist parties, during the summer season at least, will have been booked into those nearest to the town.

Perhaps the most interesting excursion to be made from Balatonfüred is that to Nagyvázsony, where there is the medieval castle built by general Pál Kinizsi, one of Matthias Corvinus's supporters. The castle is a fascinating if rather bleak affair, for much has been demolished over the centuries. The squat tower contains an exhibition of the fortress's history, emphasizing its role during the Turkish incursions. A lapidarium nearby has several handsome fragments of relief, one illustrating medieval horses being of particular interest to the guides.

Pál Kiniszi was, it seems, a giant of a man renowned for his physical strength and courage, but he also clearly was a deeply religious patron of the arts. The Gothic church in the village, dating from 1481, was built at his request and he also established a monastery, now ruined, nearby. The church has an attractive plain white façade crowned by the simplest of towers and supported by a pair of wide buttresses. Inside, there is spidery vaulting, but all the furnishings seem to be Baroque. The sacristy door is Gothic in inspiration at least and there is a pleasing relief of St Stephen receiving his crown from the Mother of Christ over the altar. Not far from here, the former Baroque palace of Count Zichy has been converted into a hotel, with seventy-two beds at the time of writing, and is as pleasant a place as any to put up at. The village also contains a series of farm houses which must rank as some of the most attractive in Hungary.

From Balatonfüred, the road to TIHANY, a small peninsula with a church and abbey, should be followed. Although Tihany has been developed rather enthusiastically as a tourist resort, the village still has something of the air of a fishing settlement. Dating from the Iron Age, it was first fortified by the Romans. In 1055 King Andrew I of Hungary established a Benedictine abbey here which was later fortified and successfully defended against the Turks.

The Baroque church was erected by the Benedictines after a fire in 1683 destroyed much of the abbey. It was completed in 1754 only after a second fire in the 1730s had destroyed their nearly complete efforts to reconstruct it. The present church is attributed to Josef Tietharth and has a severe façade enlivened by a rather ornate doorway. Inside, the church's chief glory at first glance would seem to be the woodwork, which is entirely the work of Sebestyén Stuhlhoff (1725–79), who is said to have taken over twenty-five years to complete it. Of even greater beauty is the Romanesque crypt, which survived the fires and Turkish assaults. Its dark masonry contains the tomb of King Andrew I and dates from the last two decades of the eleventh century. The crypt's solid masonry and plain columns impart a sense of peace to the structure, which is a refreshing contrast to the Baroque figures in the chancel and nave, even if they represent the best of their kind.

A museum in the abbey relates the history of the region from the Stone Age to the present time, while a lapidarium in the cellar contains some Romanesque and medieval carvings.

Opposite the church there are a number of walks through gardens, and next door is the terrace of the Rege pastry-shop (delicious refreshments as well as a fine view).

The north-western part of the peninsula contains some high ground referred to as the Lavender Hills, at the summit of which are the sparse remains of several Romanesque settlements. Often only a church ruin suggests that there were any settlements at all here at this time.

Tihany is not that far from BADACSONY, the centre of the region's wine industry. Again a railway line divides the town. The area nearest to the shore has been extensively developed for bathing, while that nearer the hills seems almost exclusively devoted to wine. Wine museums, tastings and cellars line the road to the west here. The eighteenth-century 'peasant Baroque' Szegedy-Róza house contains a literary museum devoted to Balaton poetry, while above on the hill with extensive views over the vinyards is the house of the great Hungarian poet Sándor Kisfaludy (1772–1844) and the Kisfaludy Inn. There can be few more pleasant ways to spend the early evening than to watch the sun setting over the volcanic soil of these hills with a glass of dry Bádacsőnyi Kenyelü and a plate of paprikas for company. These gentle hills seem to complement perfectly the mellowness of the wine.

If Badacsony is the centre of the wine-producing part of Lake Balaton, KESZTHELY is the largest town in the area and is rich in imposing architecture, of which the Louis Seize Town Hall and the Festetics Palace are the most important.

The palace, built by the Counts Festetics in the middle of the eighteenth century and then extended in the later part of the nineteenth century, is chiefly notable for its magnificent Baroque library. Whereas the Baroque south wing of the palace is attributed to Christopher Hofstadter, the library is believed to have been the work of Johann Ranz and Andreas Fischer. It contains over 52,000 volumes, including many rare manuscripts dating from the seventeenth century. The rest of the palace is a haphazard museum with several rooms containing Rococo and Biedermeier furniture.

The Baroque parish church nearby was erected in the 1740s and was built on an earlier Gothic one of 1386. This explains the frescoes dating from the sixteenth century to be found in the nave.

Despite a distressing amount of post-war development, it is uplifting to find that the Szabadság Inn, frequented by travellers since the late eighteenth century, is still a hotel with a reputation for fine cooking and polite service.

Of the five lidos, the Szigetfürdő, with its ornate and colourful towers approached over a small bridge, is probably the most pleasant spot to bathe at along the lake, although it has been modernized recently and has lost a little of its mid-nineteenth-century charm.

Two miles along the coast from here, at Hévíz, is the largest hot-water lake in Europe. Its area is 50,000 square metres and the spring breaks forth from a thirty-five-metre deep funnel-like hole, so that the temperature is a warm 28°C even in the winter. Bathing is popular all the year round and the State Balnearic Hospital accounts for the many people who take a 'cure' during the late autumn here. The water allows tropical and sub-tropical flowers to grow, while its high concentration of chemicals gives it the reputation of being successful in the treatment of muscular ailments.

This mecca of rheumatics is a suitable place to conclude a tour of Balaton, although in a guide of this size it has only been possible to mention the highlights of this remarkable lake, which understandably enjoys the affections of all Hungarians and outshines the smaller and less impressive waters of neighbouring Austria.

The route back to Budapest lies through Székesfehérvár, a picturesque old city half-way between the lake and the capital. Alternatively, the north-western route to Vienna takes us through Szombathely to Fertőd, the château of the Esterházys, and the Austrian frontier beyond Sopron.

SZÉKESFEHÉRVÁR, the Romans' Herculia or Alba Regia, was in medieval times the spiritual centre of Hungary. Until 1527, the kings were crowned in the town and most members of the royal family were buried there. Between 1543 and 1688, the city fell into neglect under the Turkish occupation and most of the medieval architecture was destroyed, but the routing of the Turks led here, as in so many other settlements in the country, to a flourishing of Baroque architecture, so that the old town has a picturesque and rambling street plan dotted with many charming examples of eighteenth-century architecture, usually of the Zopf, or late Louis Seize, variety.

The centre of the town is the Szabadság tér. The large Council Hall consists of a western wing built in 1690 and an eastern wing of three storeys constructed at the end of the eighteenth century in a late Baroque style.

In the same square stands the more spirited Bishop's Palace, designed by Jakob Rieder and built between 1790 and 1801. The façade, with its pairs of Corinthian pilasters, is rather Neo-Classical, the entire front being crowned with a massive coat of arms. The interior contains rooms in empire and Biedermeier styles and the library possesses over 40,000 volumes (apply to the porter).

At the eastern end of Szabadság Square is a lapidarium with several medieval objects dating from the destroyed eleventh-century royal basilica, where kings were crowned and buried. A sarcophagus described as Venetian-Byzantine is reputed to have been the tomb of Stephen I, the first King of Hungary.

Wandering along the Március 15 útca brings us to another treasure of the city, the Cistercian church, constructed in the 1750s. Its Baroque interior is rather upstaged by the magnificent Rococo cabinets in the sacristy. A former Jesuits' chemist's with a Rococo interior is nearby at the sign of the Black Eagle, as is also the nineteenth-century Vörösmarty theatre (with a café opposite).

Nearby is the town museum or István Király house in the Gagarin Square. Old photographs, models and the usual post-1945 reconstruction exhibits are displayed here. Not far from the Arany János útca is the cathedral. The building is Baroque and both the sanctuary and the main altar are the work of Franz Anton Hillebrandt, whose name we have encountered in Vienna (p. 37). It strikes a note of a grander order, serious but lavish.

The ceiling of the nave is decorated with scenes from the life of King Stephen I. In the crypt are to be seen the red marble caskets of the Hungarian King Béla III who ruled from 1174 to 1196. Near the cathedral stands the Gothic St Anne chapel, which was built in about 1470. It is an impressive building whose three high Gothic windows are accented by a curious lantern on the roof. A small but intricate rose window has been cut through the thick masonry of the west end. The interior, a single space vaulted by thin ribs, is sombre.

In the Petőfi Sándor útca rises the former Baroque church of the Carmelites, which contains a series of superb frescoes executed before 1770 by Franz Anton Maulbertsch, illustrating various scenes from the New Testament. The chancel contains a work by the eighteenth-century Bavarian sculptor Hauser and some contemporary Baroque stalls. Next door in the former seminary of the Carmelites is a museum of ecclesiastical art.

The Serbian Orthodox church in the Rác útca is also worth visiting. It is an eighteenth-century building, Baroque in style, and probably the work of a certain János Kerschoffer. The choir is semicircular underneath a half-dome, with ceiling frescoes illustrating scenes from the life of Christ and John the Baptist. The Rococo icon screen is one of the best of its kind in the country. There is a strange incongruity between this and the Baroque exterior, especially noticeable after a few moments have been spent contemplating the Byzantine style of the rest of the interior.

If, instead of returning to Budapest, the traveller wishes to go back to

Vienna from Balaton, efforts should be made to visit Szombathely and Fertőd, where there are other treasures.

SZOMBATHELY, the Savaria of the Romans, is another city with a late eighteenth-century character to its centre. The square at the heart of the settlement is Berzsenyi Dániel tér, which predictably enough is dominated by a Bishop's Palace, the work of Menyhért Hefele and dating from 1779. Maulbertsch and Dorfmeister were responsible for the frescoes inside, although experts say that neither artist excelled himself here. Hefele left his stamp on Szombathely in a way few other Hungarian architects were able to in other places. He was responsible not only for several of the buildings around the Bishop's Palace but also for the cathedral to the north, the conservatorium opposite it and the cathedral school – a case of '*Si monumentum requiris circumspice*' which is virtually unrivalled in any Central European city of this size.

The remains of the Roman basilica of St Quirinus, including a beautiful mosaic floor and some sections of Roman military road, are to be found in a lapidarium between the school and the cathedral. Sad to say, though the Hungarian guides seem quite proud of it, a 'modern espresso' has been built in this 'historic setting'.

In the Majakovszkij tér south of the main square, there are the remains of a temple dedicated to the worship of Isis. Savaria seems to have been the northernmost centre of the Isis cult and fragments of the temple are displayed here along with some thousands of other related objects. Those interested in archaeology should also visit the Savaria Museum, which is in the eastern part of the inner city near the railway station. The Franciscan church nearby, originating in the fifteenth century but rebuilt somewhat licentiously in the seventeenth century, is also worth a glance.

Before leaving Szombathely – it is not really a place to stay too long in – it should be pointed out that in the north-western part of the town is a botanical garden containing 2,000 species of trees and shrubs which are a pleasant distraction from the noise of the city centre. Thirteen kilometres south of here is JÁK, an even more pleasing escape (buses from main square) boasting the finest Romanesque church in all Hungary, with a magnificent portal but many tourists and guides.

West of Szombathely, on the Austrian frontier, is KŐSZEG. A small town of barely fifteen thousand inhabitants, it is the highest town in

Hungary (300 metres above sea level), almost in the foothills of the Alps.

We enter by way of the 'Heroes Gate', erected in 1932 to commemorate the 400th anniversary of the great siege, when a handful of Hungarians held up a force of Turks twenty times its size for over a month. The medieval Jurisich tér, named after the defenders' leader, is the site of the Baroque St Imre's church, constructed in the early seventeenth century. Some of this church dates from medieval times and the detailing is both Renaissance and Gothic. Next to it stands the altogether more restrained Gothic St James church dating from 1400 and evoking Teutonic earnestness. Here the mixture is partly Baroque and partly Gothic, but the splendid wall paintings are fifteenth-century.

The Town Hall nearby is Gothic in origin but was rebuilt in the Baroque period at the same time as the house opposite, whose sgraffito work dates from 1668. The narrow streets which lead from here to the castle are all worth exploring. An old drawbridge leads to the massive inner fortress which houses a museum and a very pleasant wine cellar.

The Strucc Hotel on the corner of Köztársaság tér was built at the turn of the seventeenth and eighteenth centuries and is the obvious place to stay, despite its modernized interior. Its rooms have views onto the many bastions and towers which survive from the castle's still impressive line of fortifications. Above, a high Calvary church with three steeples built between 1729 and 1735 looks down onto the town and its surroundings. At dusk, as the light recedes across the hills towards the Alps, the streets are almost deserted.

From here, with Austria so clearly visible, the last of Hungary's varied treasures beckons, if only to remind one of the great families who built the country into such a powerful force in the years after the Turks were routed. Few names conjure up Magyar nobility with such force as that of Esterházy, and so it is fitting to leave Hungary paying our respects to the great Esterházy palace at FERTŐD.

It is of course no longer the property of this once wealthy family. In Vienna and America, there are rooms adorned with photographs from before the last war of the castle and that last generation of Hungarian princes. Sometimes they are riding horses, sometimes they are picknicking, but in the background the impressive building is always the same. Often proudly referred to by Hungarians as the Versailles of

Central Europe, it is not quite as grand as either the palaces of the Sun-King or Maria Theresa, but as the palace of an aristocratic family it is without rival in Hungary.

Built between 1720 and 1766 for Prince Miklós Esterházy, most of what is seen today was designed by the architect Anton Erhard Martinelli. Martinelli, it may be recalled, designed the Town Hall in Pest (see p. 76). The rounded wings, however, are attributed to Miklós Jacoby (1733–84), and the transition to the central section has rightly been criticized for being discordant. The happier one-storey ranges which round off the court were erected in the 1760s by Johann Ferdinand Mödlhammer.

We enter by a splendid iron gate into the court. Although the palace suffered considerable damage in the Second World War, it has been splendidly restored. The guides offered by the palace administration are more than adequate and great care will be taken to explain the details of the two-storey ceremonial hall of the prince and princess and the delightful series of Chinese rooms.

Part of these have been given over to a Haydn memorial museum. Between 1761 and 1790 Haydn was the court conductor of the Esterházys and the theatre at Fertőd was one of the centres of Rococo Europe, witnessing the first performances of many of Haydn's works. The state rooms were and still are a magnificent setting for that composer's music, even if the theatre and part of the temple complex in the gardens vanished forever in the last years of the war, sacrificed to the shrapnel of a new invading army.

Like so many great houses in Central Europe, the absence of any resident family gives the building a maudlin, empty atmosphere and it is only during the summer when concerts are regularly organized in the palace that something of its former glory is recovered. If we are lucky, we shall leave Hungary with the music of Haydn ringing in our ears.

10

PRAGUE

Prague, the golden city. Few places live up to their flattering sobriquets as well as the capital of Czechoslovakia. It is without doubt the most beautiful city in Central Europe. There are some who would say that it outshines even Florence and Venice – a sacrilegious claim, maybe, but it would be difficult to choose between the charms of say the back streets beyond the Accademia or the streets around Santo Spirito in Florence and the gas-lit lanes of the Kleinseite.

Rare for a part of Europe which has experienced so much destruction this century, Prague survived the ravages of the last war largely intact, effectively bombed neither by the Allies nor by the Luftwaffe. As a result, the quantity of its medieval and Baroque buildings is unrivalled elsewhere in the world. Neon-lighting and advertising have rarely intruded into this picturesque ensemble, and though the restoration of its many crumbling buildings is painstakingly slow, it is, in contrast to what neighbouring Austria is doing, remarkably sensitive.

The city lies most picturesquely in a broad basin on both banks of the Moldau, which in Czech is called the Vltava. Its foundation is ascribed to the seventh-century heroine Libussa, the first Duchess of Bohemia, and Ottokar II (1253–78) granted it a municipal charter. During the reign of Charles IV (1346–78) the university was founded and much of the city along the right bank of the river was built.

During the Thirty Years War, whose origins can be traced to the dramatic defenestration of two Catholic councillors from a window of the Hradčany castle on 23 May 1618, the city was occupied twice. It has been rightly said that there are few darker pages in the world's history than those in which the state of Bohemia after the Thirty Years War is recorded. Almost every part of the country was devastated during that war, and a population of three million dwindled to less than 800,000 by the end of the war. The great Bohemian aristocracy was decimated, and Prague took two centuries to recover its former glory, for the nobles who replaced those who had perished were more interested in living near the court in Vienna than in Prague.

This decline continued in the eighteenth century, when Maria Theresa centralized the government of the Austrian empire, so that it was only with the birth of Czech nationalism in the early nineteenth century that Prague began to recover something of its former glory.

With the collapse of the Habsburg empire in 1919, Czechoslovakia and particularly Prague enjoyed a rebirth of cultural activity which, though extinguished by the Nazis in 1939, lasted sufficiently long for the city to be seen as a second Paris. To a certain extent the natural artistic talents of the Czechs proved irrepressible even after the last war, when the city again enjoyed, at least until 1968, a flowering still described as the 'Prague Spring'.

Since then, there has been a feeling of hopelessness among many Czech intellectuals who, like 'thinkers' in any totalitarian regime, feel suppressed and threatened, as chance encounters with former university professors working in tobacconist's, or writers forced to clean windows for a living, show. But one would not wish to belittle the artistic achievements of Czechs today, and there is in the three opera houses of the city evidence to suggest that the country's traditionally rich development of the arts continues nevertheless.

If the luggage-search at the frontier has not taken too long, the morning express from Vienna will have wound its way through the Bohemian forests to arrive in Prague in time for tea.

The western railway station is in itself a triumphant affirmation of the Czech spirit for design and its past glories. An art-nouveau building, it is immediately more imaginative in conception than the splendid old stations of Hungary, and of course in a different league entirely from most stations in Austria.* The lower part of the station has recently been modernized, but the former ticket hall, with the coats of arms of the cities the station was once a link with, stands out between Czech national

---

*The traveller who would like a more picturesque *entrée* into the capital, though at the cost of several hours, can leave the north Prater railway station of Vienna in the rustic three-carriage train for Břeclav to reach Prague via Brno in Moravia, arriving at the rather quaint iron-columned former state railway station. This is conveniently situated a few minutes' walk from the Powder Tower, which is glimpsed in the evening light as soon as leaving the station.

heroines rendered in white stucco. Quite who these noble ladies are I have never been able to find out, but they are clearly at least royalty, for their expressions betray almost unanimous disapproval of the more voluptuous *femmes fatales* below, who grace an inscription boasting '*Prag mater urbium*'.

Emerging from the long aircraft hangar of a ticket office, a small park leads directly to a narrow street called Jeruzalémská. This passes on the right a gaudy nineteenth-century synagogue, opposite which rises an even more flashy Ringstrasse palais, before emerging under the tower of St Henry's church. It is the first of many black towers to be encountered in the city, most of which have this picturesque triangular outline. The church, likes so many in the city, is invariably closed except on Sunday mornings, but easily seen are a number of impressive tombstones which adorn its façade. One particularly memorable wizened old knight who passed away in 1566 stares across the tramlines at the queues for rotten apples in the market.

The large yellow nineteenth-century palais which looks faintly theatrical is the headquarters of Czech television. To its left a narrow street soon leads to the Powder Tower, and if time is limited the old town can be immediately inspected from here (see p. 150).

The long boulevard called Na příkopě, running left from the Powder Tower's fantastic fifteenth-century sculptures, however, leads to the principal square of the city, the Wenceslas Square, or Václavské náměsti.

This long square is the centre of the new yellow Neo-Classical town above the older parts of Prague and is a busy thoroughfare. The theatre at the far end was formerly reserved for productions in the German language, the Czechs having their own theatre in the older part of the town nearer the river. It is yet another creation of Helmer and Fellner and its delightful gold and red velvet interior still gives more than passable performances of Mozart operas in German, although the majority of works tend to be in Czech.

The pompous classical building next to the theatre is the Bohemian Museum, erected between 1885 and 1890 by the architect Schulz. Its interior contains a handsome staircase which ascends to a so-called Pantheon, an imposing hall destined once for festivals and now occasionally used for chamber concerts. It is still adorned by eight life-size bronze statues of persons celebrated in Bohemian history. The rooms around it contain documents associated with the Thirty Years War, as well as reconstructions of old Bohemian apothecary rooms which are themselves small museums of porcelain and woodcarving. On the second floor there are geological and palaeontological collections.

The Wenceslas Square contains what is probably the most agreeable place to stay in the city, the art-nouveau Hotel Europa. Those who long for the latest comforts of modern luxury hotels will find its cosy shabbiness rather upsetting, but there is charming service and the café of the hotel must be one of the greatest period pieces in Central Europe, even though the only available newspapers in English seem to be three-week-old copies of the *Morning Star*. The art-nouveau glass of the dining room has recently been restored and should be seen even if one is not staying at the hotel.

Before embarking on the long and absorbing task of exploring the old town, a small detour should be made from the square along the Sokolska třida which passes in front of the museum to the beautiful Charles church. The church is a mixture of Gothic and Baroque, the interior having been modernized in 1720 by the great German Baroque architect Kilian Dientzenhofer. The dome and the octagonal star vaults have rightly been called one of the most spectacular achievements of medieval builders.

Returning to the Wenceslas Square, one should head for the medieval Powder Tower, through which lies the old town.

The Powder Tower itself is a building of considerable interest. It was erected as a gate tower in 1475–84 but restored in the 1880s when the Národni Dům, or People's House, was erected in a flamboyant art-nouveau next door. The tower is situated on the former city moat, or Graben, which is now called Na příkopě. This road, which runs around one side of the old quarter, is rich in Baroque façades, although some have been ravaged by recent shop-fronts. But the former Palais Piccolomini still retains some lovely Baroque detail dating from 1738, peering out between hardware shops.

The People's House itself is a suitable place to stop for coffee, although the interior, with its sumptuous art-nouveau, is not the jolliest place in Central Europe. Despite the fountains and extraordinary lighting, there is an inescapable feeling that this grand old café has seen better times. There are still a handful of clients who look as if they have frequented it since Kafka's day, but otherwise the comfortable sofas are deserted save for the ever-increasing numbers of third world students who learn the tenets of communism through scholarships to study medicine or chemistry at the Charles University.

It should perhaps be pointed out here, as this is where the problem may be first encountered, that if coats are worn they must be given to the attendant on duty unless the heating in the café has failed, when during the winter months it will be more than necessary to keep them on.

Refreshed, if perhaps a little maudlin at this glimpse of past glories, we pass the Čedok tourist office at the back of the People's Palace, where hotel rooms and (less easily) rooms in private houses can be booked, and enter the old town.

Down the Hybernská, past the Neo-Classical church, which sounds an odd note amid all this Baroque and Gothic and once belonged to an Irish order of Franciscans (Hibernians), we come to the fruit market Ovocný trh. Here stands a theatre known as the 'Tyl', a pleasing early Biedermeier building which witnessed the first performance of Mozart's *Don Giovanni* in 1787.*

Behind it in the Železná ulice is the Carolinum, or Charles university, which still houses some of the smaller faculties. It has a fine oriel window on the side facing the market. Several of the rooms inside (admittance is difficult – try bribing the porter) have retained their Gothic character, including the vaulted hall passageway and the lecture rooms. The largest of these witnessed the 'disputations' of John Hus (*c.* 1373–1415), the celebrated reformer.

Hus, who was rector of the university in 1402, carried the teachings of Wycliffe into the heart of Bohemia, incurring the wrath both of the German nobility, who saw that this great orator was supported mainly by Slav Czechs, and also that of the orthodox clergy. Hus's support for Czech nationalism and the Czech language aroused tremendous enthusiasm, but he was denounced and despite a safe conduct burnt at the Council of Constance in 1415. The wrath which greeted the news of this event led to the Hussite wars, as the spirit of the reformation swept over the land in the form of civil war.

From the Carolinum, we take the Havelská, where because of their windows or gables, most of the houses repay close attention.

* Tickets for the Tyl are best obtained through the ticket office. At the last moment seats seem suddenly to appear from the side booths to fill the stalls gangways before the curtain rises.

At the end of this street stands the beautiful church of St Martin-on-the-Walls, a name referring to its proximity to the old fortifications. The church has stood here since the thirteenth century and is essentially a Romanesque construction which was adapted to Gothic during the second half of the fourteenth century. Although it was restored during the first decade of this century, it remains in atmosphere remarkably medieval and serves today as the evangelical church of the Bohemian Brothers. On the nearby Uhelný trh, the house at the corner with the arches is believed to be where Mozart lived in 1787. A plaque and a crumbling relief over the main façade commemorate this.

From here the Skořepka leads to Betlémské nám., where the twin white gables of the Bethlem chapel seem rather new for a building purporting to be medieval. This is because the original chapel was demolished at the end of the eighteenth century and what we now see is the work of Jaroslav Frágner, carried out to the original plans but during the 1950s. The reason for this unique and in its own way remarkable piece of reconstruction of what is at first glance a far from distinguished building is that it was here that Jan Hus held some of his earliest services in Czech rather than Latin.

The Husová, which runs from here, contains the large Dominican church erected in 1339–71 by Drzice and Arnost von Pardubice but later given a Baroque interior by František Spaček in the 1730s. The showy stucco decoration of the interior dates from this time and contains sculptures by Matthias Schönherr. The Husová itself is one of the oldest streets in Prague and is rich in gables, although the narrowness of the street make them difficult to appreciate.

On the right down the Karlová is the Malé nám., or small square or ring, a welcome space adorned by a faultless series of buildings whose pediments and gables make as pretty a skyline as can be seen in Central Europe. At the centre of this square is an iron-surrounded Renaissance fountain dating from the sixteenth century. To the left of this, the Petzold house has a late Renaissance façade with sgraffito decoration, while behind the fountain is the Judge's House, with a classical portal attributed to Johann Kranner, who is believed to have built it in 1798. There are several cafés here where, despite a service which is almost Balkan in its slowness, a pleasant half-hour can be spent taking in these restful surroundings.

The Malé nám. leads directly to the most important square in the old town, the Starométské nám., formerly referred to as the large ring. Graced at one end by the tower of the Town Hall and at the other by the twin towers of the Teyn church, this must be one of the most beautiful squares in the world. Without waiting to examine each of the jewels which make up the whole, the thing to do now is to ascend the tower of the Town Hall. Far less exhausting than that of St Stephen's cathedral in Vienna, it is sufficiently low to provide at close quarters a view of the roofs and gables which are so elusive from the narrow street.

Across the river rises the barrack of a palace which is the Hradčany castle, embracing the Gothic cathedral of St Vitus. On the horizon there are some alarming concrete blocks of flats, but these sinister things should be ignored and the picturesque sights immediately below examined more carefully.

As well as its tower, the Town Hall is graced by a magnificent astronomical clock. The work of Nikolaus von Kadaň, dating from about 1410, the clock has been restored several times. The Gothic detailing and statuary of the clock belong partly to the beginning of the fifteenth century and partly to the early sixteenth. The allegories of the twelve months are, however, only an 1864 copy of the original.

Next to this is a fine piece of middle-pointed Gothic around the door to the Town Hall. This dates from 1475 and is believed to have been the work of Matěj Rejsek, a mason who also worked on part of St Vitus's cathedral. His name is also associated with the beautiful 'Erker chapel' beneath the tower, an exquisite oriel window, dating from 1389 but adorned with coats of arms from a century later. The chapel was destroyed during the war but has been partly restored. At the corner stands a copy of a Gothic Madonna. The main wing of the building next to this is nineteenth-century Gothic revival.

To the right of the Town Hall, the square opens up dramatically towards the Baroque façade of St Nicholas's church, an important work of Kilian Dientzenhofer dating from the 1730s with sculpture by Anton Braun. Originally built by the Benedictines, the church now belongs to the Czechoslovak state and is rarely open to the public. Inside, the frescoes are the work of the Bavarian painter Cosmas D. Asam and recall the legend of St Benedict and St Nicholas.

Near the centre of the square stands a rather incongruous, straggling group of statues built in 1915 to commemorate the 500th anniversary of the death of John Hus. It is a strange mixture of realism and art-nouveau, but whatever its merits as an individual work of art, it cannot be seen as a happy addition to the square.

To the east of this, in front of the twin towers of the Teyn church, rise the picturesque gables of the early Gothic Teyn school. The gables are curiously reminiscent of some Venetian *scuola* and are later than the rest of the building. The highly ornate Rococo palace to its right is the former Goltz-Kinsky palace, built between 1755 and 1765 to K. I. Dientzenhofer's designs. Today it contains the absorbing graphic collection of the Czech National Gallery.

The Teyn church, so often covered in scaffolding, has been under restoration for years, but if progress continues at the present pace it may soon be possible to see more than just the twin pointed towers crowned by four graceful turrets and the high-pitched roof which was added in 1460 shortly after George Podiebrad was crowned King of Bohemia here.* It was he who caused the façade to be adorned by a large chalice, the symbol of the Hussites whose church this was. But after the battle of the White Mountain (1620) the chalice was replaced by an image of the Virgin. With a little luck, it should at least be possible to see the round-arched north doorway, dating from 1390. This imposing baldachin arch, with its delicate tracery, is attributed to Peter Parler, the great medieval craftsman. The lower right console contains two beautiful sculptures of the evangelists Mark and John.

Inside, the church seems at first to be rather cluttered. The Gothic vaulting and arcades are filled with high altars, of which that under a Gothic baldachin in the north aisle is the most interesting. The work of Matěj Rejsek, it dates from the last decade of the fifteenth century.

Attached to the last south-eastern pier is the red-marble tombstone of the celebrated Danish astronomer Tycho Brahe (d. 1601), who was invited to Prague in 1599. In front of this sombre figure, clutching in one hand a globe and in the other – quite wisely, given the turbulence of the times – a sword, there is a magnificent Baroque candelabra. These and a pewter Gothic font are the chief treasures of the church, although there is some Gothic wooden carving on several of the side altars which should not be overlooked.

From the Teyn church, we return to the Town Hall, perhaps lingering

---

*The door numbered 601 has recently been open at six o'clock in the evening. This leads to a courtyard at the end of which a further door brings us into the dark and sombre interior.

over some Slovak wine at a nearby bar before taking the Karlová, where almost immediately to our right a quartet of Titans struggling to support a heavy Baroque portal remind us of the presence in this city of another great Baroque architect whose dramatic sculpture we are already familiar with: Fischer von Erlach (see Chapter 2). In the few minutes spent wandering around the old town, it has been possible to admire the achievements of the two great Dientzenhofer architects and recognize a lighter less exuberant Baroque. Here Johann Bernhard Fischer von Erlach's palace takes us back to the exotic world of Prince Eugen's Winter Palace in Vienna with something of a jolt.

The lavish mass of the Clam-Gallas Palace at the end of the narrow Husová has a profusion of relief carving which is unmistakably Viennese. For years, its blackened façade has been covered in scaffolding and its fine Carlo Carlone frescoes around the splendid staircase are almost impossible to see, but even in permanent restoration the building has a forceful personality unmatched by any other Baroque palace on this side of the river.

The Gallas family exists no more – one of the very few of the *'erste Gesellschaft'* to die out – but at the beginning of the eighteenth century, when this palace was built, the family was to spawn not only ambassadors to England but also viceroys of Naples. This dazzling pile is as fine an epitaph for them as any funerary monument.

From here the Karlová, which is usually being dug up for tramlines, leads to the Charles Bridge. Before crossing this most spectacular of bridges, a slight detour to the right will bring one to the remains of the former ghetto. Once divided from the rest of the old town by walls, the ghetto was a focus for trade and intellectuals. During the reign of the reforming eighteenth-century Joseph II (see p. 23), the walls were demolished and Jews began to play a vital part in the public life of the city.

The Křižovnická which leads to it ironically takes us past a veritable barrack of Catholicism in the form of the Clementinum. Its massive pilastered façade is the work of Francesco Caratti, an architect who in Prague seems to have developed an unpleasant taste for the monumental. It is expressive of the power once enjoyed by the Jesuits in the country. Its libraries are rich in barley-sugar columns, with a tower for star-gazing and courtyards for masquerades in which various *Dei ex machina* would chasten those weak in faith. Today, the only chastening comes from the sullen porters, who insist on making it as difficult as possible to see either the refectory, mathematical room or library.

Beyond the Clementinum is a wall behind which trees enclose a small elevated garden littered with tombs. This is the Jewish cemetery, perhaps one of the best-known and certainly most bizarre sights of Central Europe. Laid out in the fifteenth century, it was the principal Jewish burial ground of the city until 1787, since when no more graves have been added. The selective eye of the camera captures the melancholy decay of this place more than a long sustained glance, although even without any knowledge of Hebrew the visitor will find several of the tombstones merit close inspection for their decoration. Of the 20,000 to be seen, the oldest dates from 1439, while the most valuable all date from the eighteenth century.

It may be tempting to linger here, with the sunlight filtering through the trees, but there are more cheery sights to be explored over the Charles Bridge. The slight curve of the bridge, with its distant pinnacles and the Baroque dome of St Nicholas's beyond, cry out for galloping horses, but the days when it was possible to ride across are long past and we should be content to walk slowly under the watchful eyes of the statues of St Francis Xavier and his pious companions.

The most notable of these is the bronze statue of St John Nepomuk, the patron saint of Bohemia. He stands in the middle of the bridge and is the work of Matthias Rauchmuller of Nuremberg, who excuted it in 1683. Between the sixth and the seventh pillars on the right is a slab of marble with a cross, marking the spot where the saint is said to have been flung from the bridge in 1383 by order of Wenzel IV for refusing to betray what his wife the empress had told him in the confessional. According to legend, the body then floated for a considerable time in the river with five brilliant stars hovering over its head.

As well as the memory of these events, the bridge also affords incomparable views of the Hradčany castle, with its Baroque façades, and, to the left, the stately and recently renovated National Theatre. At night, the view is even more picturesque, while in winter the steam rising from the freezing water adds even more to the impressiveness forged here by masonry and nature.

Under the tower, past a pretty gabled building which once housed the first coffee-house in the city, is the so-called 'Small Side' or 'Malá

Strana' ('Kleinseite'), 150 acres between the bridge and the Palais Černín of haunting beauty.

The celebrated Three Ostriches Inn (in Czech, U tri pstrosm) is near the bridge to offer a cool glass of Czech beer or a good dinner. Among the leafy Čertovka Kampa to the left of the bridge, the most interesting building is probably the Baroque Palais Nostitz, designed by Francesco Caratti in 1670 with his inevitable giant order of pilasters. The palais, like many others on this side of the river, is an embassy. Nearer the Dražickeho nám. is the Maltézské Square, with the Gothic former church of the Maltese knights.

But these are only distractions from the gloriously arcaded square of Malostranské náměsti. The north side of the square is dominated by the Smiřicky and Sternbeck Palaces, heavy humourless façades concealing the memory of ancient conspiracies. A lighter note is struck by the east side of the square's Kauserstein palais, a work of 1700 attributed to Alliprandi. But all these are just a child's bricks strewn at the feet of the genius of Christoph Dientzenhofer's St Nicholas church.

The most ambitious Jesuit church in Bohemia, St Nicholas is largely the work of Christopher Dientzenhofer, the father of Kilian, the most original architect of his age, of whom little is known except that he died in Prague at the age of sixty-seven in 1722. The restless curves of the façade show the influence of Borromini and Hildebrandt, especially his Piarist church in Vienna (see p. 46). The dome and presbytery are both the work of Kilian Dientzenhofer (1689–1751) and also suggest the inspiration of Hildebrandt and Rome.

Inside, the space wanders in a series of dazzling strides which never seem predictable, as entablatures cut into circular spaces and the nave pilasters refuse to remain subordinate to the wall. Palko and Kracker's frescoes, if not of outstanding quality, only reinforce the rather giddy impression of this spectacular interior.

Less than five minutes' walk to the north-east, past the Gothic St Thomas's church at the corner of this square, is another remarkable building, the Palais Waldstein. Erected in the third decade of the seventeenth century, it was long thought to be the work of the Milanese architect Giovanni Marini, but would seem now to have been largely the design of Andrea Spezza. In size and conception it is uninhibited Baroque, but in design the style is Renaissance, culminating with a magnificent three-bay loggia overlooking the garden. Regrettably, the open hall here no longer contains the horse (stuffed) on which the great General Wallenstein rode at the battle of Lützen (1633), but the gardens are still adorned by a series of seventeenth-century bronzes.

From the Malostranské nám., there are two routes up to the Hradčany castle area. Both at the time of writing are gas-lit and so perhaps can best be enjoyed in the early evening. The first leads from Thunovská, past the back of the Thun Palace on the Nerudová, along the steps known as Zámecké schody. Unfortunately the rear elevation of the Thun Palace is nowhere near as dramatic as the one on the Nerudová, but this, with its stone eagles and bulging entablatures – the work of that most daring architect Jan Santini (b. 1667) – can be seen on the way down, or by going up the Nerudová itself. The views are better along the steps, but some may prefer the road, where a magnificent pair of gables crowns the façade of No. 233.

Those with time to spare may also wish to turn left after the Nerudová and descend to the Tržiště to take in the Lobkovicz Palace (1703–7), now the German embassy, boasting an elegant top storey by Palliardi (1769), and nearby, the Palais Schönborn (the American embassy) with its high garden pavilion (1643–56), remodelled by Santini and guarded by a brightly uniformed American marine.

This mopping-up of Baroque bits and pieces is quite exhausting and so, before going on, a refreshing glass of mineral water or beer may be enjoyed at the U Mécénase back in the square, a vast vaulted beer cellar packed with the cherubic faces of Czech conscripts.

When the Hradčany is finally climbed, the view into the long gardens of the embassies should be sufficient to convince anyone that a diplomat's life has its compensations. Tables for a garden party can usually be seen at the American, while the garden of the British embassy residence boasts at the time of writing a fine set of croquet hoops.

Such distractions aside, it is time to contemplate the power-house of Czechoslovakia, for just as the old kings of Bohemia fortified the Hradčany to preserve their power, so too has every leader of the country this century worked and lived within the walls of this rather relentless-looking castle. If the time is right – midday or three-thirty in the afternoon – we shall be just in time for an equally relentless demonstration of modern Czech discipline. With a slow pounding of boots on marble, a khaki-clad guard of honour goose-steps into the courtyard before, at a tap of an NCO's rifle-butt, sweating and nervous, these hapless conscripts fall into their sentry boxes. Their magnificent wooden rifles have silver moving parts which glint in the sun, but the entire spectacle is both grotesque and absurd, leaving behind a rather unpleasant taste.

Grotesque, too, are the dagger-thrusting Titans above the main gate, 1912 copies of originals of 1768. Passing underneath their watchful gaze is somehow peculiarly disconcerting, but distraction is at hand in the shape of the Matthias Gate, a pleasingly Italian affair derived from a Serlio copybook and erected by Giovanni Filippi at the beginning of the eighteenth century. The monumental and beautifully executed flag-poles should not be overlooked, if only because they are the work of that most ingenious inter-war architect, Josef Plečnik (1872–1956), who in the twenties was commissioned to restore and modernize the castle, with what success will become evident. The rest of what is now seen is all rather uninspired Nicolo Pacassi, who was commissioned by the Empress Maria Theresa to complete the castle between 1762 and 1768.

Going through the arch, a glimpse into the interior right and left reveals the unmistakable white marble of Istria, a rarity in this part of the world which Plečnik had imported to express his own brilliant de-tailing. It is a Mediterranean language that this architecture speaks, and it is not surprising that the Czechs have for years hated it.

The courtyard beyond is more unrelieved Pacassi, although a seven-teenth-century fountain at the centre affords some distraction from the pedantic consoles and pilasters. The meanness of this space is a perfect foil to the next courtyard, in which rises the Gothic cathedral of St Vitus, a soaring mass of pinnacles and towers. The marble surface of the court along with the plinth of the statue of St George (1373), by the Kolozsváry brothers, are again the work of Plečnik. The statue itself is a copy of the fourteenth-century original which is now in the Czech National Gallery. These things can be taken in at a glance before entering the cathedral, which rises chaotically above all this order. Begun in 1344, it was finished only in 1929 when, after a break of over 450 years, the nave and principal tower were completed.

The buildings around the church make it difficult at first to take the entire structure in and one can only pick at parts of the façade. The south transept, crowned by the most beautiful tracery hinting at French flamboyant, was constructed between 1366 and 1419 by the gifted Peter Parler. It has three noble pointed arches whose gates have bronze alle-gories of the months of the year.

Inside, despite the impressive height, the nave vaulting is rather lifeless and it is to the choir that one's attention is drawn. At its centre, within a set of Renaissance railings, rises the imposing Monument of the Kings, executed in marble by Alexander Colins of Malines in 1570–73 for Rudolph II and erected over the hereditary burial-place of the Bohemian monarchs. Beneath it repose Charles IV (d. 1378) and Wenzel IV (d. 1419) as well as several other monarchs, though not Elizabeth, the princess who became the mother of England's dashing Prince Rupert after marrying Frederick the Elector Palatine, the Winter King of the Bohemians whose defeat at the battle of the White Mountain in 1620 destroyed the cause of Bohemian Protestantism.

It is worth dwelling on this tragic event while pondering the remains of these kings and queens, who can never have foreseen how their culture would be wiped out in 1620 and the destiny of their land placed into the hands of foreigners – Austrians who neither comprehended nor sympathized with its former institutions.

The Wenzel chapel, which is the first on the right of the choir, is still reputed to contain the helmet and chain-mail coat of the saint as well as his gentle statue, executed by Peter Parler's nephew in 1373. The chapel, which was constructed between 1347 and 1366, is inlaid with precious stones and decorated with ancient frescoes of the Prague school. The ring on the door is reputed to be that grasped by the saint when he was slain in 935 by his brother Boleslav. Adjoining this chapel is the Martinic chapel, containing the remains of a former imperial councillor, whose defenestration (see p. 162) was the immediate cause of the Thirty Years War.

On the left of the choir is the chapel of Saints Simon and Jude, with a painting of 1368, but here the ambulatory, with its wide range of treasures, soon distracts the eye. First comes the Gothic Ladislaus oratorium, borne by florid vaulting of 1493. Then beyond, like some shipwrecked silver treasure trove, is Fischer von Erlach's bombastic tomb for St John Nepomuk of 1736. More self-effacing is a capital carving of Adam and Eve at the end of the choir, the work of Peter Parler, while above, along the triforium arcade, run twenty-one busts of members of the royal family in the fourteenth century, partly the work of Peter Parler's craftsmen.

In the nearby Sternberg chapel are the tombs of Ottokar I (1230–53) and II (1253–78) by Peter of Gmund, while at the back of the high altar is the tomb of St Vitus. Another chapel dedicated to St John the Baptist contains a candelabrum which is reputed to have belonged to Solomon, although later experts have pointed out that the base is in fact twelfth-century.

After the cold air of all this Gothic masonry, the courtyard outside on a hot summer's day blinds one like a furnace. In one corner of the court, however, a cool fountain plays in front of an unassuming entrance where a small column carries nothing more than a shiny gold ball. This sort of architectural joke is a typical piece of Plečnik. It marks the entrance to the largest and grandest secular Gothic interior in Central Europe, the great Hall of Ladislaus, which was constructed in the last two decades of the fifteenth century. The sense of light and space is pleasantly refreshing after the darkness of the cathedral, and there are no furniture or wall fittings to distract the eye from the energetic forms of the Gothic vaulting.

From here a number of rooms open out of the hall, of which the two in the north-east wing of the palace are of most interest. One of these contains the coats of arms of the seventeenth-century servants of the king, while the courtiers' hall nearby, known as the Old Judiciary Chamber, contains vaulting which matches the elegance of the Ladislaus Hall. This room also contains a sober classical tribune dating from 1563 which dwarfs both in size and quality a rather Strawberry Hill Gothic throne below. Until 1847, this room served the Bohemian Diet, but the nearby Statthalterei or council room witnessed more dramatic events. It is rather unprepossessing for a place of such historical significance. But as we gaze out through its window over the towers and gardens of the city, it is perhaps worth recalling the events which led to what must be one of the most infamous acts of personal violence in history.

The differences between Catholics and Protestants reached a head in Bohemia with the succession to the throne in 1618. The Catholic councillors had arranged for the Archduke Ferdinand, a determined persecutor of Protestants, to succeed King Matthias. To head this off, Count Thurn and the other Protestant nobles met to deal with the Catholic councillors who had been appointed by Ferdinand over their heads. Ulrich of Kinsky proposed that the royal councillors should be poniarded in the council chamber, but Thurn's suggestion, that they should be thrown from the windows of Hradčany palace, prevailed.

Early on the morning of the memorable 23 May, these representatives of Protestantism, their rapiers drawn, their breastplates gleaming in the sun, proceeded to the Hradčany. When they reached the council room what contemporary chroniclers refer to, with surprising understatement, as a 'stormy discussion' arose. Martinic and Slavata, the two Catholic councillors, were accused of being traitors and worthless disciples of the Jesuits. What followed is perhaps best described in the words of the seventeenth-century historian Skala Ze Zhore:

'No mercy was granted them and they were both thrown dressed in their cloaks with their rapiers and decorations head-first out of the western window into a moat beneath the palace. They loudly screamed *"Ach, ach oweh!"* and attempted to hold on to the narrow window-ledge, but Thurn beat their knuckles with the hilt of his sword until they were both obliged to let go.' *

This act of violence precipitated the Thirty Years War, which was to lay the country so completely to waste.

From these tumultuous events, a few steps outside, behind the cathedral, lead to the Romanesque basilica of St George, its rather Dalmatian-looking towers dressed in an early Baroque façade. The towers date from the year 970 and the interior, which has also had to cope with Baroque additions, is a calm barn of a building with massive round piers and depressed arches. In the crypt the piers are shorter and thinner, with seventeenth-century vaulting, while the south entrance to the church boasts an undistinguished Renaissance gateway.

From St George's, the road descends to the right along the Jiřská. There may be some who will be tempted to return to the castle and wander among the paintings in the bleak white rooms belonging to the National Gallery, but though there is much here to match the treasures in Vienna or Budapest, at the end of the Jiřská is the entrance to the palace gardens which, as well as offering memorable views, contain some of the most remarkable garden architecture erected anywhere this century. Walking along, the eye is constantly amused by marble temples and obelisks, all beautifully finished, if rather monumental. Their strange Mediterranean forms are curious legacies of Plečnik's imagination, and they culminate in a dramatic flight of stairs, at the bottom of which rests a large water basin. The gardens and distant domes beneath are a happy contrast to the long humourless barrack-like façades

---

* It remains to add that neither of the unfortunate councillors who fell into what might be termed a dung heap perished, a circumstance Catholics later attributed to a miracle.

which, save for the odd Etruscan gesture imparted to them by Plečnik, are almost impossible to admire.

Almost opposite the first entrance to the Hradčany, a café with a terrace of leafy trees will serve food and drinks. The impressive three-storey palais facing this, with its three central bays raised over a Serlian arch, is the Archbishop's Palace, dating from the sixteenth century but clothed in the language of Louis Seize in the 1760s by Jan Wirch. The Hradčanské náměsti behind is full of other impressive palaces, of which the Schwarzenberg's sgraffito rustication immediately catches the eye. It dates from the 1540s and has a rather Neapolitan swagger about it. Inside is an interesting if propaganda-orientated collection of militaria. The courtyard in the summer, however, is the scene of hilarious medieval mimes involving impressive displays of swordsmanship and a dramatic skill which can keep spectators of any nationality on the edge of their seats. The shows are a thoroughly Bohemian affair, with the Czechs' natural talent for acting and clowning brilliantly exposed through a series of fortunately fairly simple plots.

At the centre of this square stands a rather dull Baroque monument to the Virgin Mary. Opposite the Palais Schwarzenberg is the modern art gallery housed in the Palais Sternbeck, a picturesque building attributed to Martinelli and Alliprandi.

From here the Palais Martinic, with its seventeenth-century gables, leads the way to the narrow Kanovnická which, passing a gate to the castle from which overgrown paths invitingly fall below, eventually leads to the Kapučinská, another precious gas-lit lane.

At the end of this stands the remarkable Loreto church, whose façade (1720–22) is the work of the Dientzenhofers. Its long irregular façade is full of fantasy and is the perfect antidote to the monstrous pile of the Palais Černin (1669–97) which towers opposite it. This wretched build-ing, with its hideous gigantic order and relentless pediments, is pre-dictably the work of Caratti. Though its garden front is relieved by two enormous Serlian arches, the entire structure is as irrelevant to its sur-roundings as a space-station would be to Venice. Needless to say, those who commissioned it soon grew weary of being besieged by its earnest-ness and even before the collapse of the Habsburg empire it had been relegated to its only possible use, that of a barrack.

But to return to the Loreto church. With what humour the Dient-zenhofers must have relished creating a façade which in every way mocks the massive pedantry of Caratti. Inside, the church is a riot of Baroque stucco and frescoes, uninhibited in a way which only the temporary presence here of Christ's birthplace *en route* for Loreto could perhaps justify.

Concealed behind the church however is even greater treasure, an imitation of the celebrated Santa Casa of Loreto executed between 1626 and 1631 by Giovanni Orsi and Andrea Allio, with well-proportioned twin Corinthian half-columns.

From here, the Pohořelec leads past several late Renaissance buildings and the light Rococo Palais Kučera to the Strahov monastery, almost at the highest spot of the town and commanding exceptional views of the cathedral.

The abbey was founded in 1140. In the courtyard are the former church – the order has been suppressed – and the library, with an effete façade on the fringes of Neo-Classicism from the 1780s by Ignac Palliardi. The interior of the library and the former abbey garden would both merit two asterisks on a pre-war guide, although both seemed at the time of writing to be inaccessible, so that neither the magnificent stucco work of Orsi nor the beautiful bookcases of Palliardi could be as much as glimpsed. The gardens generally are less difficult to enter, but the splendid view of the cathedral from there is often denied by a shabby man in a blue suit, impossible even to bribe.

Returning to the Hradčany along the Uvoz, it is tempting to branch off to the right through the acres and acres of orchards which in season envelop the hillside, so that a few minutes' walk among them instantly banishes the city.

Those interested in ethnography should take these blossomed paths, for at the end of them is the Villa Kinsky, with a beautiful collection of ethnographic costumes, introduced by a taped commentary usually running slow and so presenting a lugubrious description of the museum's exhibits.

But if architecture as well as nature is wanted, it is perhaps better to follow the U Prašného mostu to the Mariánské Hradby, at the northern end of which stands the exotic Belvedere, a harmonious Renaissance arcaded loggia erected in 1536 to the designs of one Paolo della Stella. An attractive Renaissance fountain stands in front of the arcades, whose gentle symmetry is brilliantly set off by the maverick roof, reminiscent in shape of a Turkish tent.

From this eccentric structure, various paths run through the former Chotek Gardens to a pagoda café where, overlooking the Moldau, with a cool breeze blowing, sunset over the golden city can be enjoyed as its melancholy beauty falls asleep in the glow of green gas-light.

11

BOHEMIA AND THE SPAS

The treasures of Bohemia are varied and vast enough to fill a large book. Every town is rich in Baroque building. Almost every hill or rocky crag seems to be crowned by a picturesque castle, while between each settlement, great and small, rolling hills or endless pine forests sweep across the horizon. But it is generally less well known, though evident to the traveller, that Bohemia is also the most industrialized part of Central Europe. The province was the purse of the Habsburg empire before the nineteenth century on account of its silver mines, and because it was rich in other natural ores it became during the industrial revolution the Central European equivalent of the English midlands. There is still much left of this, and even from the renowned spas there are few views on which a red and white factory or power-station chimney does not intrude.

Environmentalists see poison and pollution at work in every forest here and the number of trees which seem to be dying or simply to have fallen down is legion. But unless the traveller visits the immediate environs of a power station, he or she is unlikely to be made aware of this depressing problem, which the Czechoslovak government has only very recently decided to face.

· THE SPAS AND NORTHERN BOHEMIA ·

The easiest way to visit the spas and north-western Bohemia is to take one of the expresses from the former Franz-Josef station in Prague to the delightful town of Cheb (or Eger, as the Germans call it). Because the train (which usually leaves at the convenient hour of 11.20 a.m.) is heading for Germany, it is tolerably fast, comfortable and, even more important, almost empty. A restaurant car is invariably attached and while good food is sometimes difficult to find in Prague, I have never known better service and cooking on a train than that provided in these blue carriages. Of course the clientele can be a little eccentric: a Cuban engineer drowning his sorrows over the Bohemian climate with glass after glass of delicious Pilsen beer, or a family of stiff Prussians returning to Berlin, or the inevitable chatter of various Czechs, often in differing stages of gentle inebriation.

The train runs at a steady thirty-five miles an hour, passing the abandoned wooden railway station of Vysehrad, crossing the Moldau, with a view of Hradčany, before slowly leaving behind the art-nouveau villas and façades of the suburbs. Within minutes, despite the slow pace, narrow valleys with fast-rushing streams and rivers, deserted save for the occasional fisherman, open up.

After about half-an-hour, the train passes the impressive castle of KARLŠTEJN, rising on a precipitous rock. It is the largest and best known of the scores of ruritanian schlosses which crown many dramatic hill-tops in Bohemia. Under a cloudy sky, it has a rainy grey colour which is far from inviting. Erected in 1348–65 by Charles IV of Bohemia and laid siege to in the fifteenth century, the castle was little more than a ruin at the end of the last century. Though fully restored, it no longer houses, as it once did, the Bohemian regalia, and many of its treasures have long disappeared to museums in Prague. The central part of the building is the chapel, with the remains of various fourteenth-century wall-paintings depicting the Apocalypse. In addition, there is the chapel of St Catherine, a vaulted space less than twelve feet long where the emperor Charles IV would retire to meditate. Higher up is the third chapel of the castle, that of the Holy Cross, which contains a gilded triptych by Tommaso de Modena.

The guided tours which lead one around the interminable fortifications are rather depressing, and modern and insensitive lighting removes even more of the magic that was once Schloss Karlstein. Better perhaps then to admire the great pile from afar rather than break the spell by entering it. Moreover, while the castle has a reasonable restaurant with a view over the surrounding hills, its fare is unlikely to be up to that offered by the Czechoslovak railways. Even with a day in hand it would I think be better to walk round Karlštejn a few miles to the west to Lodenice and Berounka and its fantastic precipitous gorge rather than penetrate this noble mass of masonry.

A little to the north, in a tributary valley of Berounka, lies the small town of KŘIVOKLÁT, with its chapel of delicate elegance constructed between 1493 to 1522, while further up the valley lies RAKOVNÍK, with its long grey market place, gate towers and church.

After Karlštejn, the line runs on across more rolling countryside to PLZEŇ (Pilsen), a town which rises through the smoke, its cathedral pinnacles surrounded by brick nineteenth-century chimneys like an illustration from Pugin's *Contrasts*. As might be expected from a city which has dedicated itself to producing quite simply the best beer in the world, there is little of great architectural merit to be seen, apart from the Gothic church of St Bartholomew. Grassy rails lead to the old brewery buildings from the crumbling yellow station, with its dramatic Beaux-Arts roof-line and ubiquitous *femmes fatales* on the frieze.

After Pilsen, the line becomes single-track. At STŘÍBRO, an hour could be spent admiring the yellow barn of a church and the Renaissance Town Hall. Nearby lie the ruins of the once great castle of Guttenstein, where Burian of Guttenstein held Peter Payne prisoner while he wrote to the Pope and to Henry VI of England striving to get a high price for his prisoner, the 'forgotten great Englishman'.

Two and a half miles south of here are the extraordinary buildings which make up Kladruby abbey church – extraordinary, for here a link between Baroque and Gothic is forged through the brilliance of Giovanni Santini. The abbey church appears Gothic in its entirety until the eye picks out a '1712' pediment from which the transept pinnacles spring. This curious device, as a contemporary document inviting the Abbot of Melk to drop in to admire the '*amplissima in more gotico nondum visa cupola*' shows, was a source of considerable wonder to the good monks themselves. Santini's skill in cloaking a Romanesque structure with ribs and a dome and a host of statues rather in the style of Batty Langley is unforgettable, even if dampness and an occasional broken window impart a tinge of melancholy to this foundation now bereft of its Benedictines.

Over the hills the roads run to Marienbad, still a just name for Mariánské Lázně, but the train halts only briefly at the yellow classical station and, so as not to leave this excellent carriage without good reason, it is best to continue to Cheb and put up at Franzensbad for the night before returning to this spa en route for Carlsbad.

It is late afternoon by the time the train pulls into Cheb, but a couple of hours at most will suffice to see this historic town before another train takes us in eight minutes to a completely different world at Franzensbad.

However, at first CHEB is far from inspiring. The red block of a station must be the ugliest railway building in Bohemia. Outside, the streets which fall down the slight hill inspire even less confidence, lined as they are with depressing seedy buildings which may once have been a brighter colour than the smoky grey black grime which almost without exception dulls their façades. The long avenue here, named after some Czech–Soviet bond of indissoluble comradeship, should be followed, crossing over the equally dreary road named 1st of May, until the market square renews our faith in the town.

In contrast to everything between it and the railway station, the ensemble of seventeenth- and eighteenth-century buildings which now open up before the eye is one of the treasures of Central Europe, rivalled possibly only by the in many ways similar squares to be found in the German-speaking parts of Transylvania. The square falls down from the comfortable Hotel Hvězda on the right to a series of small timbered houses. Opposite the hotel at the corner of the Březinova is the former hotel, excitingly starred in every guide written before 1914, called the 'Two Archdukes'. All that remains, alas, of this once illustrious establishment are the well-preserved gold heads of the two princes, sons it would seem of Maria Theresa, which adorn the façade.

The Březinova street is in itself an object of considerable charm, but walking down the square to the fountain with its statue of Roland, past *trompe-l'œil* pilasters, the Jatečni leads left to where several seventeenth-century houses of equal quality can be inspected. No. 457 has a fine coat of arms, while further along there is a noteworthy yellow façade crowned by an effigy of a knight gazing benevolently between the gentle embrace of several undersized twin pilasters.

At the end of this road is another striking façade, green with white stucco scallop shells above the windows. A narrow road to the left leads to the thirteenth-century Franciscan church, invariably shut. Opposite, the chapel of St Clara by Christopher Dientzenhofer seems to have been converted into some kind of bleak lecture theatre.

From these rather maudlin remains, the Růžová and Jakuzská lead back to the square, where among a clutch of timbered houses the Kavarna Špalíček offers refreshment.

On one side of the café stands a confident Rococo façade of red and gold with a splendid series of excellently carved stucco faces beaming out above the first floor. Next to it is a Gothic door of noble proportions, while at the bottom of the square is the town museum containing the room where Wallenstein, the great general of the Thirty Years War, was assassinated by Devereux. This is a gloomy place. On one wall a portrait of Wallenstein hangs, while on another there is an eighteenth-century depiction of the bloody scene immortalized by Schiller's play.

From here the picturesque Kammena runs down past the Dominican church, usually shut, but with a pleasing façade. To the right a path ascends up to the deanery church, a plain fifteenth-century building restored by the Baroque architect Balthasar Neumann. It has an impressive Gothic portal with fine cusps over the door and a still faintly discernible plaque commemorating the jubilee of the Austrian emperor, Franz Josef, in 1908. The glass inside all seems to be garish modern, and a notice reports that the entire building was restored in 1966.

In front of the church, Baroque statuary, possibly by Neumann, leads down to a seedy but picturesque square behind which, to the left, is the castle, situated on a rock above the river. It was erected by Frederick Barbarossa after his marriage in 1149 to Adelheid of Vohburg, but was last lived in during the seventeenth century. The principal tower is built of blocks of black lava and is believed to have once been part of an earlier castle of the margraves of Vohburg. Inside, the two-storey chapel dates from the twelfth century. The lower storey is Romanesque with zigzag piers recalling Alsace, while the storey above is pointed Gothic. The adjoining room, the former banquet hall where Wallenstein's officers were murdered a few hours before the general, is marked only by the arched remains of the windows.

From the castle a leafy promenade leads back to the Dobrovského and eventually to the square.

Despite its obvious charm, in recent years Cheb has not been a place to spend the night in, and the regular train service to FRANZENSBAD (Františkovy Lázně) should now be used to enjoy the early evening in what is perhaps the best preserved of the great spas of Bohemia. The picturesque route crosses a long high viaduct into some woods before halting after a few minutes at a faded yellow station. This sets the tone for the entire spa, which without exception is made up of buildings coloured the same nostalgic *Kaisergelb* (imperial yellow). Theatres, hotels, sheds, villas, all bask in soft yellow, relieved only by some white detailing and an occasional green shutter or balcony. At first glance not a single house seems to be later than 1913 and there are no streets of hideous post-war development to trail through before reaching the town centre, as there are in other Bohemian spas.

From the station, an avenue runs straight to a park lined with former hotels. The roads are usually deserted even in summer. Itinerant musicians carrying their instrument cases through the park seem to be the only inhabitants during the early evening.

Unfortunately, as the western visitor soon discovers, where once every second house would open its doors to the traveller, nearly all the guest houses and hotels have been converted into '*dûms*' – homes for the members of various state factories or unions. Finding a room is thus not as easy as in the west, where spontaneity is still catered for. None the less, Franzensbad is far from the busiest place in Bohemia and the chances are usually better than evens of finding somewhere civilized to stay.

Through the park, past the bandstand with its elegant wooden patterns, the path runs to the left of the Catholic church (locked except on Sundays) and past the former Hotel Kreuz, with its creeper-covered balcony, onto the main road of the spa. This is another leafy avenue which boasts on the left the Čedok office, where accommodation can be arranged, and on the right a splendid house where Beethoven stayed in 1812. The black and gold plaque in Teutonic script records the precise date, while inside, an empire mirror and an unusual portrait of the composer, clearly installed shortly afterwards, are as touching a memorial to him as anything to be found in the countless Beethoven museums of Austria and Germany.

Further down from this house is the Hotel Slovan, one of the few boarding houses which are open to western travellers. Although drastically restored in the seventies, the eccentric caryatids on the staircase ceilings have been lovingly preserved.

At the end of this avenue is the chief drinking well, the so-called Francis spring, named after that severe emperor who was the last Habsburg to wear the crown of the Holy Roman Empire (see p. 53). The spring stands under a Greek Doric rotunda filled with gleaming polished brass pipes. On one side runs the colonnade whose columns provide very necessary shelter from what seem in June to be constant thunderstorms. During the morning the columns are lined with walkers sipping water from porcelain jugs with long spouts, but in the evening they are generally as quiet as a Greek temple. The only permanent character is a snarling bust of Lenin, whose demonic expression is not in the slightest mollified by the lush flower-beds surrounding him.

On the other side of the spring is a large hall known as the casino, though gambling rarely takes place in its grand saloons. Instead it serves as a general meeting place for lectures and rallies. It is an unfortunate fact of life in Czechoslovakia that even on holiday the ominous rhetoric of communism continues to thunder its phrases out of strategically placed loudspeakers. In Franzensbad, this usually starts at about 7.45 a.m., diluted by sequences, interminably repeated, of some Tchaikovsky piano concerto.

This can be escaped by following the road round the back of the casino to the evangelical church, past the faded signs of old pension houses, which were named after towns in the Austrian empire. The road running along the edge of the park from here leads to the gaudily restored Russian church which, like most Russian churches, boasts a picturesque assortment of domes. Beyond it, on the Kollárova, is an impressive conservatory restaurant belonging to one of the *důms*.

At the end of the Kollárova is the theatre, a curious early twentieth-century building made up of cubist motifs which are strangely jarring in this more classical setting of park and villas. A few minutes' walk through the park leads to the former Villa Imperiale, a picturesque building, horribly gutted inside but doubtless, judging by the row of West German cars parked outside, a comfortable place to stay.

From here an avenue of oaks leads to the rather Parisian-looking former Kaiserbad, another temple dedicated to water, which bubbles between the polished brass pipes. A bust nearby commemorates Dr Adler, one of the spa's most eminent physicians, who was responsible for discovering many of the potent cures to be found in the waters around here.

Beyond these yellow baths is a small stream. The deserted grass around it is a frequent playground for rabbits, especially at dusk. Across the stream, a straight path leads uphill to a fork. The left turning brings the walker immediately into the country, for Franzensbad, unlike Marienbad and Carlsbad, is not hemmed in by narrow valleys.

The route, indicated by red and white markers, provides a series of panoramic views of the Bohemian foothills. All that is lacking, as the road runs down to village ponds and up to deserted crossroads, is a pub or hostelry – the houses are mostly quiet buildings with little to invite the stranger across their thresholds.

A second walk, in the opposite direction to this and with a café at the end of it, runs from the Ruská near the former Kaiserbad towards the railway. After passing underneath two railway bridges, the path runs uphill and is marked by a series of red hearts through the woods, which lead ultimately to a small café surrounded by trees and the scent of acacia.

From Franzensbad, there are frequent buses to MARIENBAD, that favourite spa of Edward VII who, both as king and as Prince of Wales, insisted on spending much of his summer at this unpretentious town.

Unlike Franzensbad, it lies in a charming valley enclosed on three sides by pine-clad hills. At the beginning of the nineteenth century, the region was still an impenetrable wilderness. Then the springs which belonged to the nearby abbey of Tepl were found by various eminent men of medicine to possess curative qualities, and development began. Villas shot up, hotels appeared and with the visits of such fashionable European royalty as Prince Edward this small spa became for a few weeks each year the centre of European diplomacy, as foreign ministers from Vienna and St Petersburg came to take the waters between intense discussions in their respective hotels with the private secretaries of any convalescent royalty present.

It was at Marienbad that Edward tried on occasions to detach the Austrian emperor, Franz Josef, that aged bastion of the old order, away from Germany and the steadfast alliance between the two empires which was to have such disastrous consequences for Europe in 1914.

Of all this diplomatic activity, there is little to remind us in today's Marienbad. From the station, a No. 5 trolley bus follows the Husova and then along the Cs. armady boulevard, which is bounded on the right by the park and on the left by a series of decaying nineteenth-century hotels. Above these stands the first of two poignant relics of Marienbad's Edwardian past, the English church.

It is as melancholy a sight as anything to be seen in Central Europe – its tracery bare save for a few fragments of Clayton and Bell glass left in the west end's rose window, its pews ripped out, its walls scribbled upon. At the time of writing the vestry door is conveniently absent, so that this most maudlin of Victorian ruins can be examined at will. Inside, the light shines through onto the only decorative objects to have survived intact, a memorial plaque to Edward VII, 'Emperor of India by grace of God'. Next to it some Czech wag has scribbled 'God Save the Queen'. Where once a monarch and his entourage regularly worshipped, there remains only dust and decay.

This is a sombre way to begin a visit to a spa, but the rest of the town is far from cheering. The Russian church further down the road above the English church is in rather more robust state, but its colours are so vulgar as to seriously inhibit any enjoyment of it.

From here the road leads down to the principal square of the town. Each of the small hotels has wood-panelled rooms which have remained unchanged for decades, and a small yellow theatre off to the left has retained its stuccoed interior.

To the right, along the top of a leafy embankment, rises the most impressive structure in the entire town: the long winding colonnade which, with its magnificent iron columns, could easily be the work of the ubiquitous Helmer and Fellner partnership.

Inside, the scores of walkers sipping water as they perambulate up and down cut a grotesque figure. Each one holds a small china tea-pot from whose nozzle the healing waters are periodically sucked in the way people chew on pipes. The arcade itself has been ruthlessly restored. Where once it was possible to walk on stone, there is only linoleum. Where paintings hung on the walls, there are now only ugly bronzes. As a laconic comment on this state of affairs, the face of the nineteenth-century clock has slid round, so that the numeral six is where twelve normally stands.

A fine yellow villa opposite restores some hope. It boasts the only façade in Central Europe which has a three-dimensional representation in stucco of an American steam-engine. This and an abandoned pair of kettle-drums in the centre are perhaps the more memorable sights of this colonnade, which once saw a portly King of England amble along surrounded by the excited and curious eyes of hundreds of onlookers. But then today the arcade is named after Maxim Gorki rather than a Habsburg archduke.

At the end of the colonnade there is at the time of writing a large building site. The earnest spa officials proudly proclaim that this will soon be the grandest and noblest of all the springs, but a model of the design suggests that whatever fills this hole will be completely out of tune with the classical architecture around it.

To the right of this is the bronze statue of the Abbot Reitenberger (d. 1860), who, like Dr Joseph Neyr, whose wizened features are commemorated nearby in a bronze bust, did much to promote the prosperity of the baths.

On a small square on the other side of the colonnade rises the large imposing Catholic church, an uninspired work of the 1840s, usually open during the week.

Behind it, across another square, stands the second surviving link with King Edward, the former Hotel Weimar (now the Hotel Kafka), where the monarch would put up during his sojourns here. It is almost inconceivable that the rooms of this unpretentious establishment once resounded to the talk of state secrets. The painting which once hung in its dining room depicting the 'Uncle of Europe' on one of his strolls through the colonnades has disappeared, while the memorial statues in the nearby garden depicting the Austrian emperor and the English king also seem to have been lost. Only over the main entrance does the Gothic script of old German plaque recall the illustrious personage who enjoyed rooms on the first floor during the town's Edwardian summers.

Next to the hotel is the spa museum, a curious building containing on its first floor the remains of Goethe's house – the poet still enjoys the authorities' esteem – with the furniture on which the master wrote during his frequent stays here a few generations before King Edward. On the ground floor, a bird's-eye panorama view of the spa shows the English church in all its old glory, while rooms to the right contain a thin collection of Marienbadalia, with nothing which even remotely refers to the heady diplomatic life of the town in the early 1900s. A series of portraits of the spa's doctors, earnest and well groomed, is well displayed, while behind another case are a number of old biscuit tins which once held the famous *Oblaten*, those large thin wafers which are the great speciality of the region and which even today are delicious when found at their best (that is in tins rather than packets).

From the museum, various paths run up to the Hámelika hills, passing Beaux-Arts-style baths, including the remarkable Moor's bath, whose interior is still a riot of nineteenth-century arts-and-crafts decor.

Of the many paths which thread the pine forest here, that above the Pod Panoramou leading to the Café Miramonte is perhaps the favourite.

It passes several interesting viewpoints, including one which, according to a plaque, was frequented by Goethe. Above the Miramonte, the summit of the hill offers views of the Bohemian hills and mountains. The former 'Kaiser Tower' has been rather crudely adapted to this century and, like so many things which recall empires and monarchies in this part of the world, renamed.

From here a path marked by yellow finger-posts winds its way slowly down to the Červená Karkulka, a restaurant surrounded by woods which is a favourite eating place of the spa guests, who then return to the town centre by way of the Rudolf spring.

From here the railway is also not far and next to it is the bus station, where there are frequent services to the last great spa to be seen in Bohemia, Carlsbad, now known as Karlovy Vary.*

Like Marienbad, CARLSBAD is set in a narrow valley whose pine-clad slopes are traversed by paths in all directions. But it is a far older establishment than Marienbad, the curative properties of its waters having been praised as early as 1347 by the Emperor Charles IV, who is reputed to have discovered them one day, while hunting, although there are sources to indicate that the springs here were known a hundred years earlier.

The principal ingredients of the waters are sulphate of soda, carbonate of soda and common salt. The springs rise from beneath a very hard kind of rock, known in German as the *Sprudeldecke*, a crust from which hot water rushes up wherever it is broken. Most of the older part of the town is built on this crust, under which is a vast reservoir of mineral water. The steam from this escapes through artificial apertures in the rock which, on account of the incrustations deposited by the water, need to be cleared every few weeks. It is a fashion here to put roses and crockery in the waters for a few days and then sell them, covered in the brown-yellow deposit which is formed, as souvenirs. The older incrustations are usually the most expensive, but few should cost more than a handful of crowns, and they are unique if sombre memorials of the place.

---

* If it is intended to put up at Marienbad, the following morning could be well spent walking over the hill to Krynvert, where an old château of Metternich's houses a small museum containing an early piano made in Vienna, one of whose pedals sounds six strokes of a drum.

Arriving in Carlsbad, however, is often a depressing experience. The bus drops one near the newer quarters over the river Ohře. Bleak, shabby blocks of flats, all rapidly erected and far from sensitively placed, fortify the horizon. Across the river, where the spa itself begins, there is no improvement, for the first building to be seen is a vast black concrete bunker, built no doubt during the decade of civic pride in the 1970s and purporting to house springs, though at first glance it looks like an armoured-car barracks.

Optimism returns, however, if we keep to the right of the stream and walk through the former town park. As well laid out with trees as a small college garden, it is colourfully rounded off by the former imperial and royal military spa establishment. This is a jolly white stuccoed villa with reliefs of bayonets, rifles, lances and shakos marking each wing. In front of this runs a beautiful wrought-iron colonnade, crying out for white-gloved officers to lounge under its elegant spandrels.

At the first bridge beyond this, on the other side of the stream, rises the Budvar ale house, almost the only place where a cooked meal can be had after 2.30 p.m. The clientele here take their beer seriously and it is disarmingly strong, so that by the time pudding has arrived there may well be a chorus of inebriated workers drowning their sorrows in a beery rendering of some Bohemian folk-song. Near the Budvar along the same side of the stream is another ale house with an unashamedly German façade which could have served as a set for *The Mastersingers of Nuremberg*. Opposite it begins the first of the long colonnades, an effete Corinthian order of stone, which runs further on into a quainter wooden one, filled with dilapidated souvenir shops.

At the end of this is the Čedok office and next to it is the only hotel which can cope with an unexpected visit, the Atlantic. This is a satisfactory establishment, especially if rooms have been found on the top floor, where balconies are adorned by hideous but priceless art-nouveau porcelain figures and where the views extend over the stream to the flamboyant Baroque Magdalene church. The service is variable, but the narrow dark-panelled staircase leading up to the rooms has preserved a style which, if not to everyone's taste, is unforgettable.

Across the stream from the hotel is a haughty copper-domed assembly hall and the inevitable Helmer and Fellner theatre, with a plan identical to the one they used in Vienna, though with a standard of decoration inside which would put most theatres in that city to shame.

Above this, enjoying the cramped site to the full, is the Magdalene church, a masterpiece of Kilian Dientzenhofer erected in the 1730s. The plan is octagonal, the dome oval, and convex and concave are mixed in a way which cannot dispel a lingering first impression of confusion.

At the end of the urban part of the stream, before the water continues its winding path through the woods, stand the great buildings of the former Hotel Pupp, now renamed Moskva, a shabby but comfortable establishment. Its rooms are modernized and its airy white conservatory has been painted over so that no light whatever reaches the room which once resounded to the sounds of Strauss waltzes and the whisper of treachery, for it was here that the infamous Austrian traitor, Colonel Redl, met his Russian contacts just before the First World War to hand them the entire Austrian order of battle.

Opposite the Moskva is a jolly Neo-Rococo palais called Quisiana, once a most popular pension house but now given over to the trade unions. A park from here across the river leads to the grand former Kaiserbad, a theatrical-looking building designed by Helmer and Fellner but closed to the public (a surly notice points out: 'Visits are not allowed').

The promenade, which returns to the Hotel Atlantic, passes some of the best shops in Czechoslovakia and a number of cafés. That named 'The Elephant' still retains an air of prosperity and seems to be a popular and elegant meeting place for local Czechs. A little further along the best *Oblaten* wafers can be bought in green tins proudly displayed in a cake shop invariably filled with old ladies queuing for gaudy cakes covered in meringue.

The chief glories of Carlsbad, however, not even decades of communism have succeeded in removing, and those are its countless picturesque walks.

One of the most enjoyable begins almost opposite the Hotel Atlantic on the Zámecká, where the quaint castle restaurant points the road up to the English church. Unlike its cousin in Marienbad, this Edwardian building is still used, though as an Evangelical church, and its red-brick façade and stained-glass windows are all preserved in immaculate condition. A key to visit the interior can be obtained from the priest's house next door (first floor). There is much of Victorian England left here, and the pews, memorial plaques and some sentimentally inscribed stone benches in the overgrown garden of the church would not seem out of place in a village in the home counties.

Behind the church, a small path overlooking the town below runs uphill. A memorial seat after a few minutes records the '*affezione*' of an Italian whose life was prolonged by his weeks of convalescence here. This path continues until it stumbles across the rails of what appears to be a disused funicular. To the right of these the path emerges in a small clearing at the centre of which stands an obelisk erected in 1804 to the memory of the Earl of Findlater, 'nature's friend' and a man who won the affections of the people of Carlsbad.

On the other side of the funicular line are some fine beech woods, and the path runs down to a small chapel, next to which a tree has collapsed, narrowly missing the building. Although its glass has been broken and there is no image of Christ left, a wooden book has carved on it the words in Czech which when translated seem to mean *Ecce Homo*. A smaller sign asks in German for alms for the chapel's upkeep.

Nearby, at the crossroads of all these forest paths, is an Alpine-style wooden shelter, green and cream with pretty patterned carvings and an almost incomprehensible map on one wall. A path running straight ahead from the Ecce Homo chapel leads after a couple of minutes to the so-called Findlater Temple, a wooden structure with green Ionic capitals, again bereft of its altar or any evidence that it might once have been a sacred building. Beneath it are the tennis courts, no longer lawn as they were in Baedeker's day but clearly just as popular.

Behind the Findlater Temple at the summit of the hill through the trees, a red-brick tower is just visible. This can be best reached by following the path past the temple and then turning sharp left at the first opportunity. The tower, once called the Franz Josef lookout, is typical of many such structures which mark the woods around Vienna. This one, however, is always open and offers a first-floor view over Carlsbad to the hills beyond, and – if the spiral staircase is mounted to the next floor – an even broader view encompassing the depressing blocks of high-rise housing in new Carlsbad and several wooded valleys.

From here, a path stretches down the other side of the hill towards the town. After five or ten minutes, a ruined neo-Gothic chapel appears where a plaque has survived to exhort the walker in German to pause and pray for a moment. Inside, the wooden altar and its pews, protected by an iron grill, have just about survived and amid all these ecclesiastical remnants is a pair of white plates nestling among the fragments of the stained glass. The outer wall of the chapel forms another side to the path and has on it the words: '*1882 La Vierge Marie auteur de ma guérison inespérée.*' There can be few more melancholy places in the world and only some tea at the Café Pupp below in any way distracts the senses away from this litter of past glories which seem to impinge on one at every corner.

Compared with the spas, the villages of northern Bohemia are rather more cheerful.

The small town of LOUNY can be reached by bus from Carlsbad along twisted woody valleys. It has a worthy Deanery church rebuilt by one Master Benedict (d. 1512) with effete Gothic tracery and Baroque altars. The town itself has a pretty square, with several houses dating from the late fifteenth century, and an inn which provides a suitable halt for lunch.

A few miles north of Louny lies TEPLITZ (Teplice), once a small spa town, situated prettily on the Elbe. Since the war, industrial development in the town has given it a rather weary air, but it remains an important starting point for exploring Bohemia and is on the main road to Saxony. Almost all that remains of its charming nineteenth-century atmosphere can be seen in the gardens on the hill behind the former castle of Prince Clary, whose autobiography describes most poignantly what the town looked like at the beginning of the century. Neither the walks around its castle nor its architecture rival those of Carlsbad or Marienbad, but a few hours wandering around here can be pleasantly rounded off by a having lunch or a cup of coffee in the colonnade near the Helmer and Fellner theatre.

From Teplitz a railway line runs south-east towards Prague past the extensive ruins on the right bank of the Elbe of SCHRECKENSTEIN (Střekov), a castle destroyed in the eighteenth century. Once the key to the Elbe, the castle was the scene of many a desperate struggle, and its foundation can be traced back to the year 820. The Germans were making raids into Bohemia and advice was sought as to how to stop them. According to local legend, a certain Strzek suggested the construction of a strong fortress on the river and then was asked to choose the spot and build the castle. Many stories have since arisen describing the great deeds of heroism Strzek performed in defending this site, but the chronicles of the Middle Ages reveal that the castle was to live through even more trying times. On 16 June 1426, for example, a battle around the walls saw 7,000 Germans put to the sword, together with some 500 knights and counts.

As well as legends and chronicles, Schreckenstein has also given rise to countless fairy tales, of which that of Mathilde of Schreckenstein is perhaps the most enduring. Mathilde was captured with her lover by the dreaded Kuba, an inveterate huntsman who was so enraged when the gnomes secreted the lover out of the castle that as revenge he hurled the hapless Mathilde from the battlements. On dark summer nights it is said that her cries can still be heard echoing around the ruins. As the castle was besieged no less than five times between 1621 and 1648, there are some who say that the rattle of armour and rapiers can also be heard in the nearby woods.

A few miles further down the Elbe lies the altogether less sinister town of LITOMĚŘICE, again bypassed by the railway and so virtually untouched by the civic pride of the nineteenth century. The town is renowned for its being almost a museum of Octavian Broggio (1668–1742), a gifted architect who imparted several of his more imaginative designs to the town. He was responsible for the interior of the Jesuit church and the rebuilt church of the Minorites. But it is the chapel of St Vaclav, begun in 1714 on the north slope of the cathedral hill, which gives the best idea of his work, many of whose profiles seem to have been inspired by the Austrian architect Prandtauer (see p. 61). In the nearby huddle of cottages where once coaching inns abounded are several ale houses (marked by the letter 'U' followed by the Czech name).

About four miles to the north-east of Litoměřice is Octavian Broggio's one great house, at Ploskovice. The house was later brutally enlarged for Ferdinand IV (1835–48), who insisted on an additional storey which obliterates its proportions. The melancholy garden has plausibly been referred to by Brian Knox as the 'last despairing calculation of an exquisite order'.

· EASTERN BOHEMIA ·

From Prague, the former Franz Josef railway runs to Kolín and Poděbrady, situated in the heart of eastern Bohemia, a traditional Central

European battleground. East of Poděbrady unfolds the rolling landscape which witnessed near Kolín the only serious defeat the Austrians ever were able to inflict on their Prussian adversaries. The great victory gained by the Austrian Field-Marshal Daun over Frederick the Great on 18 June 1757 even compelled the Prussians to evacuate Bohemia.

KOLÍN itself is a dull place. Many of its oldest houses were rebuilt after a fire in 1734, although the Deanery church of 1360–78, being partly the work of Peter Parler, should not be overlooked. Chancel and nave have been described as 'two tragic acts joined by an irrelevant *coup de théâtre*', a harsh judgement which overlooks the inspiring quality of the craftsmanship. Set above the country's version of Crewe Junction, with its detached belfry of the sixteenth century, it strikes a welcome note of artistic achievement and humanity.

Close to Kolín are two more interesting settlements, SEDLEC and KOUŘIM. The former is an old Cistercian abbey church of the fourteenth century, remodelled in the early eighteenth century by the wilful Santini. The latter preserves the best defences in Bohemia and has a low aisled Deanery church with an octagonal crypt.

But even these are overshadowed by the glorious architecture of KUTNÁ HORA, known to the Germans for centuries as Kuttenberg, a royal town established in 1308 with at least one church which can stand comparison with any in Europe. Vaclav II (1278–1305) established his mint here, and it is perhaps worth pointing out that in the fifteenth century the population of the town was identical to that of London. By extraordinary good luck it survived both the Hussite wars and a fire in the 1770s to present the traveller today with a maze of streets each adorned with oriels and Rococo fronts.

The most important church in the town is that of St Barbara, with endlessly fascinating vaulting attributed to Master Benedict – the vault was closed in 1512 after his death. It is wholly composed of segments and constantly distracts the visitor from the late Gothic wall paintings and the pulpit's fine sixteenth-century stone reliefs. Only the Renaissance confessionals and handsome choir stalls offer some stability among the soaring ribs.

Near to this, if rather intimidated by it, is the Baroque church of St John Nepomuk, designed in 1734 by Kanka. In the Kamenný Dům, or former Town Hall, is another treasure, the Vaclav chapel, with ball-flower ornament and pinnacles. The nearby Ursulin convent is octagonal in plan and is the work of Kilian Dientzenhofer. It offers a more pleasing retreat than the dull mining museum expensively created in the rooms of the Town Hall. Of the other churches in the town, the Trinity, late Gothic of the 1490s, seems to be permanently locked and has no obvious means of access.

East of here the roads all seem to be signposted to HRADEC KRÁLOVÉ, known (as Königgrätz) to military historians as the site of the decisive battle in the Austro-Prussian war of 1866, a six-week engagement which ousted Austria from her position of supremacy among the German states. The battle, which was one of the bloodiest of the nineteenth century, saw the Austrians attempt to use their theatrical frontal bayonet charges for the last time. The Prussian needle guns turned the battle into a massacre as one by one the Austrian regiments were mown down. The loss of officers was particularly high – on average a third killed, another third wounded – owing to their reckless habit of personally leading the bayonet charges. It can truly be said that Austrian bravery on that day was ill-served by the incompetence of the staff officers who repeatedly ordered these futile assaults.

As a reminder of this slaughter, various monuments on the battlefield have survived. Hradec Králové itself has an oval Baroque chapel among the remains of its old fortifications and a rather severe Gothic 'White Tower' dating from 1574, but otherwise little to detain one.

South of here lies the most beautiful town in eastern Bohemia, LITOMYŠL, another example of the beneficial effects of being by-passed by the railways. Its square still retains almost all its medieval arcades, only one of them falling victim to clumsy conversion into a cement-faced hotel.

The local Baroque mason was Jiři Béba, who seems to have been responsible for the north wing of the Town Hall and the houses in the square numbered 53 and 61. No. 110, U Vrytim, with a sturdy knight on its 1546 façade, offers refreshment. The nearby Piarist's church is the work of Alliprandi and can be dated from 1714, while the Jan Avostalis house, constructed rather grandly between 1568 and 1575, is considered one of the most important works of Bohemian Renaissance. Its loggia on the second floor reveals a world of chivalry and battle – the whole of Bohemian nobility seems to be waging war across its walls.

From Litomyšl, minor roads wind north to Náchod, with its Renaissance castle, via a broad valley which is almost a museum of Kilian Dientzenhofer churches: Broumov, Vernerovice and Hermankovice all boast examples of his art and will occupy anyone with a car for the best part of a day.

· SOUTHERN BOHEMIA AND THE ROSE TOWNS ·

Those who have seen enough of north and eastern Bohemia may wish to return to the west and to Austria through southern Bohemia and the so-called rose towns.

The sleepy countryside of southern Bohemia has also known more than its fair share of violence. The forerunners of the Schwarzenberg family, the Rosenbergs, contested almost every town here, choosing as their badge a rose and so echoing the more sanguinary conflicts of the Middle Ages in England.

At SLAVONICE, a former staging post between Prague and Vienna, the gabled square still recalls these troubled times with various contemporary inscriptions, while at nearby TELČ (good restaurant at No. 7, Cerny Orel), Renaissance sgraffito adorns many of the two-storey houses. Telč itself is notable for the fourteenth-century castle of the Hradec family, which contains a pleasing old chapel, and the unique concentration of seventeenth-century façades which give the town the atmosphere of a stage set.

From Telč, a bus service frequently runs to JINDŘICHŮV HRADEC, whose castle contains a spectacular three-storey arcade and a rotonda by an unknown Italian architect clearly impressed by the theatrical possibilities of his commission. The gardens are untended, but the whole effect is impressive.

From Telč, it is only a few miles to the finest rose in southern Bohemia, the great gardens and palace of ČESKÝ KRUMLOV. The town itself is not without interest and a couple of days could be spent enjoying its varied treasures.

The principal gate to the town is a massive essay in Serlio. Past this the streets twist off to right and left. Those houses to the east shelter the remains of various seventeenth-century monastic buildings before a bridge most picturesquely crosses the Moldau. This leads eventually, after some inns best selected according to taste and instinct, to the town square (Čedok office on the right), a plain space only partly enlivened by the Town Hall and the nearby nineteenth-century Hotel Růže (comfortable). The picturesque 'Káplanka' next to the town church has an oriel and vaulted rooms which seem hardly to have altered at all since 1520. The nearby church of Svaty Vit (St Vitus), however, with its empty triple nave, is less inspiring. But from it there opens out a magnificent view of the castle with its thirteenth-century tower. The immense rectangular mass of stone, with its late Gothic windows, again evokes Anthony Hope.

Inside, its cold maze of rooms seems a most unfriendly home for a wealthy princely family, and its staircases are cramped and ugly. The guide is clearly most impressed by the Rococo chapel dedicated to St George and the blue and pink long gallery. But it is the theatre which is most memorable. Its battered eighteenth-century gold stage is still intact.

Outside, the gardens seem to stretch as far as the Austrian frontier. Less than seventy years ago, a private army dressed in white and blue guarded the castle's approaches, while an equally numerous army of gardeners attempted to meet princely demands and grow pineapples between the hedges.

No account of Krumlov would be complete without reference to the legend of the White Lady, a hapless princess married to a monster of a man in the Middle Ages. Needless to say, her apparition is still a regular sight to some of the older villagers, heralding impending catastrophe and still, despite the rhetoric of communism, impressing some Czechs more than the combined teachings of Lenin and Marx. Her uneasy steps are all that remain of the lost order which ruled Krumlov for so long.

From here a road winds west to Prachatice, with more sgraffitoed houses, Husinec, once a home of itinerant musicians, and other villages which still have traces of a pre-industrial revolution existence. But if the dollars are running out, the road south leads past the fortified town of Rožmberk (Rosenberg) and a ruined monastery into the less gentle but also less melancholy hills of Upper Austria.

12

MORAVIA AND SLOVAKIA

East of Bohemia stretch the hills and plain of Moravia. The border between Bohemia and Moravia lacks natural obstacles and indeed the Moravian is indistinguishable from the Bohemian, language and religion being largely the same. Its three historic urban centres, Znojmo, Brno and Olomouc, are all built along the old south-west to north-east road which has for centuries linked Central with Eastern Europe. The land is rich and fertile, and if the Moravians are in any way different from the western Czechs it is due to this abundance of fertile land, which gives them a more happy-go-lucky approach to life.

More than any other inhabitants of Czechoslovakia, the rural Moravians cling to their brightly coloured ethnic costumes. The large estates which almost exclusively made up this part of the Austrian empire have long disappeared, but in their wake they have left a series of castles which are almost unrivalled in any other areas of Central Europe apart from Bohemia.

The capital of Moravia, BRNO, or Brünn, the so-called Leeds (or, as some writers prefer, Manchester) of Czechoslovakia, lies at the centre of the province, well connected by road and rail, and is the best place to begin enjoying the Moravian lands.

The city lies at the foot of the Špilberk, or Spielberg, the old quarters surrounded by a Ringstrasse constructed on the site of earlier fortifications. Of the medieval town walls, only one gate remains, to the south-east, while most of the older houses are to the north and east of the cathedral.

From the station, the Husova třída leads off to the left towards the castle, beyond which is a former Augustinian monastery dating in part from the fourteenth century. The castle foundations are littered with casemates which earned the Spielberg a rather sinister reputation in the nineteenth century. What Siberia was to Russia and Botany Bay to England, Brno's Spielberg was until 1857 to the miscreants of the Habsburg Empire. Among the distinguished inmates of these dungeons were the truculent Colonel Trenck, commander of the half-savage Pandours, who died here in 1749, and Count Silvio Pellico, the Italian poet who was imprisoned here in 1822–30 and who described his sad experiences in *Le mie prigioni*, a work which so outraged liberal thinking in Europe that it is no exaggeration to say that this more than anything else contributed to the prison's closure in 1857.

At the foot of the castle hill, the Husova třída contains the exciting buildings of the Applied Arts Museum, designed in the twenties as a *tour-de-force* by the great Czech architect of this century, Jan Kotěra. It is flanked by other buildings of the same period but of less distinction: former schools, technical institutes and other institutions which all testify to how seriously the Austrians took higher education in the decades before Sarajevo.

The narrow Starobrnmenska leads from here to the principal square of the city, the náměstí 25 února, bright with Baroque façades and dominated by the former Palais Dietrichstein, attributed to the local Baroque builder Moric Grimm, a man with some taste for decorative detailing. Behind this rises the cathedral, built in the Gothic style in the fifteenth century but, as a result of the Swede's artillery during the Thirty Years War, restored in a style closely resembling Rococo, fussy and uninspired. The other church on the square is the seventeenth-century Capuchin church, in whose crypt lie the mummified remains of the hapless Colonel Trenck.

Nearby, the house at No. 10 Starobrnmenska has a fine Renaissance doorway, while at the end of this street, the old Town Hall faces onto the square, with its 1577 tower and late Gothic portal leading to the 'Brünn dragon', a crocodile skin suspended in the main corridor which has enjoyed the affections of the townsfolk for centuries.

From here the Vitězství leads to the Svobody nám, the second square in the old town which contains a commemorative column erected in 1680. There are also several cafés and drinking establishments, wine being preferred here to Bohemian beer.

In the nearby street leading off from the square, unromantically named 9 Kvetna, is the invariably shut church of St James, an elegant medieval construction built between 1314 and 1480 and rather similar in atmosphere to the church of Maria am Gestade in Vienna (see p. 30). The glass, some of which is nineteenth century, was described earlier this century as 'superb' and is certainly as good as any Victorian glass to be found in Central Europe. In the ambulatory of the choir is the monument of Field Marshal Count Radwit de Souches (d. 1683), the courageous defender of the city against the Swedes in 1645. The north aisle contains a wooden crucifix dating from the first half of the four-teenth century.

Further along the 9 Kvetna is the church of St Thomas, a fourteenth-century building with an early Baroque portal and an altar piece by Franz Anton Maulbertsch.

Leading from the right of this street runs a small road back towards the square, passing in the Chorazova the early Baroque church of the Jesuits, richly decorated with paintings and Baroque altars, but since the order's expulsion from communist Czechoslovakia after the war, in a sad state of decline.

Behind this are the town's two theatres. The modern, ugly and charmless one is named after the great composer of Brno, Leoš Janáček (1854–1928), who would doubtless have preferred the familiar Helmer and Fellner neo-Baroque affair next door which he grew up with. This opera house has the unique distinction of being the first theatre in the old Austrian empire to have been fitted with electric light.

For all the delights of its old town, Brno is not really a place to linger. The new town is uninspired and omnipresent, and though excellent rooms can be acquired at the Grand Hotel in the třída 1 Máje, those travelling by car or bus might prefer to head a few miles north and find rooms in the villages around PERNŠTEJN castle, a ruritanian building with an exotic skyline and a chapel partly Gothic and partly Renaissance in style. The building sits in the usual Central European position on a low spur between two tributary streams. Its cellular vaulting is dated 1522, and though some restoration work has been done, the entire place wears a look of neglect, perhaps inevitable for a building which has not been lived in since 1945.

To the south-west of Brno are the Italianate *logge* of MORAVSKÝ KRUMLOV – its regular tiers of orders guarded by soldiers who have occupied this sixteenth-century Schloss for the last two decades, although another part of the building has now become a museum of modern art with several interesting examples of Moravian art-nouveau, including works by Alfons Mucha.

From here, the road runs west to the remains of the great Benedictine abbey at TŘEBíč. Founded in 1101, in the eighteenth century this once wealthy establishment was reduced to little more than a rather imposing courtyard. In the north part of the church, the masonry is impressively cut, while the eighteenth-century vault of the nave has restrained wafer-thin ribs undecorated but perversely Baroque. The crypt is dark early Gothic, earnest and gloomy, reminiscent of Pannonhalma in Hungary.

To the east of Brno lies another fine palace on the road to Velehrad, at a place called BUČOVICE. It was constructed by Pietro Gabri of Brno to plans drawn up by that celebrated expert on fortifications, Pietro Ferrabosco di Lagno. The elegant courtyard is articulated by Ionic, Corinthian and Composite columns, giving the place a southern almost Italianate appearance rare on this side of the Carpathians. At the centre of the courtyard is a fountain of 1635 portraying a young man with the Golden Fleece. The imperial hall off the courtyard is equally Latin, with naked stucco figures embracing various escutcheons and a series of landscapes depicting the goddess of hunting, Diana.

To the east of here, at Strilky, the road rises north to KROMĚŘíž, a great house of the Liechtensteins, who more than anyone in this part of Central Europe were responsible for the demise of the style of architecture just admired in Bučovice. Owning more land than any other family in Moravia, the Liechtensteins were in the perfect position to have built castles and palaces which reflected the latest taste sweeping through the court at Vienna after 1627. As late as 1838, a German traveller to the province could remark that of all the nobilities of Europe that of Austria had lost least of its feudal power.

Before examining the splendours of Kroměříž, it is perhaps apposite to recall what another nineteenth-century traveller thought of the typical aristocratic owner: 'Humane in his conduct, patriarchal in his habits, unostentatious in his luxury, magnificent in undertakings, the kind protector of his peasantry, the judicious patron of arts, letters, and manufactures, such is the true old Austrian nobleman.'

The most judicious patron of the arts the Liechtensteins produced here was the seventeenth-century Prince Karl Eusebius, who seems to have believed it to be his sacred duty to leave beautiful objects of eternal remembrance. Money existed only for this purpose, so it is not surprising that in the course of his building projects he had a rather stormy relationship with several of his architects. The Erna brothers from Brno and Giovanni Tencala were his chief builders, but the unfortunate Tencala's domes had a habit of collapsing, so that the hapless architect was continually being fired. But at Kroměříž, a town sacked by the Swedes in 1643, the presence of a Liechtenstein prince as the bishop in 1690 enabled the town's fortunes to be glowingly restored. The castle was rebuilt from the ruins of the former *burg* and its gardens were given a 250-yard colonnade which is one of the most impressive structures in the country. Each arch of this relentless Doric order is marked by a Roman bust, so that no less than forty-six of these classical worthies contemplate the Moravian hills. The Schloss itself contains the former bishop's library and a collection of paintings with, among other old masters, a Van Dyck portrait of Charles I with Queen Henrietta.

South of here runs a road down to the Austrian frontier, where a little to the west lies the second important city of Moravia, ZNOJMO, or Znaim.

The settlement dates back to the time of King Ottokar I, who founded a town here in 1226 on the left bank of the river Thaya. It was here that an armistice was concluded between Napoleon and the Archduke Charles after the carnage of the battle of Wagram (see p. 5). The old fortifications were dismantled as a result of this but they have been replaced by promenades, as at Graz.

The cathedral church of St Catherine which stands at the centre of the city has Romanesque features and some particularly fine paintings on its nave walls – pale blues and greens still to suffer the restorer's heavy hand. From here the route to the castle of the margraves of Moravia leads through a brewery to the exquisite two-storey Gothic chapel dedicated to Svaty Vaclav. The lower chapel is sometimes locked and 'orthodoxized' but one can still obtain a rather shifty-looking guide with a key from the first house on the left in the Malá Mikulasska street.

Around the nearby Town Hall (which dates from 1445, although there is little to suggest such antiquity today) are a number of other old houses. On the main square, No. 7 with its Tuscan columns and No. 10 with its caryatids are worth looking at carefully. Near No. 13 is a café with a fourteenth-century interior, only partly modernized.

Between Znojmo and the Austrian frontier are several valuable Baroque buildings which, perhaps because of the proximity to Vienna, seem to have been able to command the talents of the very first division of Baroque architects. Hildebrandt's one work of unquestionable authenticity in Moravia is the convent at Louvka, a mass of yellow stucco visible for miles and now a barrack. At first glance, the building seems to have something in common with Hildebrandt's great work along the Danube at Göttweig, but the outline here is gentler and less exotic.

At VRANOV on the Thaya, also a few miles from Znojmo, it is Fischer von Erlach's genius that can be seen in the Schloss, designed in 1690–94. Situated in low-lying rather damp woods, it employs Fischer's favourite oval motif for the 'Ancestors' Hall', whose deep windows are cut into the ceiling and flanked by a modest order of pilasters. The splendid chaos of Rottmayr's frescoes were added a couple of years later. In the sun, the light fills every corner of this space, which because of its scale is considerably more intimate than the oval rooms Fischer created in Vienna. From here river and park run to the Austrian frontier, where the sinister barbed wire, sentry-boxes and fences would be inconceivable to the world which created Vranov.

A few miles east of Vranov lies another spectacular castle, LEDNICE, or Eisgrub, a neo-Gothic Schloss of the Liechtensteins, with an excellent English architectural library, a 500-yard-long conservatory and a magnificent park.

The journey back to Brno and thence to the last city of Moravia, OLOMOUC (Olmütz), is an hour and a half by bus or car which threading these sleepy hills encounters a rather grander landscape further north.

The city has a garrison aspect even today, when Russian soldiers fill the barracks and fortifications built for a corps of the Austrian army. Though taken by the Swedes during the Thirty Years War, it successfully withstood a siege by Frederick the Great in 1758. At the centre of the great eastern road to Krakow and Galicia, it is, as one might expect for a garrison town, always rather crowded. As well as soldiers and traders, it is full of students from the university (founded 1573), which, although moved to Brno in the eighteenth century, was refounded after the war. As well as sieges, Olomouc has known several other events of historical significance for Central Europe. It was here during the tumultuous events of 1848 that the Austrian Kaiser, Franz Josef, was crowned.

Although its older quarters boast several Baroque fountains and a number of interesting churches, it is difficult to describe Olomouc as beautiful. The Town Hall in the main square is a wedding-cake structure, all minarets and gables, relieved by a rather more serious fourteenth-century Gothic portal and a chapel oriel of 1491.

The cathedral, dating from 1107, was enthusiastically re-Gothicized in the 1880s, although the remains of a fourteenth-century vaulted cloister are to be seen to its north.

The square in front of the cathedral extends on its east side past the fine façade of the former Palais Liechtenstein, an early work of the 1660s by Lucchese and only just Baroque. Near here rises the Jesuit church of 1712, slim and severe, while to the south-west is the Dominican chapel of St Alexis, dating from 1380, with a dark cloister vaulted in 1483. The fifteenth-century Franciscan church is also worth trying to enter, if only to see the rather demented nineteenth-century woodwork which fills every corner.

In the picturesque roads which wind from here to the Town Hall, between the murky clothes shops and occasional tobacconists stuffed with Havana cigars are a couple of cafés and wine bars.

Not far from the Town Hall rises the battlemented thirteenth-century south tower of the church of St Mořic. Its north tower is fifteenth-century and its nave, despite the dramatic skyline, plain and high. The east end, however, is more inspiring, with a Renaissance front from which flow a series of free-standing steps dating from 1564.

Perhaps the most curious structure in the city is that to be found in the upper market square, for of all the Baroque columns and monuments to be seen in Olomouc the early eighteenth-century Trinity Column here is the most eccentric and brilliant. It was erected 'to the honour of the divine trinity' ('*deo triune veroque*'). Eight rows of steps, containing eight steps each, lead up to eight doors, opening into a small eight-sided chapel. This is surrounded by a grating to which cling stone angels holding lanterns. Above, a sort of obelisk rises to the height of 114 feet adorned by groups of stone figures of bishops, saints and angels, perhaps best described as possessing 'oriental quaintness'. At least one nineteenth-century traveller to this square has questioned how anyone could think it suitable for the 'noble simplicity of Christianity'.

Such questions were not, however, the only concern of nineteenth-century writers. Far more seem to have been moved by another feature of Moravia, the extraordinary beauty of the Moravian girls. Hardly any travel book written during the last century failed to mention this, and while perhaps the traditional Moravian beauty is still to be found in her village, dressed in ethnic clothes inherited from her grandmother, it is surprising that the ravages of the twentieth century in Central Europe have allowed this attractive sight to flourish in the city as well. But if the German stock of this city has declined, the frontiers to the east have remained open and there is certainly Polish and Slovak blood flowing in their veins.

East of Olomouc, road and railway run to Žilina, a bleak industrial landscape but the gateway to the Tatras and Slovakia.

Although Bratislava, the capital of Slovakia (see p. 202), lies on the Central European plain, Slovakia itself is a mountainous country and the Slovaks are a hardy race of hillsmen, never quite at home in a city suit. They are, as Mrs Phillimore pointed out in her book *In the Carpathians*, one of the most lovable races of Europe – kind and hospitable, with a zest for enjoyment which makes the Czech seem an anaemic depressive in comparison. In the country, society is still clannish and rather patriarchal. Village weddings last for days and gallons of alcohol are consumed in a feast of singing and dancing.

Slovakia is also a land of colour, where houses and dress are brightly tinted so that villages bathed in the light of a Carpathian sunset seem to almost glow with purples, reds and golds. As might be expected in such a country, the sort of fabulous architectural treasures to be found in Bohemia and Moravia are not so common, and although today the Slovaks are in every way the Czechs' 'equals', their cultural development was retarded for centuries by their environment and also the insane Magyarization policies that their Hungarian masters pursued here during the days of the Habsburg empire. For if Vienna, which ruled Bohemia, allowed the Czechs free use of their language, the Magyars, who were the self-appointed master race of Eastern Europe, permitted no such privileges, and Slovaks were relentlessly forced to learn the impossible Hungarian tongue. Thus no Slovak middle class could prosper, and until the last fifty years one could speak of a peasant race with some justification.

From Žilina, a railway follows some picturesque scenery to Poprad, which is situated at the foot of the high Tatras. The hundred-odd miles is accomplished by an express train in about two and a half hours, and on a clear day is one of the most delightful train journeys in Europe, with narrow valleys, rapids and ruins marking every turn. As the train negotiates the low-lying Tatra mountains, tunnels lead to the dramatic defile of Strečno before reaching Ružomberok, a town situated prettily above several mineral springs. It is a quiet place, perfect for excursions to the Matras, the next tier of Carpathians, between the Fatras and the Tatras. Two miles south of here is the Liptovský kriz, an eighteenth-century church made of wood, capable of holding more than 600 worshippers, although not a single nail seems to have been used during its construction.

Beyond Ružomberok, the railway suddenly offers a fine view of the chief summits of the Carpathians. The line crosses the watershed here between the Baltic and the Black Sea before descending to Štrba, from where a dramatic view can be had of the highest of the Tatras, once named after the Austrian Emperor Franz Josef and then after the first president of the Czechoslovak republic, Masaryk, but now simply called the Great Tatra, or Vysoke Tatry.

Štrba is the highest station on the main line and is connected to a number of smaller resorts by funiculars and cog-wheel railways. The station here is invariably crowded with East German, Russian and Czech walkers. Rucksacks and maps are brandished, Thermos flasks waved, and anyone not wearing regulation walking boots is subjected to rigorous and bemused scrutiny.

One of the small railways with its bright red carriages runs from here to the lake of Štrbské Pleso, a desolate haunting place in the shadow of the Tatras whose peaks, rising sheer almost from the trees, have even in the heat of summer a menacing aspect. A typically styleless modern hotel with a reasonable restaurant on one side of the lake in no way detracts from the overwhelming sense of isolation. Thunderstorms occur here with terrifying force.

From Štrbské Pleso, which, unless its melancholy beauty seizes the traveller, can be enjoyed quite fruitfully for a couple of hours, another narrow-gauge line runs through the dark pine forests to STARÝ SMOKOVEC, an old Saxon settlement but since the end of the war inhabited exclusively by Slovaks. This is the Tatras dressed in the spa-cum-resort façades seen in Bohemia. Large wood-panelled hotels, all in that style of Neo-Baroque-Alpine which was *de rigueur* in 1912, rise out of the woods. Some have been given art-deco interiors in the thirties, others have been more recently restored. In contrast to Carlsbad and Marienbad there is a lively atmosphere here and there are no urban developments of the sixties to mar the views. This is the place to put up for a few nights. The Grand Hotel, which should be booked in advance, is, with its faded parquetry, still the most luxurious establishment in the Tatras.

From here professional climbers can be hired as guides for more difficult ascents, while the local office of the Carpathian tourist club will provide maps should expeditions be contemplated beyond those suggested by the finger-posts.

A narrow-gauge railway ascends in five minutes (on foot it takes forty-five minutes) to the picturesque Hrebienok, from where signs unpromisingly marked Sliezkýdom can be followed for a pleasant afternoon's walk underneath the very highest peaks. Behind us rise the mountains and their lakes, once thought to be the 'eyes' of some sea. In front, below, the valleys fall away towards Kežmarok and Hungary.

Another railway runs from Starý Smokovec to TATRANSKÁ LOMNICA, also essentially a nineteenth-century settlement made up of villas and hotels, although behind some green hedges near the station lie some curious *Kaisergelb*-coloured buildings; elegance neglected, with red facings and richly carved wooden pavilions. At first sight these give the impression of a Himalayan railway station, but an open door, at the time of writing easily penetrated, leads to dusty rooms with encaustic tiles lit from above – clearly once the steam baths of some grand duke on holiday in the Tatras.

Although lower than Smokovec, Tatranská Lomnica has great charm and offers a number of finger-posted walks which, if less dramatic than those described above, offer calm and the almost intoxicating smell of pine.

The days when months were free to spend aimlessly wandering among this, nature's greatest gift to Central Europe, are long past, and no one but the most committed walker will wish to dwell longer than a few days here. Some will question even that amount of time, especially if they are used to the superior comforts of Switzerland or even the Tyrol. Society and fashion have passed the Tatras by, but the mountains retain their majesty and those who seek unspoilt forests and peaks off the beaten track will find these grey castles of rock a welcome escape.

In the flat lands below, a most interesting excursion can be made for a few hours to KEŽMAROK, the Kesmark of the Saxons, a sleepy little town with sweet-shops selling pastilles as hard as granite. It is one of the oldest towns in Slovakia, having been granted a royal charter in 1380. Near the imposing red Protestant church designed by Hansen, the architect of the Vienna Parliament, is an eighteenth-century wooden church. It has quaint wooden spiral columns and is an elegant counterpoise to Hansen's rather overpowering design paid for by some wealthy merchants.

The town itself also possesses an older church with some crude but none the less attractive Baroque carvings strangely at ease inside the building's rude fifteenth-century masonry. Many of the houses which make up the main street and square are from the eighteenth century, and while not one boasts the decorative and architectural quality of such houses in Moravia, taken as a whole the ensemble is attractive. Restaurants are few, but the odd café along the main street leading to the station will offer a glass of delicious Slovak red wine, at its best as good as anything in Hungary.

On the periphery of the town's rather village-like centre is a kind of minor Ringstrasse with several buildings striking that familiar heavy note of Habsburg administration. Italianate for the post-office, a pattern-book Gothic for the school – even here the rhetoric of empire had to have its say.

Nearby, striking more feudal colours, is the former Schloss of Count Tököly, converted into a dull museum but with a medieval chapel and in its cellars a restaurant where bus-loads of Russian tourists are treated to some excellent Slovak cuisine, greatly to be preferred to the heavier dumpling-obsessed Bohemian fare.

From Kežmarok, the branch line runs north towards the Polish frontier, past brightly coloured villages, to the castle of STARÁ LUB-OVŇA, set on an eminence commanding the road to Poland. It is a sturdy fort built for battle, not show. Around it are villages nearly all of which are brightly coloured with one-storey houses, spotlessly clean and warm. During the winter, the temperature is regularly below minus 20°C, but in summer the midday sun and the cool evening make this a tranquil land of the most relaxing kind. Melancholy is banished and the Slovaks' sheer delight in living is contagious, as is shown by their weddings. The traveller who finds himself invited to one of these bacchanalian feasts should be prepared for some serious drinking if he is not to offend his host, and for some no less serious eating if he is not to offend the army of cooks which every village mobilizes to cope with such celebrations.

Invariably the festivities take place in the village hall, usually a Nissen hut erected between the wars. Its walls are plain and only a small chandelier, doubtless the last vestige of some nearby feudal lord's property, adorning the ceiling suggests that this is a room for celebration. Along one wall sit the assembled women of the village, rocking and singing some discordant hymn. Parallel to these are several long tables for the men, with bottles of beer, *borovicka* (a juniper schnapps) and plain bottles of mineral water in front of them. On a type of dais, a brightly clad band waits for the old women to stop singing before striking up a waltz or polka, at which point the young teenage waitresses, who have valiantly supplied the dozens of well-wishers with cooked chicken dishes at regular half-hour intervals, drop their plates and dance with each other with a fervour and abandon which no stony looks from their grandmothers can inhibit.

These festivities continue for the best part of the weekend, but their climax tends to come late on a Saturday afternoon, when to the shouts of all those present, the bride, in the most dazzling ethnic dress of her village, has her bonnet sewn up and attached to her hair. 'You will live long! Life will be hard! Your husband will be strong!' they all shout at the unperturbed girl, who when fully dressed stands up to be promptly hauled off by her groom, who picks her up with what might be described as an affectionate fireman's lift. They disappear, but after several hours return to join in the dancing.

From Stará Lubovňa, a narrow mountain road follows the Polish frontier through other attractive villages to the ancient town of BAR-DEJOV, which has preserved its medieval street plan entirely. The old town is essentially one large picturesque square flanked on each side by brightly coloured houses, mostly Gothic in origin with some rude classical motifs about them. At the centre of the square, which is built on a slight incline, is the church of St Aegidius, a fourteenth-century building with carved choir stalls of the fifteenth century, when the town was a wealthy establishment of merchants trading on the roads running to Galicia. The handsome Town Hall also dates from this time.

As the old farm-hands alight from buses and carts, with brightly coloured headscarves and baskets full of eggs and vegetables for the market, aprons and pleated dresses seem to be the rule. Ties are virtually nowhere to be seen, nor are soldiers or policemen, normally in evidence in any Eastern European hamlet. What high-rise buildings there are have been confined to a distant hill, and green fields rather than grey concrete are what most distract the eye.

From this idyllic scene, the road plunges south to KOŠICE, the Kaschau of the Habsburgs, still known to the Hungarians as Kassa, the second most important city in Slovakia, rivalled in its beauty only by the capital, Bratislava. An ancient royal free town on the right bank of the Hornád river, Košice still has the air of a former seat of imperial administration. Its main square is lined with administrative buildings which once preserved Hungary's hold on eastern Slovakia. Rising up in black Gothic defiance at all this eclectic bureaucratic clutter is the cathedral dedicated to St Elizabeth and rightly considered one of the finest Gothic churches in Central Europe.

It was built in 1382–1497 on the site of an earlier church and was thoroughly restored in 1877–96. It has double aisles, a polygonal choir and two towers of which the southern, unfinished, is particularly memorable. Situated on an island site, its coloured tiled roofing, pinnacles and statues over the portals are undeterred by the traffic and bustle around them. Inside, the effect is no less impressive. Most of the glass is nineteenth-century, but through the gloom the eye is seized and held by a splendid canopy of 1472, soaring some sixty-six feet high. Beyond this and some tiers of flickering candles is the late Gothic high altar, whose four wings are adorned with forty-eight German paintings on a gold ground attributed to a medieval craftsman called Wohlgemut. On the north and south-east walls there are traces of medieval frescoes, as there also seem to be in the chapel dedicated to St Stephen and St John.

Darkness and coolness are quickly dispelled by the bright sunlight outside and by the presence behind the rear façade of the cathedral of a building as imperious and dominating, though it is much later – the Košice theatre, an exuberant design which despite its traces of eastern Rococo seems to be another essay of Helmer and Fellner, though a rather more spirited one than usual. Slovak is not the most musical language to be heard in Europe, but the performances of Verdi and

Puccini which are given here rarely lack musicianship, and the strings of the orchestra have a richness of sound many western orchestras would relish.

The façades of the main street ring the changes of most nineteenth-century styles, but they hide the beauty of the place, for each narrow archway should be explored for the cool courts which lie hidden behind their rather unpretentious entrances.

Between them rises the Hotel Slovan, with its modernized rooms and mediocre kitchens. For all the abundance of vegetables to be seen in the markets here, it must be said that Košice has little for the gourmet. In the back streets there are some quaint bars selling wine, although many of them seem to be the haunts of gipsies, who seem to be in great preponderance here. Their manner is not usually hostile, but to attempt to photograph them is to invite considerable abuse and even a hail of grapes during the day and more dangerous projectiles at night.

The racial tensions which once existed here between Magyar and Slovak have largely been replaced by a growing resentment between Slovaks and gipsies, but the traveller will rarely have any hint of this, and memories of Košice will most likely be of a country town quietly setting about its business.

Košice is well connected with the rest of Slovakia by rail, and lines run to Poprad, Banská Bystrica, Hungary and Bratislava. If there is a spare afternoon, there is probably no better excursion from here than to LEVOČA, between Košice and Poprad. Levoča, at the foot of the Tatras, can also be reached from Poprad, but its chief glory is the spectacular sculptures attributed to Meister Pavel in its medieval church.

The town here was once exclusively inhabited by Germans, but since the war there have been only a handful of grey-haired Teutons left. Like Hermannstadt in Transylvania and Cheb in Bohemia, the entire settlement breathes the spirit of Teuton industry in its regular façades and rectangular squares.

The church of St James dates from the thirteenth century and with its lofty slim tower rises high above the rest of the town. Around it are the Renaissance and Gothic houses built by craftsmen who had learnt their trade hundreds of miles west of here. The Town Hall, with its arches, looks as if it could have been lifted straight from the square at Cheb. Inside, the original vaulting has survived (entrance by permission from the town office), and among the dust lie the innumerable papers of a modern bureaucracy.

From here, the road runs down to BANSKÁ BYSTRICA, where another church dedicated to St Elizabeth with a medieval altar awaits. The town is prettily situated on the Bystrica and has undergone considerable industrial development since the war. In the fifteenth and sixteenth centuries it was renowned for its dominance of the silver and copper markets of Europe, but the mines which had made the town so rich dried up in the eighteenth century and only after the First World War could a new way of economic life be constructed. Today, despite the picturesque town square, this is not a happy place, Russian air-force personnel mope around the bars and cafés and on Sundays visit the churches with a look of bewilderment rather than redemption on their faces. The mountains which surround the town on all sides have a menacing aspect echoed in the rather austere walls of the castle.

The Elizabeth church, a humble Gothic structure, contains a valuable fourteenth-century altar full of piety and grace, but in the nearby Town Hall, built in the early sixteenth century, the museum of Slovak resistance has become the town's chief shrine and the children seem to file past its grim images with far more solemnity than they would stand before any communion rail. In the Hotel Lux, by the main square, there are more earnest faces. Only in the market, on the aprons of the countryfolk selling cucumbers, does Slovak colour burst forth.

From Banská Bystrica runs a charming road which dispels these misgivings and leads through optimistic hills crowned by castles. Twelve miles south along the railway line or the road numbered 66 at the time of writing is the castle of ZVOLEN, erected by King Louis I of Anjou in 1380 and made to bear a Renaissance façade during the late 1500s. Its quaint half-timbering and absurd crenellations *alla Veneziana* conceal a maze of dark and at the time of writing rather damp rooms, most of which contain the remnants of what must have been a prosperous if not princely residence. What remains of the town which Matthias Corvinus occupied several times during his struggles with the Turk has long been eaten away by the building programmes of the post-war period, but amid this concrete clutter there are several medieval houses, although of rather undistinguished quality.

From here a branch line runs to Kremnica, after an hour of cuttings and embankments, seven tunnels and a horizon marked at almost every point by castle ruins. Despite the almost Asiatic slowness of the local train, this is a memorable overture to the equally unforgettable sights of the former imperial mint.

KREMNICA, for all its quaintness, has been involved with mining and minting precious ores for centuries. Its old walls surrounding the narrow streets still testify to the days when its wealth needed to be guarded by troops sent down the valley from Košice. The gold and silver mines are still productive, and special commemorative coins are regularly struck here, even if their value cannot match the medieval 'Kremnitz ducat'.

The patrician houses mostly date from the fifteenth and sixteenth century and are all unspoilt. The Town Hall in the main square has a museum which traces the history of the mint here since the Middle Ages, when the mines were worked by Germans summoned by Ferdinand I (1526–64).

The castle, with its impressive medieval walls, is considered the best-preserved medieval castle in Slovakia. Its defensive priorities included a well-protected chapel, which was nevertheless knocked about during the last war. Some of what remains has a rather Victorian look to it.

The people of Kremnica are, as most mining communities tend to be, of rather cheerful disposition and the few wine bars there are offer a friendly service to anyone armed with only a few words of German.

South of Kremnica, the line continues to BANSKÁ ŠTIAVNICA, another small mining community. It is not as picturesque as Kremnica, although the town is situated on terraces overlooking a deep ravine. The buildings again date from the fifteenth and sixteenth centuries but are rather more imposing than those we have seen so far.

The main church is that of St Nicholas, Romanesque in origin but with Baroque alterations dating from more prosperous times. The nearby Gothic St Catherine's is rarely open, but it is worth knocking up the priest next door to be allowed into its dark traceried interior.

The castle above is no longer a prison and can be visited. It is also worth spending a few minutes in the Dionýz-Štúr town museum, a geology/history lesson of the area which recalls the fact that gunpowder was first used in Europe for mining purposes here in the year 1657.

Despite the enormous wealth these mines yielded in the past, the only real sign of its reinvestment in this part of the world comes a few miles further along the road to Nitra at a village called Zláte Moravce. Here, less than a mile to the north, situated in a small overgrown park well laid out with exotic trees, is a classical Schloss whose even proportions and rustication strike a Bohemian note of wealth. Inside, the dusty rooms are filled with furniture from different periods, including at least two superb suites of Biedermeier, but in the autumn they can be noisy, for outside are the largest deer shoots in the country and gunfire adds a staccato accompaniment to any visit.

The road to Nitra and Trnava, both cities with important pasts, descends towards the beginning of the Central European plain.

At NITRA the hills are already clad in vines, but the only buildings of interest here are a Baroque cathedral and a small Romanesque church in the grim suburb of Párovce. As this is never open and the hotels in Nitra are not of the best, it will be more convenient to press on to TRNAVA, once named the Slovak Rome and, until the establishment of the Hungarian See at Eztergom, the most important religious centre in the country.

There is little of this past glory left and many of the churches are filled with Orthodox clutter and locked or boarded up. The cathedral, a fourteenth-century building, was given a Baroque interior and two ludicrous towers in the eighteenth century. Nearby, however, is an altogether more impressive church built by the Jesuits in 1628 to the designs of the Italian Pietro Spazzo. Austere yet hot with the fire of the Counter-Reformation, it is a generation earlier than similar buildings lying a few miles south-west, which because of the Turkish incursions could only be built fifty years later.

As well as the many Renaissance houses of note here, there are a charming Biedermeier theatre and a sixteenth-century Archbishop's Palace to be found within five minutes' walk of the Jesuit church. This can all be taken in at a glance and may have to be if the remaining few miles down onto the plain are to be covered in time to reach the Danube and the capital of Slovakia, BRATISLAVA, before sunset. The pointed towers of its castle are visible for miles around, reminding one that the kings of Hungary were once crowned here and that on more than one occasion it was here rather than Budapest or Vienna that the Habsburgs rallied their forces.

Situated on the last spurs of the Carpathians, the town has suffered considerably from the insensitive planning of post-war years, but its streets and squares have retained much charm and interest. The castle is a brief ascent from the Danube promenade called the Jesininovo Nabř. Its four corner towers date from between the fifteenth and seventeenth centuries and it is perhaps poignant to recall that in the rooms of the south-east tower, the Hungarian crown jewels admired in Budapest (see p. 75) were stored for decades. A tour of the interior is possible most days of the week. Several of the rooms have been excellently restored to give a convincing impression of what life in the eighteenth century must have been like for the town's garrison commander. Somewhere among the uniforms, pictures and Empire furniture, a small room may be pointed out as the birthplace of St Elizabeth of Thüringen. Through the pointed windows of the towers can be seen on a clear day Vienna to the west and in the sharp light of winter the great Benedictine abbey of Pannonhalma in Hungary to the east (see p. 98).

From the castle, a path winds down to the Staromestská (good wines at the Rybne nám.) and the cathedral church of St Martin. Begun in 1204 and completed in 1445, it was restored both in the nineteenth century and in the years immediately after the last war. The coronation church of the Habsburgs in Hungary until 1848, it has a tower which is still surmounted by a pyramid bearing a gilded crown. Inside, the church, for all its wealth, lacks the mystery of Levoča or Košice. Perhaps it was built too near Vienna and the more airy interior of the cathedral there. Only the chapel of St Anna in the north aisle captures the spirit of the fourteenth century.

Another chapel dedicated to St Eleemosinarius was built and decorated by Raphael Donner, who was also responsible for the rather heavy equestrian statue of St Martin of 1734, dressed most curiously in Magyar costume, outside the choir.

The Nalepkova leads east from here past various shops and nineteenth-century houses to the theatre, early Helmer and Fellner with a seductively curved frontispiece. In front of it is a bust of the composer Hummel, who was born here in 1778.

Further south the land slopes down towards the broad expanse of the Danube, where there are several other institutional buildings dating from Kaiserlich and Königlich days, including the university and the

Slovak National Gallery, which has some pleasant nineteenth-century paintings.

Nearby, the Mostova Gorkeho, a narrow street which was once the 'coronation hill' where the Habsburgs ascended after being crowned in the cathedral, runs to the river. Of all the monarchs who raised the sword of St Stephen to the four quarters of heaven, none did so amid wilder enthusiasm than Maria Theresa, who in 1741 ascended here with her child to call upon the Hungarians to save her empire, attacked by Prussia eager for Silesian territory. History recounts few more stirring scenes than this appeal to Magyar chivalry, which in turn was met with the famous cry: *'Vitam et sanguinem pro rege nostro Maria Theresa!'*, as a hundred noblemen drew their sabres to pledge their allegiance to the woman who was their king.

As the Bulgarian tugs steam slowly up towards Austria and some Czech conscripts stare bemusedly at a machine recording the Danube's level, the memory of such heroism is perhaps irrelevant, but something of old Pressburg, as Maria Theresa and the Austrians called the city, remains further north of the theatre in the narrow Radničná. Here, next to each other in uneasy intimacy, are the former Town Hall and the Archbishop's Palace. The first is a Gothic building dressed in Renaissance clothes with a Baroque tower. Inside, good stucco and wooden ceilings make up a small town museum amid the sleepy buzz of the town's administrative offices.

Nearby is the altogether more imposing Archbishop's Palace, erected in the 1770s. In its dazzling hall of mirrors, the Peace of Pressburg was signed between Napoleon and the Austrian emperor Francis I after the battle of Austerlitz in 1805.

From here the road continues past several picturesque gables to the Gothic Franciscan church dating from the thirteenth century, with a chapel dedicated to St John which recalls the great Gothic interiors of Prague in its beauty and may have been the work of Peter Parler.

The Michalská, a pedestrian promenade beyond, culminates in the last remains of the medieval fortifications, the Michael Gate. The street is full of gift shops, second-hand bookshops and cafés all inserted into a series of façades which have changed little over the last hundred years. Unfortunately the same cannot be said for the narrow roads above it, where a flyover has been constructed at the second-floor level of some narrow Rococo houses, one of which, a pink clock museum, cannot be taken seriously after such abuse.

From the Michael gate the Bastova leads to the left, where stands another Gothic church, dedicated to St Clarissa, usually locked. The narrow streets which wind back from here to the Nalepkova are sufficient distraction for more than one day, and the Carlton Hotel on the other side of that square, known as Hviezdoslavovo náměstie 7, is as good a place to rest as any before the train, bus or boat return to the west.

With its Germans (though these are now only a few), Hungarians and Slovaks, Bratislava continues to show that, even perched on the sharp edge of the iron curtain, something of the old Habsburg mixture of blood has survived to live peacefully on into the next century.

13

SLOVENIA, ZAGREB, TRIESTE AND THE AUSTRIAN RIVIERA

Graz is the southernmost German-speaking city in Europe. Beyond it lie the hills of Slovenia, the limestone plateau, mercilessly swept by the savage *bora* wind, and Trieste, for centuries Austria's great port on the Adriatic. All have been linked by the southern railway (Südbahn) since the 1850s, but today no direct train exists between the Austrian capital and Trieste; and from Graz it is almost essential to break the journey in Ljubljana, the capital of Slovenia, and savour the last peaks of the Alps before descending to the sea.

From Graz, the line runs to the Jugoslav frontier in about half an hour before crossing the Drave at Maribor (Marburg), the former capital of lower Styria, a dreamy town but undistinguished and culturally always overshadowed by Graz to the north and Ljubljana to the south.

Pragersko, further down the line, is still the junction for Budapest, though trains are infrequent. The scenery becomes now rather hilly and the line passes through the former Roman spa of Celje. The town has a museum full of interesting archaeological fragments dating from the time of the Emperor Claudius, the founder of Colonia Claudia Celeia.

From here the railway passes Zidanimost ('Stone Bridge'), the junction for the line to ZAGREB, the attractive still partly gas-lit capital of Croatia whose architecture and parks ring the changes of nineteenth-century Austria-Hungary craftsmanship. In many ways, Zagreb is the last 'Kaiserlich and Königlich' city in Jugoslavia. The Croatians who live here still speak a dialect riddled with German phrases. One of the most loyal of the Habsburgs' peoples, for centuries the Croats formed some of the best troops in Europe, fighting first against the Turks and then in 1848 against the Hungarians. But, as can be seen as soon as one arrives, their culture ran deeper than the martial arts.

From the imposing classical railway station, displaying an immaculately kept blue steam engine as a memorial to the late Marshal Tito, gardens and museums extend towards the inner town. The first building of note on the left is the Edwardian Hotel Excelsior, whose rooms and service have been rightly considered the best in Jugoslavia. In the middle of the gardens, the first building is the yellow *fin-de-siècle* Secession, or artists' house, which houses temporary exhibitions. Behind this is the brick Strossmayer Art Gallery, named after a bishop of Zagreb who left a valuable collection of Old Masters to the city.

Beyond, past a beautiful old bandstand, the road leads to the main square of the city, the Trg Republike, the former Jellačić square, once adorned by Fernkorn's statue of the great Croatian Ban. In 1848 Jellačić led the Croats to save the Habsburgs from the revolutionary Hungarians. To the right of the square is the extraordinary Gradska Kavarna, a coffee-house where long distinguished faces still smoke pipes and discuss politics. The interior of the café is from the fifties, and these faces almost seem to be of the same decade.

From here the Bakačeva leads up to the cathedral, though anyone wanting to lunch should not overlook the Vlaška ulica to the right, where a modest sign marked 'Ćevapi' leads to the best grilled meat balls (*ćevapčići*) in northern Jugoslavia.

The cathedral is a fine late Gothic edifice dating from the fifteenth century but restored extensively in the 1890s. From the west end of the cathedral, a path runs down to the picturesque market before ascending through a gas-lit arch known as the Kamenita Vrata, or Stone Gate, where there is a shrine for prayers, to the Rococo church of St Margaret. From here there are gas-lit streets to the nearby Strossmayer promenade. This runs back down to the Republic Square. Alternatively, lanes run uphill towards the thirteenth-century St Mark's church, with a brightly coloured roof like that of St Stephen's in Vienna. Here there are several works of the great Croatian sculptor Meštrović to be admired, while in the nearby Mesnička there is the Meštrović museum filled with statues of his later period between the wars. Also near here is the Grada, or Town museum, with some Biedermeier paintings portraying Croatian society.

In the Opatička behind St Mark's, there is the fashionable Old Watch restaurant, a remarkable – given that this is a communist country – nostalgia-orientated establishment with excellent food and a clientele which must include some of the most elegant young people in Central Europe. Elegance and music, often performed with considerable skill, can also be found in the opera house, designed by Helmer and Fellner but with an interior which even by their opulent standards takes some beating. There can be no more enjoyable way of rounding off this brief excursion into Croatia.

Forty miles west of Zidanimost along the ravine of the Save, is LJUBLJANA, which is announced by some rather disappointing blocks of flats, rising underneath the last peaks of the Julian Alps. The station, all red and yellow plastic, is a squalid place full of drunken Bosnians queuing for hot-dogs, but the main avenue running straight from the station is impressive if only because most of the buildings have a well-groomed look of civic pride about them.

For years Ljubljana was just a small market town – it developed late as a result of the southern railway route to Trieste. It never could boast either the historical or cultural traditions of Croatian Zagreb. The Slovenes can be a dour race, tall, Alpine Slavs whose small numbers – there are barely one and a half million who understand this language – have given them a reserve which at first contact seems like surliness. Perhaps because of this insecurity, several architects who were Slovenes sought to express their racial identity through architecture during the early years of this century. The main road which leads from the station is full of these efforts. An art-nouveau square on the left contains façades adorned with flowing lines and the language of Jugendstil, which recalls that of another Slav race attempting to establish its identity at the same time, the Bohemians. These buildings were designed by Max Fabiani, an architect we have come across in Vienna's Kohlmarkt (see p. 12).

Further down, on the left, a brightly coloured red and yellow bank dressed in the jazzy patterns of some ethnic design attempts to achieve the same effect, although the nationalist note it strikes is more strident. The more restrained art-nouveau Union hotel opposite offers comfortable rooms, and, even if the interiors have been brutally restored in recent years, a coffee-house where it is possible to sit in peace for a few moments.

At the end of this long road from the station rises a red Baroque church, Franciscan and Roman with a faded *trompe-l'œil* interior and a catulpa tree in front of its west-end steps. It is the first evidence of a southern Latin influence and comes as a pleasant surprise after so much northern art-nouveau.

In front of this church are three curious bridges, two for pedestrians and one for motorized traffic. They are the work of Plečnik, the Slovene architect whose talents have already been seen at work on the Hradčany in Prague (see p. 159) and in Vienna. Here, in his native town, he set about rebuilding the old classical bridge, giving it a Mediterranean idiom in the form of sculptured hour-glass motifs. Where the local white limestone proved too expensive, he applied carving techniques to artificial stone and even concrete. Almost at every corner in this part of Ljubljana one of his eccentric lanterns with their archaic motifs, derived partly from Istria and partly from the Etruscans, peers out between the Biedermeier and Ringstrasse buildings.

Across the small river, a tributary of the Save, is the long colonnade Plečnik built for the market. The market itself as well as the architecture is of considerable interest, for the goods on sale rival in their exotic variety of herbs, mushrooms and fruit those seen in Budapest. The relentless series of columns are another indication of how passionate the interest in classical architecture was between the wars in Central Europe.

Nestling behind this, snug in its Salzburg profiles, is the domed and very Austrian Baroque cathedral, with some handsome Baroque stalls and stucco work. From here a promenade leads alongside the river to a restaurant marked by the sign of a black cat, called 'Maček'. It overlooks the river and is a suitable halt before following the winding streets behind up to the castle. The houses here have courtyards and ornate Baroque façades which all seem to have been inspired by the grander but almost identical houses of Graz. But whereas there the old fortifications of the castle hill have been converted into a series of gardens, here the narrow paths peter out into untamed woods.

The castle has been partly restored, although work seems to progress at such a slow pace that another thirty years may be needed before the entire complex is opened to visitors. At present the modern-looking white tower offers extensive views across the mountains up to Austria and south across the Ljubljana plain to the last foothills of the Alps and the beginning of the limestone plateau. The blue high-tech spiral staircase inside the tower is typical of the confidence the Slovenes feel in their present schools of architecture, and it must be said that there is considerable talent to be tapped by the planners of this province, who perhaps for the first time in their history have had nearly five decades of almost stable economic and social growth. The high-rise buildings which mark the suburbs have still to reach the size and density of those depressing developments in Czechoslovakia, and despite the rise in population the foreground below still gives the impression of a small town rather than an expanding city.

The gently descending path leads back to a small square which contains a quaint old patisserie, unchanged since the war. Its plain white interior belies the quality of the cakes, which are made by an old baker who studied his craft in Vienna long before the last war.

From here the river is crossed by a main road leading to Zagreb. Following the river for a few minutes along the right bank, past the low houses which were once the quarters of the German knights (among them is a Romanian wine merchant's house offering the best red wine in Central Europe), one comes eventually to a bridge with pyramids and trees, another Plečnik gesture, and the plain grey church of St Francis. Less than five years ago this rambling suburb with its untarmacked roads still resembled something from a poem of Prešerin, the impetuous but gifted nineteenth-century Slovene poet. Today the dusty lanes lead to high-rise flats for Serbian workers. They are good of their kind, but they have destroyed forever what was left of Prešerin's world.

Nearby, in a house once belonging to Plečnik, is the architectural museum. It is a moving reminder of this extraordinary but still comparatively unknown craftsman, who believed passionately in the sanctity of his craft. He died in the fifties, still cursing Corbusier. Amid his drawings and models, the hat and stick in his studio are touching reminders of a gentle soul.

The road back into the town follows a traditional route, an old Roman one, now named 'Titova'. Its half-hearted Ringstrasse soon gives way to building complexes of the seventies: supermarkets, cultural palaces, monuments to materialism rather than culture but well designed and set in spacious gardens which take the edge off much of their angularity.

On the right of the Titova, down towards the river, a small oasis of early nineteenth-century Ljubljana remains, the Congres Trg (Congress

Square), whose Biedermeier palaces saw Metternich plan the restoration of reaction in the years following the Napoleonic wars.

A small yellow classical concert hall at the end of this square is the home of the Slovene Philharmonic and saw the first performance of a Beethoven symphony as well as the conducting of Gustav Mahler before fame and fortune took him to the directorship of the Vienna Opera.

To the right of this, the bureaucracy of imperial Austria asserts itself with an ugly town hall, now part of the university. But not far away, nearer the river, the Academia Trg revives an older order in the form of the Palais Herberstein, whose dark and gloomily furnished rooms will be opened by the caretaker for a few pennies. The evening sunlight cuts through the large windows, setting the tapestries and furniture ablaze with gold. As usual, visitors are scarce.

From here it is a five-minute walk across the Titova to the Tivoli Park, the setting for that indispensable series of nineteenth-century Austrian buildings: Opera, museum and art gallery, all still dressed in varying shades of peeling 'Kaiser' yellow.

The Opera is, surprisingly, not the work of Helmer and Fellner but of two Czech architects who preferred Neo-Rococo to Baroque revival and were tunefully called Hrašby and Hruby. The interior is the usual display of red and gold, though considerably less lavish than the nearby theatres in Rijeka or Zagreb. As always in Central Europe, standards of performance vary, but the Slovenes have a natural talent for singing and when properly drilled the chorus can match that of any comparable house in the country.

The art gallery nearby is well worth a visit. None of the painters' names will be familiar, but there is evidence in these canvases of both inspiration and technique. The usual 'empire' portraits of the local gentry are followed by several rooms of late nineteenth-century portraits which would be welcome in the collections of any London gallery.

The third member of this cultural triumvirate is the Ethnographical Museum. As Slovenia has become the most developed part of Jugoslavia, the costumes on display here are never to be seen outside these rooms or at some folkloristic gala performance. Aprons are no longer worn in the hills, as they are in the villages of Slovakia or Transylvania, and the car has completely replaced the horse and cart.

It is one of the delights of Ljubljana that, within a few minutes' walk of here, along Latterman's Allee, the town can be quickly forgotten among the chestnut-lined paths of the woods. A series of Plečnik lanterns leads the way past an old villa, once the property of Marshal Radetsky, up to a hill crowned by a single-towered church. Near this an old cottage houses a museum dedicated to Ivan Cankar, a nineteenth-century Slovene writer inspired by its views over the hills. Below this, the path runs down to a small Bosnian restaurant whose charcoal grill can be smelt for miles and where the local wine and Balkan cuisine leave an impression of a culture which is no longer wholly Central European.

Between Ljubljana and Trieste, the railway runs across embankments over the Ljubljana plain, whose muddiness made the construction of this part of the line almost as difficult as that involved in bridging the Semmering Pass. On a clear day the line offers a spectacular retrospective view of the city and the Julian Alps beyond.

The Piranesian remains of an impressive viaduct blown up during the war can be seen on the right as the train ascends past Kamnik. Postoyna is renowned for its caves, of which the celebrated Adelsberg grotto, recorded in the Middle Ages but rediscovered only in 1818, is the most spectacular. In some, balls took place regularly each Whit Monday until the First World War. The spectacular illuminations of these occasions cannot be imagined, although the guide will point out a number of contemporary prints which attempt to recapture these festivities.

At Postoyna, a new bleak landscape appears as the railway penetrates the limestone plateau, or 'karst'.

This treeless landscape was perhaps best described by Schinkel, the nineteenth-century German architect, when he wrote of it on his first journey to Italy as a place which seemed to have suffered 'the most horrible revolutions of this earth'.

Further east, the single-track line to Pola and Istria takes the train through uninhabitable country still mercilessly swept by the fierce north-east *bora* wind. Here, even at the edge of its inhospitable mass, there is still something arid and forbidding about the gashes of white rock which can now be seen.

The surface is intersected by gorges and partly covered with underwood and loose stones. Numerous funnel-shaped cavities known as 'Dolines', slight depressions in the landscape, can be observed flashing past as the train gathers speed. On a clear day, the view to the east across this uneven terrain can stretch right across the heart of Istria, while to the west on the day after the end of a *bora*, a bright blue will be seen stretching from the distance into infinity as sky and, as later becomes apparent, sea meet on the azure horizon.

Depending on the time of year, the frontier formalities can be time-consuming here. For some years it has been the practice of Jugoslavs from the more southern republics to travel up to Trieste, where they exchange their bangles and pantaloons for as many pairs of jeans and packets of bubble-gum as possible. The Jugoslav authorities, alarmed at their rather shaky economy, naturally take a dim view of Jugoslav currency leaving the country and search their fellow countryfolk with considerable vigour; this, if involving no hardship to other travellers, causes some delay. However, delays can be avoided by those prepared to alight at Sežana, the Jugoslav frontier post, and take a bus from there to Villa Opicina (the Italian frontier post). Others may prefer just to sit back with a good book or watch the extraordinary scenes of mild panic which erupt about them as another illegally exported Jugoslav banknote is discovered buried in the folds of some Macedonian dress.

From Villa Opicina there follows the most picturesque fifteen minutes of railway travel in Central Europe, as the train cuts through the limestone rock and begins to descend in a sweeping curve along the coast. To the west the gaunt silhouette of the castle of Duino rises in front of the oil refinery and shipyards of Monfalcone. Fortunately for Rainer Maria Rilke, the Austrian poet who enjoyed Princess Thurn und Taxis' hospitality here before the First World War, in the months during which he wrote his *Duino Elegies* these modern eyesores had barely been contemplated.

Every year in October, scholars from all over Europe descend on Duino to hear a series of lectures on the poet, followed by a *ricevimento* for their benefit. As well as professors and writers, there is a sprinkling of that old aristocracy of Central Europe who, looking over the balcony at the blue Adriatic guarded by jagged rocks, seem more than capable of reciting from memory the verses of the first elegy: *'Wer wenn ich schrie, hörte mich denn aus den Engel Ordnungen'*. They may have nodded off during the more complex perorations of some learned professor from Barcelona, but they still know their stuff.

As the train continues to descend, a sudden gap in the rocks reveals the sea deep below, giving the impression that there is nothing but a sheer drop between the track and the ocean. In fact, there is an almost equally spectacular road beneath, constructed by the 'Duce', cutting through the rock with almost as fine views. The train rattles down past the wooden pavilion of the former Habsburg station at Miramar, as the castle floats past below.

The central station at TRIESTE does justice to this journey – elegant Grecian columns, high arches and booking hall all preserve the spirit of nineteenth-century Habsburg pride. From here a road leads to the right of the wooded square towards the sea and the *riva*. The ten-minute walk to the city centre shows immediately how prosperous the port was before the last war. Palace after palace rise to the left, proclaiming banks or insurance companies whose headquarters were once here. Across the bay, towards a Mussolini-style lighthouse, stretch the half-abandoned warehouses of the port.

With Trieste's secession to Italy after the First World War, the port which had been the unique commercial lifeline of an empire of twenty nations became just one of many Italian ports, and the slow decline began which has made Trieste, sitting on a bay which is all but empty of ships, something of a ghost city. At night the *riva*, with the curtain shutters of its *palazzi* blowing in the wind, is deserted and only the buildings along it testify to the cosmopolitan life which once flowed through its streets.

A small canal to the left terminates rather dramatically in the church of Sant'Antonio, a Neo-Classical building brilliantly situated by its architect Peter von Nobile, who designed the Burgtor in Vienna (see p. 20).

Along one side of the canal, facing the sea, is a rather jazzy twenties building which once housed the British consulate. Along the other side runs the long Palazzo Carciotti, the headquarters of the captain of the port, pulling an effete classical face with dome and portico towards the sea. Next to it is the even more chaste Greek Orthodox church, whose silver iconed interior reveals clearly how much wealth the Greek community of the city amassed in the nineteenth century. For those with brains and energy who came to the 'free port', fabulous fortunes were to be made, and the Greeks were not alone in acquiring them.

The large bank next to the church was once the Hôtel et de la Ville, where Mahler stayed when he conducted at the opera house. Its conversion, however sympathetic, into a commercial institution sounded Trieste's death-knell as a city on the circuit of distinguished European travellers, and what luxury hotels remain cannot begin to recapture its style.

Further along the *riva* is the Café Tommaseo, one of the most civilized cafés in Europe, where it is still possible to hear a waiter disputing points of Virgil with some eighty-year-old *barone* assisted by a leading critic of the *Corriere della Sera*. The asymmetry of the interior means that the mirrors between the potted plants reflect the light in an almost theatrical way, and there are times when the rooms with their crumbling ceiling and caryatids seem to constitute a stage rather than a mere café. Fortunately, because a number of heroic irredentists plotted against the Austrians here, there seems to be no danger that this magnificent institution will be harmed.

A biscuit's throw away from Tommaseo's rises the orange and red Neo-Classical Teatro Verdi, a splendid copy of La Scala in Milan and one of the few theatres in Italy to have retained its interior intact, never having suffered from fire. Performances here at their best rival those of any opera house in Italy, with the added advantage that the theatre is far more intimate and colourful than most. The audience are still shown to their seats by bicorned footmen in eighteenth-century dress and on gala nights, when Piero Capucilli or some other native of Trieste is singing, the stage is strewn with roses thrown with abandon from the countless *logge*. In few parts of Central Europe do they take Verdi as seriously.

Behind the Opera is the nineteenth-century arcade – alas damaged by fire in the twenties – known as the 'Tergesteo', containing a comfortable café once decorated with excellent nineteenth-century paintings but now rather empty after a prim restoration. From here it is only a few steps to the Piazza Unità, bounded on one side by the sea and on the other three by imposing nineteenth-century palaces of the *amministrazione*. The Lloyd palace, with its rather nervous pilasters, is a work of the Austrian Ringstrasse architect Ferstel, who seems in this design to have mellowed his usual heaviness to exploit the more southern light.

In the building next to it, past the Hotel Duchi d'Aosta, is the former hotel in which Winckelmann was murdered. Austrian police records note that the great eighteenth-century scholar and founder of art history was stabbed to death by a man of low repute – a squalid end to someone dedicated to the canons of classical beauty.

An arch through the rather heavy Town Hall leads right to a maze of ruined Venetian streets, revealing that, for all its stuffy Austrian clothes, the heart of the town is undeniably Italian. Even during the empire, this was one of the least prosperous parts of the city, a picturesque setting for the hero of some Italo Svevo novel but not for any of the fashionable bourgeois merchants. The shuttered windows are strewn with laundry and an army of cats spring from evil-smelling drains. Most of the houses are still lived in, although on the oldest of them faded advertisements for Dubonnet or '*chambres libres*' evoke a previous existence of more energy. This picturesque squalor would have been familiar to James Joyce, who lived in Trieste for many years before the First World War.

As the road ascends, a Roman arch named rather bizarrely after Richard the Lionheart, who legend says was shipwrecked here after the Crusades, appears propping up a restaurant which is open past midnight. Where once countless sailors caroused, there are now only a few pensioners enjoying their *prosciutto* and Merlot before winding their way home.

From here the road continues to rise until a garden offers a retrospective view of the harbour and the hills towards Venice. At the bottom of the gardens, laid out in true municipal style in the sixties, is the forlorn ruin of the English church, which for the last five years has been woefully neglected by the Triestine authorities, so that now, with half its roof covered in creeper and part of its interior exposed to the elements, it has become a grotesque ruin – a sight predictable in Marienbad but curiously disturbing in a city normally so diligent in the preservation of its architectural heritage.

Above the garden, the road continues to rise until it reaches a lapidarium on the right. Here, among the stones and acanthus capitals, the debris of classical orders, is Winckelmann's tomb, chaste white marble encased by his beloved Corinthian order. A relief inside depicts the scholar pursued by some heavenly graces, whose swirling robes and eager smiles seem to have quite understandably panicked this well-known misogynist into flight.

Through the railings at the end of this picturesque garden can be seen the Romanesque basilica of San Giusto, the patron saint of the city. Though not unattractive from the outside, the interior of this church is disappointing. Insensitive restoration has given the chancel a marble coat suitable for a bathroom rather than a basilica.

In front of the church a pair of Roman columns rise up before the walls of the castle, a tiresome if well-preserved citadel, containing an expensive restaurant with one of the most extensive wine lists in Italy.

From here, Mussolini-style steps descend via a fountain to the square called Piazza Carlo Goldoni, from which runs the via Imbriani. The rather unprepossessing house at No. 5 contains an untouched apartment which once belonged to the merchant Mario Morpurgo di Nilma (ring bell marked 'Museo 2 piano'). Never advertised, it is one of the city's most charming secrets, for the rooms, with their books and Third Empire furniture, have remained unrestored for nearly a century, dark and heavy curtains protecting these period pieces from the light of the twentieth century. A hapless curator will explain that the plastic coverings of the seats are essential for the preservation of the fabrics and that money is desperately needed to 'restore' the museum. Long may it last as it is, a dusty time machine free from the harshness of modern lighting and any material later than 1887.

At the end of the via Imbriani is the piazza Verdi, with a statue of the composer made from the iron of captured Austrian artillery. The original statue which the Austrians permitted to be erected on the composer's death was of white marble, but unruly elements in the Habsburg's pay insisted on demolishing it when Italy joined the central powers' enemies in 1916.

Behind it is the Bar Centrale, the best cocktail bar in the city and one which repays several visits, for there are few places in Italy where so much care is taken over their preparation. From here the large boulevard via Battisti leads up to the *stile Liberty* Café San Marco, where marble tables and art-nouveau cutlery are set among billiard tables and a frieze of masked faces. This café is still regularly frequented by intellectuals and writers, though most, it must be sadly admitted, are in their seventies.

Behind the café, a mass of abstract white stone decorated with a huge wheel window marks the largest synagogue in Central Europe. Built in the twenties by the architect Berlam (also responsible for the former British consulate), this is a spectacular building by any standards. The interior is surprisingly light and, though built for a Jewish community ten times the size of the present one, none the less continues to be well maintained.

From here any number of straight roads lead back to the piazza Unità, where rooms will with luck have been booked in the Hotel Al Teatro, an old establishment, recently restored, offering views out over the square, although light sleepers may be disconcerted by the amount of time it takes for the nearby Town Hall clock to strike the hour.

Trieste is ideal for a stay of some days for, in addition to the town, the castle of Miramar with its gardens two miles up the coast is inviting. A tram which converts itself after two minutes into a funicular leaves from the piazza Oberdan up to the *carso* or limestone plateau. Alighting at the obelisk, it is best to follow the strada Napoleonica, which runs along the cliff offering superb views of the city, the Istrian peninsula and the beginning, to the west, of the lagoons.

At the end of the strada, a road leads to the village of Contovello, on whose outskirts a bar will supply delicious red wine, beer and a local version of Parma ham. Contovello itself is a peaceful place, inhabited mainly by Slovenes who nevertheless speak perfect Italian.

From here, the road winds down back to Trieste, but a path cutting through the curves is discernible to the right and this with its steps through the green branches of the hill's trees should be followed. The sun bathes the green in a filtered gold light, and, while care should be exercised in crossing the railway line, there is no more pleasant way of descending to the sea. The path eventually emerges at the village of Barcola, now scarcely more than a suburb of Trieste. From here a seaside promenade leads in about half an hour to the white castle of Miramar.

This small carefully sited if not particularly brilliantly designed castle owes its existence entirely to the Archduke Maximilian (d. 1867), Franz Josef's younger brother. A sensitive and romantic Habsburg, Maximilian was sailing in the bay of Trieste one day when a sudden *bora* threatened to capsize his boat. He ran aground on a small promontory west of the city and in thanksgiving for what he felt was a miraculous escape proposed to build a castle on the site. At the time the work began, the 'Archdupe', as he became known, was hopelessly embroiled in the politics of the scheming Emperor Napoleon I I I of France, who appealed to him to take the throne of Mexico. This project, doomed from the beginning, became a farce when the French troops sent to steady Maximilian's uneasy throne were withdrawn. Farce then became tragedy when the revolutionaries proceeded to shoot Maximilian out of hand as a traitor to the Mexican people. Even to the last day of his life, Maximilian sought solace in the memory of Miramar, scribbling instructions to the gardeners about the arrangement of trees in the castle's park.

The park is still a maze of paths, pergolas and grottoes, best seen in the last hour of daylight. The castle is for the most part unchanged since Maximilian's day. The exterior balcony with its lanterns looks out westwards across a view which is identical to that Maximilian enjoyed. Inside, the filtered light is made all the more romantic by faintly coloured Venetian glass in the windows.

Maximilian was a great admirer of the navy and helped for years to build up the Austrian fleet into a credible force in the Mediterranean. Not surprisingly, then, several of the rooms in the castle were designed to emulate the luxury of his flagship, and both the study and the bedroom have galleon-like panelling. A guide will point out the many fascinating objects here, including the marble table, a gift from Pope Pius IX, on which Maximilian signed his formal acceptance of the Mexican throne.

Upstairs this Habsburg's privileged youth is recalled in a lavish portrait of him, clad in imperial white and surrounded by the fruits and harems of some Near Eastern pasha he had paid a state visit to. Another painting recalls the day an English frigate transferred the Habsburg empress Elizabeth from Corfu to Miramar. The painter has perceptively captured the stalwart faces of the Royal Navy escort as well as those of the more foppish Austrian officers present.

But these paintings aside, the simple open windows on this floor overlooking the Adriatic towards the lagoons are perhaps the most poignant reminder of all Maximilian strove to create. The calm is irresistible and all-absorbing, however much noise the Italian schoolchildren make in the next-door room.

From the rear of the castle, paths lead out over the roads up towards the melancholy buildings of the old Habsburg station. Timbered pavilions strewn with wistaria running along wooden columns are all that is left of this halt, still used until the 1950s judging by the old Italian timetables whose pages have been carelessly thrown about the former imperial waiting room.

Despite the wistful decay, this is not a sad place, even though Miramar enjoys a sinister reputation – it is said that all who sleep within her walls will die violently far from home. As well as Maximilian, three later occupants of the castle, an Italian duke and two American generals after the last war, have suffered this fate, and during the post-war Allied occupation of the city at least one general insisted on pitching his tent in the grounds.

But Miramar lives on happily, its walls resounding to nothing louder than the occasional Son et Lumière, and throughout Trieste, thanks to the irrepressible optimism of the Italians, there is none of the depressing decline which lays so heavy a hand over the towns of Bohemia or Transylvania.

At sunset, another of the pleasantest promenades in Europe can be made along the molo Audace opposite the Opera, a long slab of stone graced by high lanterns leading right out into the bay. The steps which fall into the sea at the end meet an inky undulating mass of water on which it seems almost possible to walk. An impressionable undergraduate once contemplated suicide here until the smell of fish being fried for the officers of an Italian frigate moored nearby eating al fresco restored him to his senses.

Along the riva past the Riviera-style Excelsior Hotel, there are several excellent fish restaurants. The Triestines, far more than the Venetians, take their food and wine seriously.

Opposite the best of these, lying anchored alongside another thirties building, the Stazione Marittima, is the last ship of the Lloyd passenger fleet, the Dionea. Lovingly preserved by a crew which invariably outnumbers the passengers, the Dionea visits the ports of Istria where once many Italians lived simply to keep the Italian flag flying along the coast of what is now Jugoslavia. (This is the fault-line between Slav and Latin, Italian and Slovene, and relations are stormy even to this day, although the traveller is unlikely to encounter any such friction.) Thanks to the Italian government's subsidy of this delightful gesture of bravura, it is possible for a negligible sum to cross into Jugoslavia, avoiding long road and rail queues. The fifties cutlery gleams, the brass fittings are all kept immaculate and a friendly if rather maudlin barman will serve the most generous cappuccinos between melancholy references to the past glories of merchant shipping on the Tilbury to Trieste route.

The Dionea leaves almost every day of the year at 8 a.m. sharp, sometimes plying to Pola (Pula), the former naval base of the Austrians rich in Roman remains, including an amphitheatre which rivals the

Colosseum. (The Hotel Riviera, where James Joyce stayed, is recommended.)

Usually, however, the boat calls at one of the Venetian fishing villages along the coast beyond Capodistria (Koper). Of these, PIRAN is the most memorable, its tall campanile visible on a clear day from the molo Audace. It contains in its square a curious array of buildings, some sporting the Byzantine forms of the Venetians, others dressed in more Austrian attire with solemn porticoes.

The campanile at present can be visited for a sum equivalent to an English halfpenny. The wooden steps seem unsafe, but the only danger is from losing one's balance at the shock of its old bells (made from more Austrian cannon?) ringing the quarters. Occasionally, the strains of a guitar can be heard echoing down from the balustrade, for the Slovenes here are incurable romantics and the view across to the lagoons and Venice is unrivalled. Below, the old walls of the pinnacled fortress rise up through the olive groves, while in some side street the silence is broken by a children's military band rehearsing a cacophanous march. Suitable sounds perhaps for the town which gave birth to the composer Giuseppe Tartini, whose eighteenth-century bewigged figure rises up in the main square, brandishing a violin.

Behind the dashing composer, the naval museum conceals among uniforms and photographs of partisans, three of the most beautiful models of wooden galleons in the world. Constructed near Ljubljana in the eighteenth century, the craftsmanship wrought on the wood must be considered equal to that of any Baroque altarpiece. These treasures are protected by glass and seem curiously unappreciated, although their like cannot be seen anywhere else in Europe.

From Piran lie scattered a series of similar settlements, each with its memorable campanile and Venetian houses. In ROVIGNO (Rovinj), the Istrian wine Terran, a deep red, like the earth in which its vines are grown, is still celebrated, although whether, as Baedeker reported in 1905, the hazel-nuts here are the finest in the world is a matter of opinion.

From Rovigno it is a bumpy bus-ride to FIUME (Rijeka), the old port of the Hungarians, a seedier and altogether less charming version of Trieste (though the Helmer and Fellner opera house boasts Klimt frescoes), or to OPATIJA, the Abbazia of the Austrians and a resort whose yellow villas and palm trees still evoke the 'Riviera Austriaca'. But here, though Austria's double-headed eagle flew in towns even further down the coast, Central Europe begins to recede and it is from Venice, not Vienna, that the inspiration is derived.

True, the Austrians built the larger hotels and even as far south as Dubrovnik have left in countless sepia family portraits hiding in dining rooms, the images of a class borne high on the service of empire. But these are the outer fringes, and Austrian rule here, though benign, was short and it is an older culture which has survived into the twentieth century.

SELECT BIBLIOGRAPHY

Armstrong, Hamilton Fish, *Where the East Begins*, New York, 1929.
Baedeker, *Austria Hungary*, tenth edition, Leipzig, 1905.
Baker, J., *Austria: Her People and Her Lands*, London, 1908.
Barea, Ilse, *Vienna*, London, 1966.
Barry, Lt-Col. P., *The Gates of the East*, London, 1906.
Corvina Guide to Hungary, Budapest, 1971.
Crankshaw, Edward, *Vienna*, London, 1938.
Cunninghame, Charles, *What I Saw in Hungary*, London, 1936.
Dehio architectural guides to Vienna, Vienna, 1954 ff.
Etherton, Lt-Col., *Through Europe and the Balkans*, London, 1928.
Gayda, Virginio, *Modern Austria, Her Racial and Social Problems*, London, 1915.
Gedye, G. E. R., *A Wayfarer in Austria*, London, 1928.
Hamilton, Lord F., *The Vanished Pomps of Yesterday*, London, 1921.
Hempel, Professor E., *Baroque Art and Architecture in Central Europe*, London, 1965.
Knox, Brian, *Baroque Architecture in Central Europe*, London, 1966.
Kohl, J. G., *Austria*, London, 1843.
Lehmann, John, *Down River*, London, 1938.
Lonyay, Count, *The Tragedy at Mayerling*, London, 1950.
Lützow, Count F., *Bohemia*, London, 1896.
Mahan, J., *Vienna Yesterday and Today*, New York, 1926.
Mitton, G., *Austria Hungary*, London, 1915.
Nicolson, Harold, *The Congress of Vienna*, London, 1944.
Newman, Bernard, *The Blue Danube*, London, 1929.
Pardoe, Miss, *The City of the Magyar*, London, 1840.
Powell, N., *Travellers to Trieste*, London, 1978.
Preyer, David, *The Art of the Vienna Galleries*, Boston, 1909.
Provost, Maxime, *My Austrian Love*, London, 1916.
Rumpold, Sir H., *The Austrian Court in the Nineteenth Century*, London, 1909.
Seton Watson, R., *Slovakia Then and Now*, London, 1931.
Stadler, K., *Austria*, London, 1971.

Stamer, W., *Continental Road Travel*, London, 1906.
Stokes, Adrian, *Hungary*, London, 1909.
Street, C. J. C., *East of Prague*, London, 1924.
Trollope, Mrs Francis, *Vienna and the Austrians*, London, 1838.
Wandruska, A., *The House of Hapsburg*, London, 1964.
Williamson, A., *The Lure of Vienna*, London, 1924.
Young, Edgar, *Czechoslovakia*, London, 1938.
Zeman, Josef, *Prague*, Prague, 1960.

MAPS

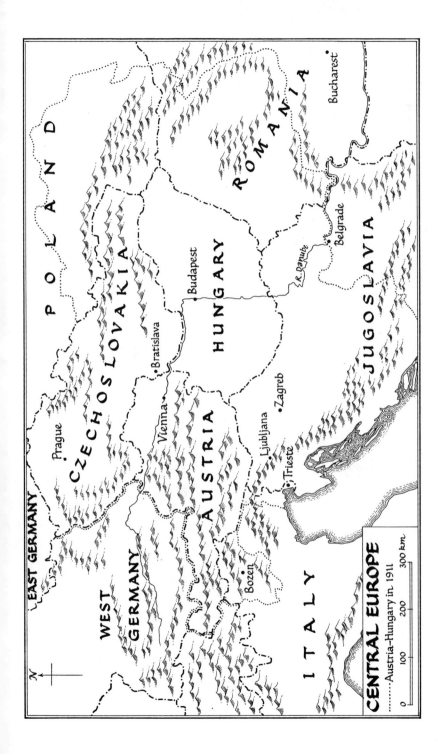

CENTRAL EUROPE

----- Austria-Hungary in 1911

0   100   200   300 km

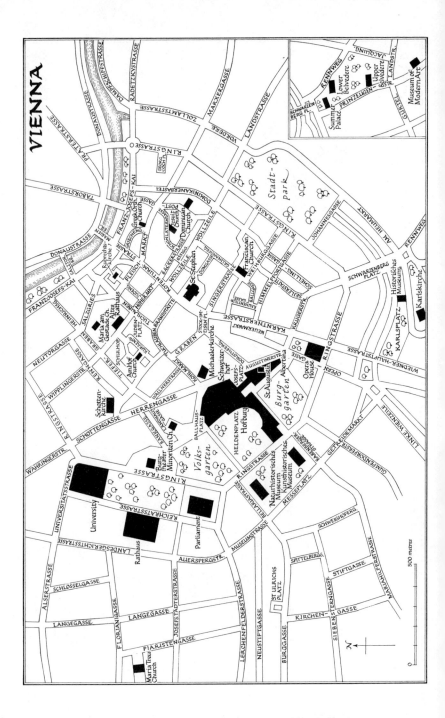

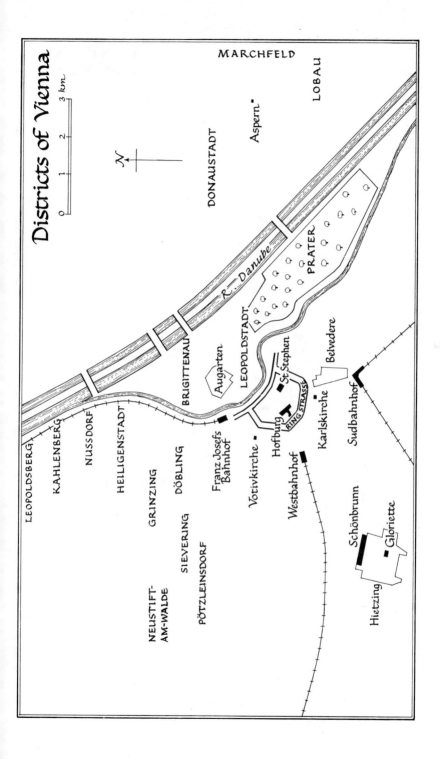

Excursions from Vienna

CZECHOSLOVAKIA

WACHAU

Krems
•Heldenberg
R. Danube
•Burg Kreuzenstein
Melk• •St Pölten
Klosterneuburg•
•VIENNA

Heiligenkreuz•
Mödling•
Mayerling•
Bruck•
Baden•

•Neusiedl am See
Rust• *Neusiedler See*
Eisenstadt• •Frauenkirchen

Klamm• •Gloggnitz
Breitenstein•
Semmering•

STYRIA

BURGENLAND

HUNGARY

Graz•

N

JUGOSLAVIA

Weissenkirchen• Dürnstein•
St Michael• R. Danube Krems•
Spitz•
Göttweig•
Aggsbach •Aggstein
Markt• •Aggsbach Dorf
•Schönbühel
•Melk Gloggnitz

0 50 km

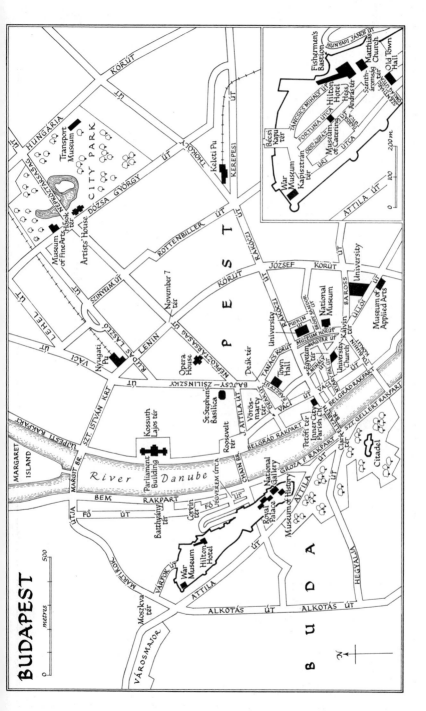

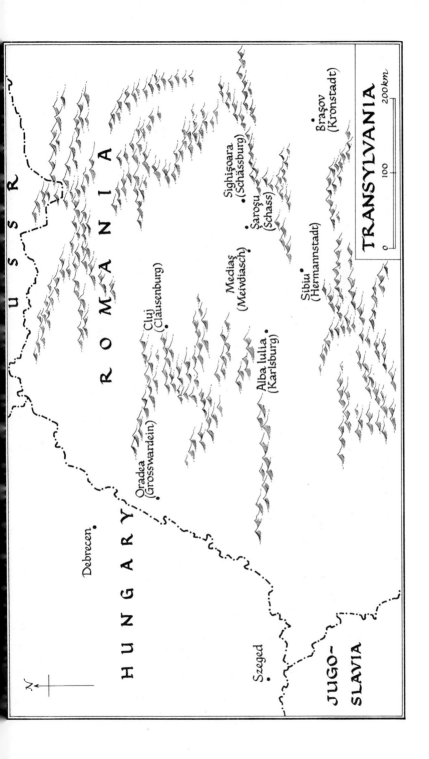

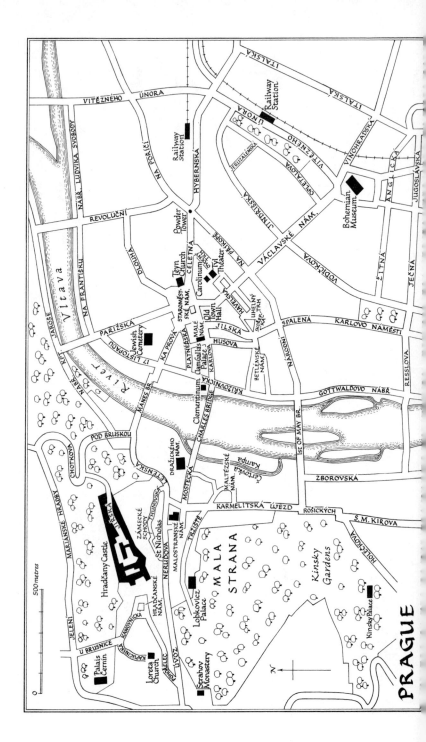

PRAGUE

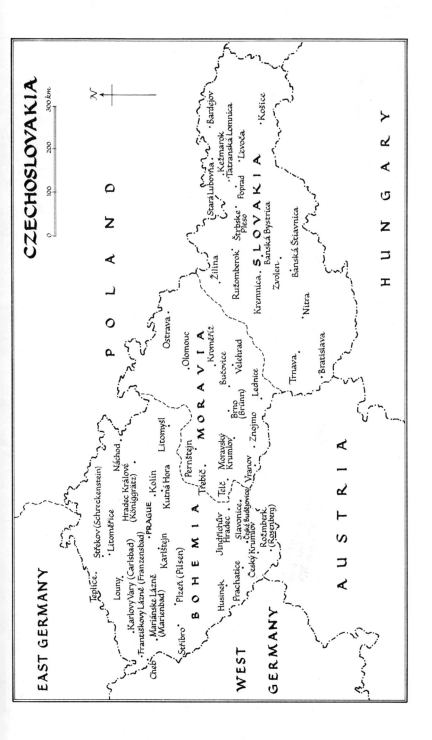

CZECHOSLOVAKIA

EAST GERMANY

POLAND

HUNGARY

AUSTRIA

WEST GERMANY

BOHEMIA

MORAVIA

SLOVAKIA

0   100   200   300 km

Teplice
Louny
Karlovy Vary (Carlsbad)
Mariánské Lázně (Marienbad)
Františkovy Lázně (Franzensbad)
Cheb
Stříbro
Plzeň (Pilsen)
Střekov (Schreckenstein)
Litoměřice
Náchod
Hradec Králové (Königgrätz)
PRAGUE
Kolín
Kutná Hora
Litomyšl
Karlštejn
Husinec
Prachatice
Jindřichův Hradec
Slavonice
České Budějovice
Český Krumlov
Rožmberk (Rosenberg)
Telč
Třebíč
Moravský Krumlov
Vranov
Znojmo
Pernštejn
Bučovice
Kroměříž
Velehrad
Lednice
Olomouc
Ostrava
Trnava
Bratislava
Nitra
Žilina
Ružomberok
Kremnica
Zvolen
Banská Bystrica
Banská Štiavnica
Štrbske Pleso
Poprad
Stará Ľubovňa
Kežmarok
Tatranská Lomnica
Levoča
Bardejov
Košice

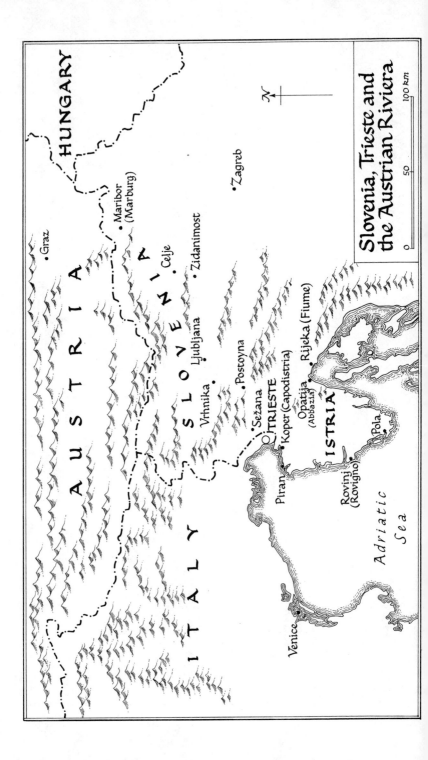

Slovenia, Trieste and the Austrian Riviera

INDEX

INDEX